Citizen Artists

Citizen Artists takes the reader on a journey through the process of producing, funding, researching, creating, rehearsing, directing, performing, and touring student-driven plays about social justice.

The process at the heart of this book was developed from 2015 to 2021 at New York City's award-winning Epic Theatre Ensemble with and for their youth ensemble: Epic NEXT. Author and Epic Co-Founder James Wallert shares his company's unique, internationally recognized methodology for training young arts leaders in playwriting, inquiry-based research, verbatim theatre, devising, applied theatre, and performance. Readers will find four original plays, 7 complete timed-to-the-minute lesson plans, 36 theatre arts exercises, and pages of practical advice from more than two dozen professional teaching artists to use for their own theatre making, arts instruction, or youth organizing.

Citizen Artists is a one-of-a-kind resource for students interested in learning about theatre and social justice; educators interested in fostering learning environments that are more rigorous, democratic, and culturally-responsive; and artists interested in creating work for new audiences that is more inclusive, courageous, and anti-racist.

James Wallert is a Founder and Co-Artistic Director of New York City's Epic Theatre Ensemble. He is an actor, playwright, director, producer, and educator. To learn more about James and Epic visit www.EpicTheatreEnsemble.org.

Citizen Artists

A Guide to Helping Young People Make
Plays That Change the World

James Wallert

Routledge
Taylor & Francis Group

LONDON AND NEW YORK

First published 2022
by Routledge
2 Park Square, Milton Park, Abingdon, Oxon OX14 4RN

and by Routledge
605 Third Avenue, New York, NY 10158

Routledge is an imprint of the Taylor & Francis Group, an informa business

© 2022 James Wallert

British Library Cataloguing-in-Publication Data
A catalogue record for this book is available from the British Library

Library of Congress Cataloging-in-Publication Data
A catalog record has been requested for this book

ISBN: 978-0-367-52926-0 (hbk)
ISBN: 978-0-367-51644-4 (pbk)
ISBN: 978-1-003-07983-5 (ebk)

DOI: 10.4324/9781003079835

Typeset in Bembo
by KnowledgeWorks Global Ltd.

Includes complete texts of four student-written plays that are changing the world:

Default

Perfect Circle

Overdrive

Nothing About Us

Contents

Figures

Introduction

"Teachers don't read introductions to books about education," a dear friend and brilliant educator cautioned me. "We're too busy. We don't have time. We crack open the table of contents, find the relevant chapters, grab the stuff we need for class, and peace out." So it is with the cautious optimism of a kid hurling a message in a bottle into the ocean that I offer a few words of preface for the educators and artists who have found a few precious spare moments to read them.

Citizen Artists details a journey through the process of producing, funding, researching, creating, rehearsing, directing, performing, and touring student-driven plays about social justice. This process was developed from 2015 to 2021 at Epic Theatre Ensemble in New York City with and for our youth ensemble: Epic NEXT. Over our 20 years as a company, the founders of Epic have established our way of working in the rehearsal room and the classroom by adopting and adapting exercises and practices from master arts educators like Eric Booth, Augusto Boal, Cicely Berry, Keith Johnstone, Rick Seer, Richard Easton, Jack Wright, Ron and Ludvika Popenhagen, and many other inspiring mentors and colleagues. It's a living breathing process that has evolved and changed over the years as more professional and student artists have joined us in the work, and I suspect and sincerely hope it will continue to do so. This book is part oral history and part snapshot of where we stand today as we look to our next 20 years and beyond.

In Part One, I outline Epic's Citizen Artist methodology by posing eighteen essential questions (one per chapter) and sharing how our artists work to address them. You'll hear directly from several current and former Epic NEXT students about how the work impacted their lives and their communities. You'll also receive some observations and practical advice from our ensemble of veteran arts educators. In Part Two, I provide seven detailed lesson plans to illustrate how this methodology can manifest itself in a classroom setting, be it middle school, high school, or university. In Part Three, you'll find the complete texts of four student-written plays that have toured all over the United States and abroad to expose and confront the most urgent inequities in our education system.

DOI: 10.4324/9781003079835-1

Epic's home is New York City and the goal of much of our work is to transform schooling in the United States, but I think the "how," "what," and "why" of our Citizen Artist process have a utility and efficacy for global impact far beyond our "where." There is a universal need for teaching in all content areas that is rigorous, joyful, creative, and student-centered. All artistic and educational institutions should commit to creating more spaces that decenter whiteness and honor different ways of knowing, seeing, and being. The plays of Epic NEXT tackle societal injustices like systemic racism, segregation, gentrification, and resource inequality that are all too common to the contemporary human experience. Dismantling these oppressive systems and the institutions that bolster and benefit from them will require a massive cultural change: the kind of change that is usually led by young people and artists. I don't anticipate that many readers will use this book to replicate a full youth development program exactly like Epic NEXT, but it is my hope to provoke and inspire some deep reflection on how we can all better invest in the next generation of artists, thinkers, leaders, and change-makers.

The world needs more Citizen Artists.

I offer this book up as a resource and a call to action for educators interested in fostering learning environments that are more empathetic and democratic; for theatre-makers interested in creating work that is more courageous and anti-racist; and for social justice professionals interested in advancing youth-driven solutions to our world's most intractable problems.

Part I

The Citizen Artist methodology

1 How do we transform art into activism?

No one would ever think to call this space a theatre: a low drop ceiling with harsh fluorescent lighting, burnt orange and brown vinyl floor tiles, folks crowded around long folding tables placed in-between a surprisingly large number of massive load-bearing concrete pillars scattered every few feet throughout the windowless room – classic 1970s New York City school cafetorium design. It was 8:15 am – an hour at which no actor should ever be awake, nor any play ever performed. Yet, on this crisp spring morning, in this dull dank room, we were there to put on a show.

I had brought 5 high school students to an event sponsored by the New York State Education Department for more than 200 educational leaders representing 27 school districts from all across the state. These superintendents and principals were there to begin the process of creating integration plans for their districts. At this moment in time, New York State has the most racially and socio-economically segregated schools in the nation,[1] and New York City Public Schools still remain more segregated than they were before the landmark 1954 Supreme Court case *Brown v. Board of Education*[2] in which the justices ruled that "Separate but Equal" schools were unconstitutional. The students were invited to perform their original 30-minute play, *Laundry City*, an exploration of the effects of educational segregation. There is no discernible front to this cafetorium, but from the base of one of the pillars, a facilitator from New York State squawks a few barely audible words of introduction via a microphone plugged into a portable speaker, "Please welcome Epic Theatre Ensemble." Jeremiah, a high school senior wearing a T-Shirt with the words, "I am Epic" written across the front, steps into the center of the room, without a mic, and speaks directly to the audience:

JEREMIAH: School segregation,
  That systematic placement,
  Race and class, don't make me laugh.
  That shit goes deeper than thin cloudy glass.
  Right past society's foundation,
  Back to America in the making.

DOI: 10.4324/9781003079835-2

The original sin: Race.
The original sin: Race.
The original sin: Race.

Olivia, Davion, Nakkia, and Nashali appear at the four corners of the space to pick up the verse.

OLIVIA: Just a social figment, it controls this place.
   Causing fear of my pigment, scared to look in my face.
   Looking down at me like I'm a disgrace.
DAVION: Knowing that nobody wants to admit it
   But this country's ruled by fear.
   Move your hands, stop covering your ears. Open your eyes.
NAKKIA: See that shit is so embedded that if you don't rise,
   Six feet under is where you're headed-buried alive.
NASHALI: By the lies, false hopes, false causes, false endorsements: crazy ride.
   This is a rollercoaster and yeah you on it.
   So tell your mama not to take off her bonnet.
JEREMIAH: Just sit, relax, and enjoy the show cause we own it. Laundry City.

With no transition, the actors shift from verse to prose, physically and vocally transforming to play a series of characters in a Brooklyn community affected by rezoning. Nakkia and Davion play the duo of a nervous Public School Principal and his subtext translator, "KEEPING IT 100."

MR. MADISON: Soon we will be admitting new students to our school.
KEEPING IT 100: The white students are a-comin'.
MR. MADISON: Nothing will change.
KEEPING IT 100: Everything's changing.
MR. MADISON: This is happening because of the rezoning going on in Brooklyn.
KEEPING IT 100: This is happening because white people are colonizing Brooklyn.
MR. MADISON: This is a great opportunity to make our school great again!
KEEPING IT 100: This is a great opportunity to snatch that white money!

The performers weave through the audience performing scene after scene, transforming from character to character. Nashali plays a mother trying to understand the situation at her daughter's school. She speaks to us in Spanish.

MRS. MALAVÉ *(English translation):* What does this mean? White people moving in? Here? Of all the places? We're quiet. We don't even get news coverage whenever a little boy is shot out here. What will they bring? Higher rent. More and more white people. I'm gonna get kicked out. I can't. This is the only place I know. I grew up here- been here my whole life. Mami and Papi are gone, God rest their souls, so I can't even ask them for advice. What am I gonna do? How will this affect Jeylin? Her school? Maybe the government will finally help them. Is that who takes care of the schools?

In the crowd, you can see some shoulders start to rise up a bit and some others start to relax. A scene title gets called out: "A Separate but Equal Bedroom." Jeremiah and Nashali step forward. We see one brother dividing the room with a long strip of tape over the other brother's objections.

POORELL: Yo, my mans!
RICH: OK, you see this line? That's my side. This is your side. Got it?
POORELL: What the hell are you doing?
RICH: Rezoning.
POORELL: What?
RICH: This side is safe. That side is dangerous.
POORELL: Are you serious? You selfish prick!
   (POORELL pushes RICH)
RICH: See! That's what I'm talking about! Your side is too dangerous! I don't feel safe.

Figure 1.1 Melysa Hierro and Jeremiah Green, Jr. rehearsing the "Separate but Equal Bedroom" scene from *Laundry City*.

Source: David Naranjo/photo courtesy of Epic Theatre Ensemble.

The show culminates in a town hall. The students had done meticulous research to craft a finale that made room for dozens of nuanced perspectives on this complex issue. Throughout the scene, several of the performers' lines are punctuated with "Mmmmm!"s, "Thank you!"s, and even an "Amen!" from members of the audience.

MR. WELLS: What is your definition of integration?

PHILLIP: I'm not really sure what we mean by integration. What I've seen when we talk about integration, it is about Black and Latino kids going to white schools to become better. That isn't integration, that's- in my view-assimilation.

AMY: I consider integration when you do the hard work of valuing what each person brings to that setting. Integration is where we learn to understand each other and appreciate each other and nobody's story or history is more important than another's.

JOE: I think where we get confused is conflating the quest for adequate educational opportunities with a quest for integration. The theory of action was if you import basically white middle class students, they would then advocate for all of the students in the school. They had more social and political capital and they would essentially serve as the saviors for the Black and Latino students in the school. I think that's racist. I think it's classist. I don't believe in the savior complex- that you need to have folks swoop in and save the poor Black and Latino children. I believe that Black and Latino folks have agency and power that have been untapped.

SARAH: For me, it's not that certain communities are less powerful; it's that certain communities haven't been given the floor. How do we give people the floor? Segregation was intentional. Integration has to be intentional. Segregation was forced. Integration has to be forced.

PHILLIP: Who says the goal is integration? I think for me the goal is about having high quality schools.

TANYA: If integration made money somehow, then America would do it.

SARAH: I think the worst part about segregation is that people end up feeling like there's something wrong with them. The worst part of segregation is young people feeling like they're stupid, they're bad, they're troublemakers, they're not worth it. That's the worst part.

The 5 actors portray 18 different characters throughout the course of this last scene, but the final question of the play is delivered by the students as themselves.

DAVION: Is separate but equal fair?

ENTIRE ENSEMBLE: Is separate but equal fair?

As their last line echoes through the cafetorium, the five citizen artists join hands and bow. The crowd rises for a standing ovation. The space feels different. It is 8:45 am and 200 people know that the room in which they are standing is now very much a theatre.

The students take in the love for another moment but then gesture for the audience to retake their seats.

OLIVIA: At Epic, we like to have a conversation after every performance and we always ask our audience the same first question: Imagine that two weeks from now, one morning you wake up and find yourself thinking about *Laundry City*. What is it that will be going through your mind: a line, a character, an idea, a question? What do you think will resonate with you over time?

The post-show discussion is especially lively and long. It runs an hour – twice as long as the play that sparked it. The facilitator from New York State jumps back on the mic to thank the students and direct the district teams to return to their work sessions. I gather the cast to take them back to their school (it's a weekday). A superintendent from Upstate New York comes over and asks the students if they can come by his table to take a look at his district's integration plan and share their thoughts. They do. We start to head out again when a superintendent from New York City's Upper West Side asks for some feedback from the students about her district's plan. The students go over to her table. After several more invitations are proffered, we are eventually invited to stay through lunch so that the cast could review and respond to each of the 27 district integration plans. I make a quick call to their Principal who agrees to excuse them from the rest of their morning classes.

About an hour into this process of consultation, Jeremiah asked if he could speak to me in the hallway. This is the dialogue from that scene in the hall, as I remember it:

JEREMIAH: Jim!
JIM: What's up?
JEREMIAH: I'm feeling emotional about all this.
JIM: Oh yeah?
JEREMIAH: Yeah, I feel like an activist.
JIM: You *are* an activist.
JEREMIAH: No, I mean, I feel like I'm in a room full of people who can actually change things and they're listening to me.
JIM: Yeah.
JEREMIAH: That's intense!
JIM: Yeah!
JEREMIAH: O.K. I'm going back in.

I was feeling pretty emotional myself after that exchange but once the initial warm and fuzzy glow faded, I began to reflect on the half empty portion of the glass (as I am sometimes wont to do) that Jeremiah had placed in front of me.

Dude, you're only *NOW* feeling like an activist?

How did I fail him like that? I had worked with Jeremiah for four years. My company, Epic Theatre Ensemble, had been in residence at his high school since 2003. I had regularly come into Jeremiah's English, History, and Science classrooms in partnership with his teachers to guide students in the exploration of the relationship between individuals and their society. Working with Epic each year for four years in what we call our Citizen Artist Sequence, these students write and perform theatre productions that are supposed to inspire empathy and awaken civic engagement. During that same time, I was leading after-school programming where students analyze a Shakespeare play, debate its social and political questions, and weave their own writing into the fabric of the script. Jeremiah had been a star participant in all of this work. He created and performed plays about social justice in his school and in his community. He explored deep political questions through his art. He learned to share his thoughts, feelings, and ideas with his peers. Why was he only now feeling like an activist? What was it about that particular moment that made Jeremiah feel like an activist? I mean, isn't all art political? Isn't the creation and performance of a play in and of itself a revolutionary act? Shouldn't all young theatre-makers think of themselves as activists?

Apparently not.

From my perspective as a theatre practitioner and arts educator working in New York City for the past 23 years, I feel confident saying that as a field, theatre has not been very effective at promoting its own value as a tool for social justice. In the mad scurry to sell season subscriptions and single tickets to a bunch of plays, we've done a miserable job of making the case for any real, tangible, essential value of theatre. As much as I'd like to think that simply practicing my art is, in itself, a form of activism, I have to acknowledge the fact that the general public certainly doesn't view it that way. So what *do* most folks think of the theatre and the people who make it?

I have some thoughts.

Five common misconceptions about the American Theatre that are nearly always true

Alas, I believe that most Americans, if they're being honest, hold the following five beliefs about theatre:

Theatre is boring

Or at best, going to the theatre is not nearly as enjoyable as watching movies or television. In 2007, *New York Times* critic Charles Isherwood in his review of the Tony Award winning production of the Pulitzer Prize winning play *August: Osage County* gushed, "This isn't theater-that's-good-for-you theater... Watching it is like sitting at home on a rainy night, greedily devouring two, three, four episodes of your favorite series in a row on DVR or DVD."[3] A couple of things to unpack here from the lead theatre critic of the paper of record: his first implication is that theatre is something you should take part in not because it's enjoyable but because it's somehow good for you, like taking multi-vitamins or eating kale – a kind of cultural colonic. His second implication: great theatre is that which most closely replicates good television shows or movies.

If we look at Broadway programming and casting choices in the decade since his review, they would seem to align with Mr. Isherwood's standards of theatrical quality. Of the 23 productions playing on Broadway in the summer of 2019, 13 were based on movies and 3 more were revivals of classic Broadway shows with movie versions easily available for streaming (*Oklahoma!, Chicago, Phantom of the Opera*). Many of the casts of these productions were led by actors primarily known for their onscreen work.

I challenge Isherwood's notion that great theatre is like a great television show or a great movie. The opposite isn't true: watching bad plays is nothing at all like watching bad movies or bad TV. Watching a bad movie can be a lot of fun. There's a whole sub-genre of movies and TV about bad movies (*Ed Wood, The Disaster Artist, Dolemite is My Name, Hail Caesar, Bowfinger, Mystery Science Theatre 3000* to name just a few). You can laugh at the acting, the dialogue, the poor production values: onscreen these things are hilarious. Enduring a bad play isn't fun for anyone. The actors, the crew, and the audience are all stuck in the same room together breathing the same uninspired air, resenting each other, and waiting for it to be over so they can escape their dreary confines and have a drink.

Great theatre isn't like a great movie or great TV. There is nothing else like experiencing great theatre. It's totally unique. It's thrilling. It's radiant. It's ephemeral. It has the power to change minds and lives. It's difficult to describe in words so let me repurpose a line that U.S. Supreme Court Justice Potter Stewart used to describe hardcore pornography and apply it to great theatre, "I shall not today attempt further to define the kinds of material I understand to be embraced within that shorthand description, and perhaps I could never succeed in intelligibly doing so. But I know it when I see it."

Theatre is expensive

According to Broadway League, the average paid admission to *Hamilton* has been $285[4] with a top ticket price of $1150[5]. When he said, "It's the story about America then, told by America now,"[6] Lin Manuel Miranda was referring to the choice to cast actors of color as the Founding Fathers, but the economics of *Hamilton*'s box office clearly tells the story that "America now" has a staggering wealth inequality problem.

The average Broadway ticket price in 2018–2019 was $145.60[7]. In 2017, the average single ticket price for all U.S. not-for-profit theatres was $39.34[8]. Even on the low end, that's a pretty rich bet for working-class Americans to make. We are pricing our way out of accessibility and relevance for the majority of people living in our country.

Theatre is white

Primarily made by white people for white people. The numbers don't refute this. According to a report by the Asian American Performers Action Coalition, in the 2016–2017 season, 67% of all available roles in New York City that season went to Caucasian actors, 86.8% of all plays were written by Caucasian playwrights, and 87.1% of all productions were directed by a white person.[9] In 2018–2019, 74% of Broadway's audiences were white.[10] All of these numbers reflect a ten-year trend of *increasing* diversity in New York theatre. In one of the most diverse cities in the world, this is what improvement looks like?

Outside of New York, the national diversity figures are also distressing. 68% of the total national membership of Actors' Equity Association, the union for professional actors and stage managers, is white. 77% of stage manager contracts on Broadway and Production Tours went to Caucasians – over three years there were only six contracts given to African American stage managers. African-American members of Equity reported salaries 10% lower than the average salaries of their white counterparts.[11]

When white arts leaders are questioned about the whiteness of their predominantly white arts institutions, they will sometimes use the phrase "artistic quality" as a smokescreen to hide the fact that their hiring practices are embracing and maintaining racial and income-based segregation. Some white arts leaders try to mitigate their institutional diversity issues by creating an education program that serves Black and Brown kids. There is often very little overlap between the teaching artists that get hired to work in a large theatre company's education program and the artists that are hired to work on that same theatre company's professional stages. "We have a very diverse education program" is the white artistic director's version of "I have a lot of Black friends."

Theatre is impoverishing

Practiced by artists who do it solely for "the love of theatre." While it's true that most theatre folks don't earn much money making theatre (The 18,422 union members who worked on an Actor's Equity Association contract in 2016–2017 had median earnings of $7,730),[12] this notion about their poverty being inspired by "the love of theatre" is a myth perpetuated by theatre producers, perhaps to make themselves feel better about not paying a proportionate share of the revenue from those insanely expensive tickets to the artists who make the shows. Every professional wants to make a living wage, but theatre artists are warned from an early age that they are easily replaceable and trained to be grateful for the opportunity just to practice their craft.

This weeds out a lot of talented young artists who can't afford to forgo an income and ensures that the majority of future theatre artists and theatre arts leaders come from a privileged class of folks whose lives and careers are subsidized by family wealth. "Paying your dues," a colloquial name sometimes given to this free labor system, is often done by those who don't have to pay for anything else.

In Epic's early days as a company, we were cautioned by the leadership of Actors Equity Association that we were paying our actors too much and that we should reduce our salaries because, "we like it when theatre companies like you stick around for a while." We have managed to stick around for 20 years and have always been at or near the top of the Off-Broadway pay scale. Only in the theatre would a union representative actively try to negotiate a lower salary for his members. There's no business like show business!

This love/poverty myth is also occasionally co-opted by successful television and film stars who temporarily forgo their Hollywood paychecks for a few months to gain "artistic street cred" in the form of critical praise and awards. "The love of theatre" is often invoked by these luminaries (and their PR firms) to provide cover for their dogged pursuit of sparkling notices and golden baubles. As one somewhat famous television actress wife once privately lamented to an Epic colleague and I about her more famous movie star husband's Tony Award snub, "I mean, what's the point of doing a play if you're not going to get an award for it?" Theatre: can you feel the love?

Theatre is dumb

Pajama Game, Follies, Xanadu, SpongeBob SquarePants: The Musical, reasons to be pretty, Slave Play, Dance of the Vampires, The Roar of the Greasepaint the Smell of the Crowd, Drat! The Cat!, Hanky Panky, Moose Murders, Whoop-Up, Ankles Aweigh, Mrs. Wiggs of the Cabbage Patch, The Bad Boy and His Teddy Bears, Taller Than a Dwarf, The Fox Holes, A Very Wise Virgin, His Honor: The Barber, Are You a Crook?, Arabesque, A Chinese Honeymoon, Plantation Revue, Little Miss Fix It, The Twelve Pound Look, Kiss Me Quick, My Wife Is Not Stylish, The Great White Hope, Take Me Back Behind the Barn, Higgledy-Piggledy, The Five Frankfurters, An Aztec Romance, Hip! Hip! Hooray!, Texas Li'l Darlin', Eunice and the Confirmed Bachelor, Getting Gertie's Garter, The Origin of the Cakewalk, and Flahooley.

These are all titles of productions that have at some point appeared on Broadway. Actually, all but three of them are titles of Broadway productions; three of them I just made up. Can you guess which three are mine? (Check the end of this chapter to find out the answer[13]). If you're struggling to identify which three titles are too stupid or too sexist or too culturally insensitive to be real, then perhaps it's not unreasonable to wonder if stupidity, sexism, and cultural insensitivity are baked into Broadway's brand. By way of citation: Broadway's nickname is "The Great White Way," one of its most famous and beloved musicals features the lyric, "I'm just a girl who can't say no," and as for evidence of its stupidity – there is so much low hanging fruit that I doubt most of you need me to provide you with an example. For those that do: *Mamma Mia!*

From 2016 to 2019, there were zero plays on Broadway about the U.S. education system, but two staged versions of Julia Roberts movies. Zero plays in the same period about U.S. immigration policy, but four Motown jukebox musicals. There hasn't been a play on Broadway in the past two decades about the rapidly worsening epidemic of American mass shootings – unless you count the 1999 revival of *Annie Get Your Gun*.

I believe the reason many Americans don't think the theatre is the place for an idea is because it is very possible to regularly attend the theatre in this country and never come across a play or a musical that expresses an original thought that is relevant to most Americans' lives. There's a long theatrical legacy of populating our country's most prominent stages with plays and musicals that serve no purpose other than to amuse and distract the audiences that can afford to pay the high prices to see them, to "employ" the artists of privilege who can afford to make the work without receiving a living wage, and to normalize and perpetuate an industry steeped in notions of white supremacy and artistic plutocracy.

So...?

So all of that really sucks. It's depressing. How can we, as theatre-makers, feel good about the choice we made to pursue our passion rather than feel bad about the choice we made to skip law school?

As I write this, the United States is waging a losing battle against the spread of COVID-19 and the American Theatre is in the midst of a great pause. At the same time, the civil unrest resulting from the murders of George Floyd, Breonna Taylor, and far too many other African-Americans has drawn more white people into conversations about systemic racism and restorative justice. White arts leaders around the country are gradually realizing that a "return to normal" is not an acceptable goal for many of their constituents. I believe there is an opportunity to make real and lasting change in our field, but statements of solidarity coupled with a mindset of polite reform won't get us there. We need to accept nothing short of radical transformation or abolition. But what do we transform or abolish first?

Maybe the answer lies with Jeremiah and the half-full part of his glass. How can we fill that glass to the brim? How can we be intentional about developing artists who have the desire and the ability to use their art for activism? How can we encourage young folks from historically marginalized communities to take up the tools of playwriting and performance to advocate for themselves and engage audiences in deep explorations of vital essential questions? How can we create a theatrical forum that encourages artists and audiences to re-envision the way that governments and large societal institutions function? How can we help young people make art that changes the world?

I have some thoughts.

If we're going to save and transform our industry, we shouldn't look to Broadway for leadership. Commercial theatre producers are beholden, first and foremost, to their bottom lines. It's a free country and Broadway is allowed to make a buck, of course, but let's not hold our collective breath waiting for Walt Disney and Scott Rudin to lead us to the Promised Land. If there is a messianic Broadway producer out there who wants to prove me wrong, I'd be thrilled, but I think that systemic change is more likely to be driven by artists and arts managers working in the educational and not-for-profit sectors. We can start the ball rolling by acknowledging our past complicity in oppression and building new institutional models that reject the prejudice, greed, cynicism, abuse, and willful cultural ignorance that have been norms for the contemporary American Theatre. We need to unlatch our intentions, ambitions, and activities away from all of that mess and remember that there is another tradition of theatre that predates season subscriptions and VIP premium ticket pricing; a tradition that is responsive and accessible; a tradition that espouses the belief that a thriving socially conscious theatre is an essential component of a just society; a tradition that elevates the griot, the rakugoka, the bard, and the town crier; a tradition that empowers the bravest and brightest young artists to challenge the failures of the status quo and point the way to something better.

We can champion the creation of art that is relevant, representative, and affordable for everyone in our communities. We can proudly assert the value of our profession by demanding that young artists from historically marginalized communities get paid a reasonable wage for the work they make. We can challenge oppressive systems by placing youth and their art in front of people with power. And once everyone has had a chance to experience the art, we can provide the time and space for people to talk to one another about what it means to them and what actions they want to take next.

Epic NEXT

Epic NEXT is a multi-year youth development program designed to identify and nurture a new generation of diverse arts leaders. Teen artists from Epic's partner high schools self-select to enter our five-week summer intensive as "Tier 1" students. Professional theatre artists mentor Tier 1 students in the development of their craft as well as in leadership, civic engagement, and college readiness. The first summer culminates in a play the students devise around a series of current social justice concerns.

"Tier 2" training is designed to replicate elements of the college experience. Students spend a week living on-campus in the dorms and taking

LEVEL	STUDENTS	FOCUS
ALUMNI APPRENTICE	4-8 University students	Arts mentorship
TIER 3	2-8 rising 12th Grade students	Peer leadership
TIER 2	10-16 rising 11th and 12th Grade students	Playwriting Directing Verbatim Theatre
TIER 1	16-25 rising 10th and 11th Grade students	Improvisation Acting Devising

Figure 1.2 Organizational chart for Epic NEXT.

theatre classes at an out-of-state university. When they return to New York City, they receive instruction in playwriting, directing, and verbatim theatre technique. The second summer concludes with the creation of an original short play about educational justice that is built to tour.

"Tier 3" students serve as peer leaders for the Tier 1 and Tier 2 cohorts. Alumni apprentices return from college to work closely with the Epic professionals to learn the fundamentals of teaching artistry and arts mentorship.

The process of researching, creating, rehearsing, revising, and performing the Tier 2 touring shows will be the primary focus of this book. Figure 1.3 is a breakdown for a typical five-week creation process for Tier 2. Our span of day is generally 10:00 am–4:30 pm.

These Tier 2 student researchers/writers/artists are commissioned by a university or community-based partner to focus on a specific aspect of education policy or pedagogy. They research the subject, interview the stakeholders, weave together transcribed selections from the interview material with their own original writing to form a script and perform the play to content-connected audiences around the United States and internationally. After each performance, the student artists facilitate a conversation with the audience about the questions and themes in the play. In five years, the plays of Epic NEXT have received 182 performances in 30 cities in 3 countries for 47,000 audience members including teachers, principals, superintendents, school board officials, education policy researchers, and legislators.

Out on tour, I will occasionally hear comments like, "I can't believe Epic makes things like that with high school students," which I think could imply a misunderstanding that one of our teaching artists can just walk into any high school classroom and crank one of these things out. I think it's important to provide the full context of our Epic NEXT training process so it's clear that this methodology and these plays are the product of a much larger investment in the future of the American Theatre.

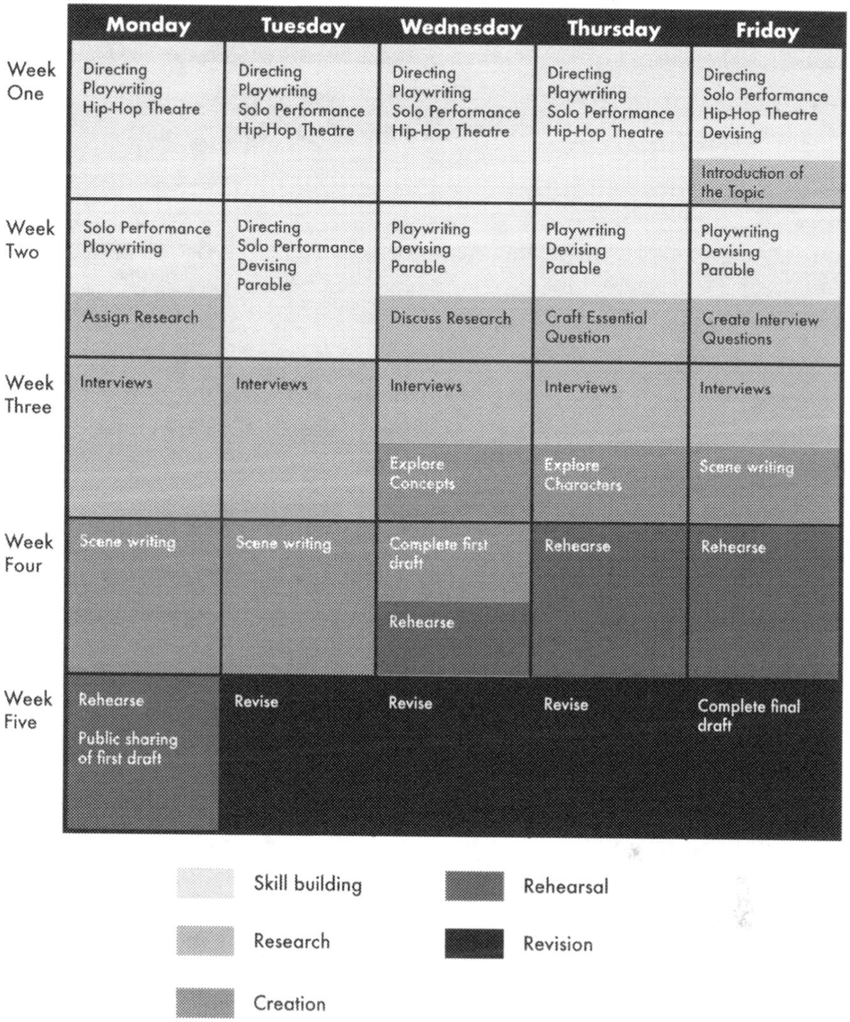

	Monday	Tuesday	Wednesday	Thursday	Friday
Week One	Directing Playwriting Hip-Hop Theatre	Directing Playwriting Solo Performance Hip-Hop Theatre	Directing Playwriting Solo Performance Hip-Hop Theatre	Directing Playwriting Solo Performance Hip-Hop Theatre	Directing Solo Performance Hip-Hop Theatre Devising Introduction of the Topic
Week Two	Solo Performance Playwriting Assign Research	Directing Solo Performance Devising Parable	Playwriting Devising Parable Discuss Research	Playwriting Devising Parable Craft Essential Question	Playwriting Devising Parable Create Interview Questions
Week Three	Interviews	Interviews	Interviews Explore Concepts	Interviews Explore Characters	Interviews Scene writing
Week Four	Scene writing	Scene writing	Complete first draft Rehearse	Rehearse	Rehearse
Week Five	Rehearse Public sharing of first draft	Revise	Revise	Revise	Complete final draft

Skill building Rehearsal

Research Revision

Creation

Figure 1.3 Calendar for a typical five week Epic NEXT creation process.

Epic NEXT production history

10467 (2015) – commissioned by the Campaign for Educational Equity

Why do we stand down when we should stand up?

New York State has one of the most inequitable public education systems in America.[14] The students of Epic NEXT worked with the Center for Educational Equity at Columbia University's Teachers College to create a passionate work of theatre that awakens audiences to the problems at hand and catalyzes action toward a new vision of equity in our public schools.

Why do we stand down when we should stand up in the battle against educational violence? And how do we conceive and construct a new value system where someone's zip code doesn't damage their educational opportunities?

Laundry City (2016) – commissioned by New York Appleseed

If integration made money somehow, America would do it.

Over 60 years after Brown v. Board of Education, New York City is one of the most segregated school districts in the United States. Conceived, written, and performed by NYC Public High School students, *Laundry City* is a hilarious and provocative exploration of what "Separate but Equal" means to us today.

Building Blocks: Colorful Minds (2017) – commissioned by Queens College

The average of mental power in man must be above that of woman.
Charles Darwin, 1871.[15]

This timely play uses theatre, dance, movement, and stand-up comedy to examine how Science, Technology, Engineering, and Math (STEM) are taught in Public Schools and the impact this pedagogy is having on diversity in the STEM workforce.

Overdrive (2018) – commissioned by The Public Good at Teachers College, Columbia University

Everybody is a genius, but if you judge a fish by its ability to climb a tree it will live its whole life believing it is stupid.

How many jobs demand that employees come up with the right answer on the spot, from memory, while the clock is ticking? How often are we forbidden to ask coworkers for help? How common is it for working professionals to be given a secret pencil-and-paper exam? The student researchers/writers/performers of Epic NEXT interviewed a diverse group of education stakeholders about the role of Standardized Assessments in Public Schools. Their findings will surprise you. *Overdrive* is a 25 minute touring play that powerfully poses the question: do we truly measure what we value and value what we measure?

Nothing About Us (2018) – commissioned by New York Appleseed

Nothing about us without us is for us.

Nothing About Us is a rigorous, passionate, and hilarious exploration of educational segregation written and performed by those most affected and least consulted: NYC Public High School students. What does separate but equal mean to us today? Transformation, empathy, and youth voice drive the conversation in this 30-minute touring play by Epic NEXT.

Default (2019) – commissioned by The Public Good at Teachers College, Columbia University

> The master's tools will never dismantle the master's house.
>
> Audre Lorde[16]

What difference does it make to students if their school's curriculum reflects the history, experiences, and knowledge of their communities and families? *Default* is a funny and moving original play created by the youth researchers/writers/artists of Epic NEXT that examines the impact that Ethnic Studies courses and Culturally Relevant Pedagogy have on students, teachers, administrators, and families.

Perfect Circle (2019) – commissioned by Legal Momentum and Legal Services NYC

> Why do we allow adults in schools to pretend that there is a real distance between their own attitudes and those of the bullies?

In a recent national survey, one in four students say that they've been bullied in school,[17] but 70% of NYC Public Schools reported zero incidents of harassment, bullying, or discrimination.[18] In *Perfect Circle*, the youth researchers/writers/artists of Epic NEXT look at the local, state, and federal protections in place for students and explore why bullying is so persistent when everyone says they're against it.

Epic NEXT Film Festival (2020) – Due to the outbreak of COVID-19, our youth ensemble transitioned from devising plays to writing and directing short films. The Epic NEXT Film Festival features 22 short films that explore how systemic racism manifests itself in education and the arts.[19]

Commissioning Partners:

Center for Ethnic, Racial, & Religious Understanding at Queens College
The Century Foundation
Diverse Charter Schools Coalition
Harlem Education History Project at Teachers College, Columbia University
Muhlenberg College
New York Appleseed
NYC Department of Education
NYU Metro Center
Patricia O'Rourke
Shino Tanikawa
Jacob Ming-Trent

THE FIFTY STATE CONVERSATION (2021) – presented in partnership with The National Coalition on School Diversity and Dodd Human Rights Impact at The University of Connecticut

On May 17, the anniversary of Brown v. Board of Education, participants from all 50 states, Washington DC, Puerto Rico, and the US Virgin Islands join online for a screening of *Nothing About Us* and a national conversation about segregation.

Notes

1. Kucsera, John with Orfield, Gary. "New York State's Extreme School Segregation Inequality, Inaction and a Damaged Future," 2014. https://civilrightsproject.ucla.edu/research/k-12-education/integration-and-diversity/ny-norflet-report-placeholder/Kucsera-New-York-Extreme-Segregation-2014.pdf
2. https://archive.nytimes.com/www.nytimes.com/interactive/2012/05/11/nyregion/segregation-in-new-york-city-public-schools.html?action=click&contentCollection=Education&module=RelatedCoverage&pgtype=article&region=Marginalia
3. Isherwood, Charles. "Mama Doesn't Feel Well, but Everyone Else Will Feel Much Worse." *New York Times*, December 5, 2007. https://www.nytimes.com/2007/12/05/theater/reviews/05august.html
4. https://www.broadwayleague.com/research/grosses-broadway-nyc/499521/48884/
5. Cox, Gordon. "Hamilton' Ticket Prices Hit $1,150 During Holiday Week." *Variety*, December 26, 2017. https://variety.com/2017/legit/news/hamilton-ticket-prices-1202648756/
6. Weinert-Kendt, Rob. "Rapping a Revolution." *New York Times*, February 5, 2015. https://www.nytimes.com/2015/02/08/theater/lin-manuel-miranda-and-others-from-hamilton-talk-history.html
7. https://www.broadwayleague.com/research/research-reports/
8. https://www.statista.com/statistics/197363/us-non-profit-theatres-average-ticket-price-by-theatre-budget-size/
9. http://www.aapacnyc.org/2016-2017.html
10. https://www.broadwayleague.com/research/order-research-reports/
11. Actors Equity Association. "Looking at Hiring Biases by the Numbers," https://actorsequity.org/news/PR/DiversityStudy/
12. 2016–2017 Theatrical Season Report (https://actorsequity.org/aboutequity/annualstudy/2016-2017-annual-study.pdf)
13. *The Fox Holes, Take Me Back behind the Barn,* and *Eunice and the Confirmed Bachelor* were the titles that I created – copyright ©2019 James Wallert.
14. Rebell, Michael A., Wolff, Jessica R., and Rogers, Joseph R., Jr. "Deficient Resources: An Analysis of the Availability of Basic Educational Resources in High-Needs Schools in Eight New York State School Districts," Campaign for Educational Equity, December 2017. http://www.centerforeducationalequity.org/media/centers/cee/EssentialResources2017-FINAL1.9.18.pdf
15. Darwin, Charles. *The Descent of Man, and Selection in Relation to Sex.* John Murray. 1871. p. 564
16. Lorde, Audre. "The Master's Tools Will Never Dismantle the Master's House." Sister Outsider: Essays and Speeches. Ed. Berkeley, CA: Crossing Press. 110-114. 2007.
17. National Center for Education Statistics. "Student Reports of Bullying: Results from the 2017 School Crime Supplement to the National Crime Victimization Survey" T6. 2019. https://nces.ed.gov/pubs2019/2019054.pdf

18. Neason, Alexandria. "NYC Says There's No Bullying in 70 Percent of Schools, State Says No Way," *The Village Voice*, September 1, 2016. https://www.villagevoice. com/2016/09/01/nyc-says-theres-no-bullying-in-70-percent-of-schools-state-says-no-way/

19. The Epic NEXT Film Festival can be found at: https://www.youtube.com/playlist?list=PLQErtALNiTIJj9YGOybQrwaC-R9r7i1cu

2 What is a Citizen Artist?

Epic's first official day of operation was September 11, 2001. My colleagues and I had spent that spring and summer fundraising, renting (and painting) an office in midtown Manhattan, finding performance venues, securing school partners, and preparing for our first season as a theatre company. In our original mission statement, we asserted that artists were best positioned to translate the struggles of history into lessons for the future. After the World Trade Center towers fell, we were forced on that first day as a company to decide what living our values in the midst of a national crisis would look like.

MELISSA FRIEDMAN, EPIC FOUNDER/CO-ARTISTIC DIRECTOR: The founding of Epic was in a way a hypothesis: theatre should be at the center of a healthy democracy. Artists are essential workers. We help process big human events in a way that draws people together in community and gets them to reckon with big issues. With 9/11 being our first day, it tested the hypothesis immediately.

Theaters in New York City closed their doors. Productions were postponed or canceled. School had only been in session for three days. Many teachers didn't yet know their students' names, but they were going to have to help them process their confusion, sadness, anger, and fear. We reached out to our contacts at the NYC Department of Education to learn that there was no comprehensive plan to guide educators and students through these difficult conversations. "Don't talk about it" was the directive many teachers were given from their principals. On the evening of September 12, we invited a group of 20 teaching artists to our offices – an aroma of fresh paint still hanging in the air – to put together a lesson plan.

During lesson planning, it can sometimes help to articulate the bad ideas first. Improvisation, crafting monologues, and scene writing were out. We didn't want students to write or draw directly about trauma. It was believed that the lesson needed to have very clear constraints to ensure a feeling of safety for everyone in the room. Ideally, the focus should be on ensemble-building

DOI: 10.4324/9781003079835-3

and envisioning what community could mean in the future. We ultimately opted for simplicity:

- Write down a list of things you needed, wanted, and loved on September 10.
- Now write down a second list of things you needed, wanted, and loved on September 11.
- Finally make a list of things you imagine you will need, want, and love a year from now.

The students share out their lists as the teaching artist scribes the words on the board. Together the group reads the words out loud. The teaching artist facilitates a class discussion about how best to arrange the words into a group poem. Once the order is set, students are assigned lines, and the class performs the poem. Time permitting and at the desire of the classroom teacher, the students can then use the poem as the foundation upon which to build tableaux, movement sequences, or songs.

By the morning of September 13, those 20 artists were in classrooms all across the city. Ron was one of the first.

RON RUSSELL, EPIC FOUNDER/EXECUTIVE DIRECTOR: A lot of what they wanted and loved on September 10 seemed banal and self-centered, like French fries and shopping and sleep. Those things came up again in the list of what they wanted for the future, but they were combined with words like hope and peace and safety. The idea was, "I'll get back to being me, but it will be a wiser me who wants more than just my immediate needs fulfilled."

Melissa visited 25 classrooms over five days.

MELISSA FRIEDMAN: After 9/11, many theatre-makers questioned the validity of their lives and their art. "What am I doing?" Some of them chose to leave New York City or leave the arts altogether. Going into classrooms in those first few days after and having these incredible healing, creative, community-building experiences, I felt it showcased the best of humanity. The resilience. The ability to find humor. I remember feeling moments of joy. I remember thinking, "Are we the only people in New York City feeling joy today?" Everything was about finding and building community. I felt buoyed and confirmed in this belief that theatre could be something that strengthens and heals us.

By Friday, September 14, Epic's curriculum was distributed to all NYC Public Schools. It was a defining first week.

Over the past 20 years, all of us at Epic, with the support and assistance of numerous partners and collaborators, have sought to reimagine and redefine an Epic Theatre for the 21st Century that builds human bridges between Public School classrooms, professional stages, and civic centers. Throughout the pages of this book, you'll hear from several of these bridge-builders.

Some of them are members of Epic's professional ensemble. Some of them are the youth researchers/writers/performers/leaders of Epic NEXT. All of them are Citizen Artists.

JIM: ***What impact do you think it has on young people to be mentored by and to make work with professional artists?***

RON RUSSELL: Recently in the New York City Public Schools, we've been talking about Social Emotional Learning (SEL). The tricky thing about SELs is that they are metacognitive modes of thinking. Sometimes people get confused and think that you can teach SELs. I just had this conversation about "How do we teach teachers to teach SELs?" You can't teach an SEL, it's a modality, a way of working, not a set of skills. Self-advocacy, grit: these aren't things that you can directly teach. They're metacognitive lessons that young people learn by working with people who give them rigorous relevant content in an empathetic and joyous delivery system. They learn similar to the way a baby learns. A baby learns language from hearing people speak it; a baby learns how to eat by watching people eat. You really can't teach it. You have to demonstrate it. I learned this very early from my most important mentor Eric Booth in a speech he gave about the nature of self-reflection. Eric was saying that very few academic content forms require self-reflection to actually learn them. You can learn historical events without a lot of self-reflection on where you fit into them. You can take yourself out of the equation and understand the French Revolution. It's certainly true of geometry and science. The arts require you to build your own reflection and metrics of success. If you're trying to play a G on the guitar, you don't just look at where your fingers go. You know how it's supposed to sound. It might even sound slightly different than the way that your teacher did it. You develop the G that you want to hear. You work on it until it becomes second nature until it's something that you can do without the cognitive moment of actually thinking, "I'm going to play a G now". It becomes a metacognitive reality for you. That mode of learning and learning to use that mode creates a level of growth and growth mindset about what you can do, and how you can learn, and the depth with which you can analyze things that no other subject teaches. You really have to watch someone else do it. I guess you could learn guitar from reading a book, but it would be very difficult because you wouldn't have the idea of what is the standard that I am trying to achieve. What is the objective standard and what is my subjective standard that I'm applying to that? Without those standards, learning can get very rote and it doesn't impact those SELs. Without the arts in young people's lives, they don't have a lot of chances to learn that modality and that form of self-reflection. Without mentors they can learn it, but not very deeply because they're not watching someone else do it.

MELISSA FRIEDMAN: The unique value of teaching artists in the classroom has a lot to do with authenticity and the opportunity for students to have a bridge to the outside world. Artists think outside the box. Theatre artists are particularly strong in terms of empathy and being able to look at things from multiple perspectives. They can creatively problem-solve. They often bring a great deal of humor and joy and passion into the room. They're actively engaged in their own learning and development. A lot of times the teachers that students encounter in the classroom convey a sense of "I am an expert and I am disseminating information so that you can be assessed on that information of which I am an expert." Though artists have expertise in terms of their skills and experience, they also can communicate the belief that we're inventing everything and learning together. The best teaching artists are comfortable with an "I don't know." That can be a really empowering paradigm shift for young people – to embrace that "I don't know." I think having a direct connection to a professional model of working is also really exciting for students. I think the reason that I have loved being a teaching artist for 30 years is also that there's an irreverent rebellious act to it. A sense of, "I'm going to help you learn about the rules and the structure, but I'm also going to encourage you to break those rules." That doesn't really happen a lot in Middle Schools and High Schools in their everyday instruction, but so much a part of what it means to be a leader is recognizing the rules and learning how and when to challenge them and break them. It's a rebellious and irreverent act to go into the classroom. At the same time, we partner with teachers and schools – they're down with it. We're not rebelling against a specific individual school, but just the notion of school as an indoctrination tool.

GODFREY L. SIMMONS, JR., EPIC ASSOCIATE ARTIST: What's great about students working with teaching artists is they get to learn by doing the thing and they're making deep connections to their everyday lives. As a teaching artist, you're not their full-time teacher. You're just in there for the gig. There's a beauty in that. The students see, "Oh this person works and they're earning money for doing their art and they're also doing other stuff outside of this and they're onstage with me playing my dad in Hamlet." You're showing them how to master something. It doesn't have to be about mastering the art. You're sharing with them a structure, a discipline, a set of skills for creative problem solving. Teaching artists provide a constructive cognitive dissonance for people who are caught in systems where they are either oppressed or they are oppressing. There's something that teaching artists bring that's necessary to help young people grapple with tough choices.

MARILYN TORRES, EPIC ASSOCIATE ARTIST: It's very very important that people see that it is possible to have a life in the arts. It's very important that they understand what a true artist is. In their minds, they think being an artist is being a star. A movie star, a basketball star. The only way to be an artist is to be a star and being a star isn't attainable. When they interact with a teaching artist they get to see what a live artist looks like and that it isn't just about being a star. In fact, most times it's not. The artist becomes something real and attainable when you learn that your teaching artist works in TV, film, and theater; that your teaching artist is also a writer and producer. They learn all the levels of what being an artist is and all the different jobs in the field that are open to them. They learn that being an artist is how you define it and how you will use your art to impact the world. The teaching artist is a real-life example of what is possible for them. The teaching artist is the bridge between the spark of "Oh, I may want to do this" and actually doing it. When you walk in the room, they see somebody that looks like them, that sounds like them, that relates to them, that loves them. It's magical. I'm a person of color so that's very present for me. I come from a group that doesn't really matter on a bigger scale. The arts help young people to know that they matter. Their voice matters. Their bodies matter. The space they take up – a lot of young people don't feel that they're entitled to the chair that they're sitting in. They don't know how to self-advocate. So when you walk in and say, "I want to know what you have to offer," that's the beginning of them knowing that somebody is interested, that they can sound the way they sound, they can look the way they look, they can move the way they move and know that they are awesome just the way they are.

AARON KROHN, EPIC ASSOCIATE ARTIST: You're helping young people become Citizen Artists. The theatrical pursuit that is so vivid in improv of acceptance; looking to your partner; thinking they are a genius, and looking out. Look, see, find, play. Helping them do that. Getting them to realize they can be themselves and getting them to be curious and looking out – that's good acting and a healthy approach to life.

VERN THIESSEN, EPIC ASSOCIATE ARTIST: Young people often don't feel that they have a voice. They don't have a voice at home. They certainly don't have a voice at school. I think it's really important to activate and empower their voices. Words have power. Words can change a kid's life. I've seen it over and over and over again – when you allow them to find their voice through theatre, and for me as a playwright, that has primarily to do with words, you see them become powerful. I want them to find the power of theatre and to use it.

NILAJA SUN, EPIC ASSOCIATE ARTIST: There is no better way for students to deeply understand and absorb how history affects people. You can tell students over and over again that the census affects them – you can say it till the cows come home – but if they happen to do a piece on the census and they can see all of the aspects of it and then how their characters are affected, then they see how they're affected. They clearly get how they're a part of history, which is so important when you're working with disenfranchised communities where no one has told them this.

DEVIN E. HAQQ, EPIC ASSOCIATE ARTIST: It's helping them find their voice. I think more students have an "in" to that awakening through something that is artistic because it's fun and creative. It's getting them to use their ideas and then allowing them to see their ideas placed at the forefront.

MICHELLE BECK, EPIC ASSOCIATE ARTIST: I think it helps kids feel seen and when you feel seen you have more confidence in yourself. You have more assuredness on the basis of who you are. I believe we desperately need that for Black and Brown students. White students have a lot of positive reinforcement, a lot of icons to look up to. There's a support system in our society for white students that I don't see existing for Black and Brown students. It's not about making students swallow a doctrine, it's about giving them a mirror so they can see themselves and they can have confidence in themselves and they can see the value that they bring to the world.

AIMÉ DONNA KELLY, FORMER EPIC STUDENT; EPIC ASSOCIATE ARTIST: I was a Freshman in High School. I thought that all I wanted to do was be a performer. And then 9/11 happened. And then you all came into my school and told us, "Here's an outlet to actually speak about these feelings." It always felt like the students were speaking first. We were the ones sharing what we felt, what we knew, and more importantly what we wanted to say. That was it. That was the beginning of everything. I made work with professional artists. I saw that you all respected what we had to say and treated us as artists not necessarily just students. That's always stayed with me, even when I went to University of the Arts. The way that I viewed my professors – it wasn't through the lens of you all are on this tier that I can't reach; it was, we're colleagues. I've always viewed the work through that lens and that started with you all.

MARK HARRIS, EPIC ASSOCIATE ARTIST: The opportunity to work with professionals and then to be treated like professionals are holding students to a high standard. That's a pretty big benefit to students, not only in advancing their work, but also to their self-esteem and sense of worth. It's important for them to get a glimpse at what professional artists do.

ANTHONY VAUGHN MERCHANT, EPIC ASSOCIATE ARTIST: If you can start where someone else finished then your ability to progress can go that much further. On a strictly technical level, I can tell you why this joke works. I will break it down for you seven different ways from Sunday so that you don't have to reinvent that wheel. This is why it works. This is why you need to take two steps and then open the door instead of taking three steps and open the door. There are some things that are like, "Bro, I technically got you here." Let me just start you off ahead of the game.

AUBREY SAVERINO, EPIC ASSOCIATE ARTIST: Teaching artists are infused with an intense passion and excitement for the craft and for sharing that passion and excitement with students. The students get a window into the professional world of what it means to be an artist. I see students' confidence skyrocket. I see students' ability to collaborate skyrocket. Those two skills alone would benefit anyone working in any job.

DEBRA MORRIS, EPIC OPERATIONS MANAGER: Learning a craft can be so much about turning inward. In the midst of considering your own artistry, you can lose sight of your place in a larger artistic context. As you enter the industry, there is pressure to do things that have been successful for many other people. Working alongside professional artists who have legitimacy and who are singular in their approach to the work can help young people find their own identity and their own way of working.

NATALIE PAUL, EPIC ASSOCIATE ARTIST: Too often young people are told that they are so far away from where they want to be and that where they want to be is surrounded by these tall concrete walls that are unscalable with spikes at the top and when you get over that wall you have to look a certain way and have a certain family background and have a certain tone in your voice, whether it's super-chipper or inexplicably deep. All of those ideas and constructs are thrown at young artists on a daily basis. At Epic, we create a unique atmosphere that brings those walls down, demystifies what artists do, and makes it clear to young people that their dreams are, in fact, realistic.

SARIN MONAE WEST, EPIC ASSOCIATE ARTIST: My drive toward being an artist and a teacher is to dream society forward. Teaching artistry allows young people to be able to see artists actively creating their own work while learning skills that are actually being practiced in the industry. It puts breath and body behind really complex ideas and makes them approachable. For young people, it's really important to be able to see themselves reflected back to them to be able to make their dreams occupy that space.

CLARO DE LOS REYES, EPIC ASSOCIATE ARTIST: There are many ways to learn and I think teaching artistry is there to offer something to different intelligences. If you are a kinesthetic learner, if you are a different type of learner, it's going to be a welcoming space for articulating yourself in a different way without any judgment. It also opens up different topics of exploration. Only recently in this country, has there been an attempt at decolonizing the curriculum. Because teaching artistry comes from a different side of the spectrum, it brings with it a vast opportunity to bring in different source material: primary sources or interviews or found texts from sources that aren't as commonly used in school curriculum. We've been haunted by the biases of education which are directly related to the biases of this country.

JACOB MING-TRENT, EPIC ASSOCIATE ARTIST: I'm less interested if the student I'm in front of becomes an artist. I'm more thinking about the student who is going to become a nurse, or a doctor, or a police officer, or a politician, or a teacher. Working with them, building their imagination, expanding what they believe is possible – taking that into their professions will make them better at whatever they choose to do. In today's world, the world is moving so fast and changing constantly, it takes people who are flexible, who can be like water, who can be imaginative at problem solving and I think working with artists definitely can help folks do that. To be 15, 16, 17 years old and to build a piece of work that absolutely has an impact on society: if you're doing that at that age, what are you going to be able to do ten or twenty years down the road when you feel empowered?

BRANDT ADAMS, EPIC ASSOCIATE ARTIST: A teaching artist draws students into an incredibly fruitful, exciting, and important conversation and shows them that they have a place in that conversation.

ABEL SANTIAGO, FORMER EPIC STUDENT; EPIC APPRENTICE: It's genuine learning. Going to Public School all my life, I was conditioned to just be like, "Yeah. Yeah. Yeah. Yeah." Just nodding, saying yes. Being fed all this information and getting graded for pretending that I was listening. In school, no one ever asked me what I thought. But over the summers with Epic, we're given a chance to voice what we think, what we need to say and what we feel. Now I'm way more outspoken and I'm able to find my voice in rooms in college and everywhere.

DALISSA DURAN, FORMER EPIC STUDENT; EPIC APPRENTICE: It's nice to meet adults who care about you. My mentor was so attentive and aware when I was uncomfortable and taught me how to be more comfortable with myself. I thought, "This woman really cares about me and my growth as a young artist and a young woman." It was fundamental to my growth. You show these kids that there are nice people out there. It's like they're saying, "I think you're worth it. I'm gifted and talented and I see that you're gifted and talented."

XAVIER PACHECO, FORMER EPIC STUDENT; EPIC ASSOCIATE ARTIST: It changed my life entirely. I think that's why I was drawn to become a teaching artist, because I felt the effect it had on me as a student. I was seen in a way that I had never been before. I was given the reins to my own process. I had never been given the liberty to express myself in that way before. I wanted to be able to speak to someone on a personal level about what it meant to be a professional. At Epic, the learning is structured around a two-way development – something that I didn't understand went two ways until I became a mentor. Building a genuine relationship with an adult that gave me the time, because in class there's no time. With Epic, you can really take the time to know someone as an individual, what their story is, what their process is. It's a life-long journey. We're building partnerships for life.

SADE OGUNJIMI, FORMER EPIC STUDENT AND APPRENTICE; EPIC PRODUCING ASSOCIATE: I felt very important getting to work with people who were working professionals in this industry who were so interested in what I had to say. I was treated like an intellectual with thoughts. It was very engaging. It was really nice to see people of color in those positions. My friends and I would always say, "The only way to get out of the hood was to become a rapper or an athlete." Seeing all those teaching artists with Epic was the first exposure I had to seeing what you could do with art. The world felt really small at the time, but meeting all those teaching artists, my world got a little bit bigger every day.

MEKHI TUDOR, EPIC ALUM AND RESEARCHER/WRITER/PERFORMER ON *PERFECT CIRCLE:* Being acknowledged by professional artists is a one-of-a-kind experience. It makes the work so much more meaningful.

LUAN TAVERAS, EPIC ALUM AND RESEARCHER/WRITER/PERFORMER ON *DEFAULT:* You get a sense of what being an artist is. You're getting the real thing. Working with professional artists grounded me. I know now that I want to do this. I know what it takes. My techniques and my process have been built through the years working with you.

LIZETTE PADUA, EPIC ALUM AND RESEARCHER/WRITER/PERFORMER ON *OVERDRIVE:* Epic is like a family. Our mentors understand aspects of what we go through. My mentors understood where I came from. Where I was born and how you're judged off of that.

Figure 2.1 Lizette Padua performing a scene from *Nothing About Us* at the Diverse Charter Schools Coalition Annual Convening in Washington, DC.

Source: Photo courtesy of Diverse Charter Schools Coalition.

3 What is Epic Theatre?

We're sometimes asked by those not familiar with our work if Epic produces a lot of plays by Bertolt Brecht. We've actually never done one of Brecht's plays either on an Off-Broadway stage, in a developmental workshop, or in any of our education programs. When people hear Epic Theatre, they often think about early 20th-Century artists like Brecht, Piscator, Meyerhold, and concepts like verfremdungseffekt or "alienation effect," but our company's name was inspired by an idea that we think was proffered by the playwright Edward Bond (although none of Epic's Founders can find any evidence attributing this definition to Bond or anyone else, nor where or when he or they might have said it). Bond (perhaps) suggested that Epic theatre — theatre that is capable of driving true civic action — exists at the nexus where psychology meets history. Both Brecht and Bond can certainly be counted among our artistic antecedents in a continuum that includes Henrik Ibsen, George Bernard Shaw, Arthur Miller, Howard Barker, María Irene Fornés, Caryl Churchill, Anna Deavere Smith, Suzan-Lori Parks, and Dominique Morisseau.

The plays made by Citizen Artists have a job to do. In fact, they have several: to engage, to question, to challenge, to inform, to empower, to illuminate, to inspire, and *yes*, to entertain. Best-selling author and world-renowned teaching artist Eric Booth identifies a key difference between art and entertainment.

ERIC BOOTH: Entertainment is not the opposite of art — please Lord don't let entertainment be the enemy of art, be opposed to art in any way, or we are goners. What distinguishes entertainment is that it happens within what we already know. Whatever your response to the entertainment presentation — laughing, crying, getting excited — underneath the surface, it confirms. Entertainment says, "Yes, the world is the way you think it is." It feels great to have your worldview confirmed in the many dynamic, imaginative, exciting ways our entertainment industries provide. Art, on the other hand, happens outside of what you already know. Inherent in the artistic experience is the capacity to expand your sense of the way the world is or might be. The art lives in an individual's

DOI: 10.4324/9781003079835-4

capacity to engage in that fundamental act of creativity – expanding the sense of the possible – every bit as much as the art resides in the what's being observed.

A great work of Epic Theatre should allow opportunities for an audience to laugh, cry, think, learn, and talk. It allows artists and audiences to see themselves and their histories in the play, while at the same time inviting them to immerse themselves in other people's lives and other people's perspectives to make important socio-political questions come alive. With 5 actors. And no sets. Or lights. Or costumes. Ideally in 30 minutes or less.

So how should a play like that look, sound, and feel? Here are some of the qualities that describe dynamic Epic Theatre.

It's Epic if it:

1 **Engages in a theatrical exploration of an essential question**
   The process begins with a big, challenging question that, when thoroughly explored, leads to asking other big, challenging questions that require thoughtful consideration by diverse members of a community. Your essential question should be one for which the ensemble doesn't yet have a complete and satisfying answer. If your question isn't interesting to the ensemble, you're going to have a tough time making a play that's interesting to an audience. Pick a new question. If your question is one that the ensemble can quickly answer with certainty, you're going to have a tough time convincing an audience to spend much time deeply considering it. Pick a new question. Your question should inspire the ensemble and the audience to seek out and dig deep for answers. The play is an investigation: sincere curiosity is required to do this work.

2 **Demands multiple acts of transformation**
   There is no scenery, no lighting effects, no make-up or costumes in the production of these plays. The stagecraft is entirely created through the intersection of the physical instruments of the actors and the minds of the audience members. The actors transform their faces, voices, and bodies to portray a diverse set of characters. With only five performers and a rich world of viewpoints to represent, each actor has to play multiple people with enough specificity and precision to make each character distinct from every other character that actor portrays. The ensemble transforms the space from a school auditorium (often among the least theatrical structures on the planet), lecture hall, library, classroom, conference room, cafeteria, street corner, or bowling alley into a theatre. Audience members receive multiple invitations before, after, and during the show to transform their roles from passive observers to active participants in the dialogue.

3 **Makes room for and gives voice to multiple points of view**
   Honoring voices of dissent is what keeps Epic Theatre from becoming agitprop. These plays are not prescriptive or partisan. They give voice and weight to a wide range of opinions and ideally, every member of

the audience should be able to find themselves in the story. Through this process, the essential question's full complexity emerges in ways that would be impossible with the linear forms of communication more familiar to most social-justice advocacy.

4 **Is driven by ideological conflict**

These are unapologetically plays of ideas. Volatile family dynamics, blossoming romantic relationships, and deep analysis of psychological abnormalities can all be extremely exciting subjects to watch unfold in a play and they can certainly find their way into a work of Epic Theatre. However, Citizen Artists utilize these subjects as a way of illuminating different aspects of their essential question. Educational segregation can indeed have a profound impact on the relationship between a parent and a child or a couple in their first weeks of dating. High-stakes standardized tests can inflict trauma on a student that leads to severe psychological problems. In the tradition of playwrights like Henrik Ibsen, George Bernard Shaw, Caryl Churchill, Suzan-Lori Parks, and Dominique Morisseau: Citizen Artists show us how the personal informs the political.

5 **Is powered by ethical dilemma**

If ideological conflict is the vehicle for the drama, ethical dilemma is the fuel. These plays frequently examine the civic consequences of personal compromise. Many oppressive systems are made up of and supported by pockets of thoughtful, conflicted individuals making difficult, sometimes heart-wrenching, choices in the interest of protecting themselves and their families. Citizen Artists identify these stakeholders in a system and employ deep empathy to articulate the weight, conflict, and consequences of the choices they make.

6 **Analyzes and deciphers coded language**

Large institutions frequently create intricate webs of complex and specialized jargon in order to control their messages and to manage the behaviors of employees and constituents. Manners of speech quickly become manners of thought. Citizen Artists interview specialists from fields connected to their inquiry to identify common institutional euphemisms, clichés, and coded language so they can decipher the subtext and intent that lie behind the words.

7 **Shows the work**

Epic NEXT student artists build their plays in part from research conducted through audio-recorded interviews. That research is presented to the audience through the verbatim performance of selected excerpts from the interview transcripts (Verbatim Theatre is a theatrical form popularized over the last thirty years by artists such as Anna Deavere Smith, David Hare, Moises Kaufman, and companies like London's Joint Stock Theatre and New York City's The Civilians). The excerpted interview material is not hidden inside the drama or presented in a radically different context for the purposes of linear storytelling. The voices from the interviews exist adjacent to the play's "plot" and comment directly on the play's essential question, not unlike a Greek Chorus.

8   **Employs direct address**

This isn't a movie. There is no "fourth wall." We're all in the room together. The actors frequently speak directly to members of the audience and there are ample opportunities provided for audience members to engage in dialogue before, after, and sometimes during the performance. You will never hear an introduction for an Epic NEXT show that includes the cliché, "Sit back, relax, and enjoy the show." We're much more likely to invite you to lean in, engage, and chew on this for a while.

9   **Honors silence and stillness**

In a fast-paced, 30-minute play swollen with words and questions and perspectives and ideas, there can be immense power and profundity in a well-crafted frozen tableau or an extended period of silence. These can allow an audience a moment to breathe or allow an ensemble to take the audience's breath away, or in rare magical moments to allow both to happen at the same time!

10 **Encourages dialogue**

These plays are intentionally designed to spark a civic conversation. The running time is kept at 30 minutes or less to allow plenty of time for the audience to identify the themes that resonate most with them, share their own experiences, and ask questions about the creative process and the writers' intentions. It is not uncommon for an audience to engage in a post-show conversation that lasts longer than the show itself. This is a good thing. This is not your grandma's run-of-the-mill, community theatre matinee talk back. We have never once had an audience member at one of our Epic NEXT post-show discussions ask that dreaded talk-back standard, "How did you learn all those lines?". Nor has an Epic NEXT audience member ever raised their hand under the pretense of asking a question and then launched into a monologue about the play they wish they'd seen that night. My response for that stalwart of the Off-Broadway talkback is usually, "Thanks. Please go home immediately and write that play and let the rest of us finish talking about this one." The conversations that take place after a great work of Epic Theatre are not at all like that. These discussions are rigorous and urgent and meaningful and joyful.

JACOB MING-TRENT: Epic Theatre is immediate. It always feels of the moment. It's an answer to the question how do you make theatre essential? If you're in a household on a fixed budget with some disposable income, how do you convince a family to use some of that disposable income on theatre? Epic says this is immediate; this is going to have a direct impact on your life. You're going to hear ideas expressed that are going to edify you in such a way that it will be worth it to spend your time and money here.

Figure 3.1 Epic NEXT students Esmirna Matos, Miladys Sanchez, Luan Taveras, Chrisaury
Guzman, and Shaena Gibson perform *Nothing About Us* at an event for Californians
for Justice in San Jose, California.

Source: James Wallert/photo courtesy of Epic Theatre Ensemble.

VERN THIESSEN: That connection to community is everything, otherwise
all it is, is a business transaction. If you look at Broadway, it's a business
transaction. You're paying for a ticket; you're getting a piece of entertainment. Connecting art to community really has an opportunity for
artists to raise specific questions about their community and to reflect
it back to the community who are watching them. Playwrights are the
lightning rods for that conversation. We are the people that provide the
spark to make sure that conversation can happen between the artists and
the community that they're trying to speak to or reflect.

NATALIE PAUL: You have to inspire the students to think bigger. This play
is not just a play. It's going to change minds. It's going to transform
the world. The play itself has agency. The plays we create at Epic are
never casual. They might speak to the heart. They will have moments
of extreme vulnerability and humanity but the plays are always serving
a larger mission of being change agents in the world. We have a mission,
we're not just doing this for fun. We're about to change some lives.

MICHELLE BECK: An Epic play doesn't let anyone off the hook. An Epic play
is asking really hard complicated nuanced questions without any easy
answers. It's not a scoop of gelato – an Epic play is a full rich meal that
you have to masticate and digest.

4 How do we work with Commissioning Partners?

Theatre is the most beautifully inefficient art form there is. It takes a dedicated group of passionate artists putting massive amounts of time, energy, rigor, and money into a story so that a relatively small group of people can have a shared experience in the same room together. A play is not an efficient vehicle for delivering a message to a mass audience. In fact, amidst a sea of high speed, cable, 5G, streaming, instant, on-demand entertainment options, a play is a rowboat. With a leaky bottom. That you're paddling with a chicken. Theatre is not a tool for mass communication, but I believe it's the art form with the greatest potential for individual transformation. For those of us who have chosen to make theatre our lives, this prospect for profound and lasting change is what keeps us energized, but the day-to-day practicalities of the profession can sometimes feel isolating and demoralizing. Sometimes they don't show up. Sometimes they don't get it. Sometimes they walk out at intermission. Sometimes they slowly unwrap a limitless collection of cellophane-encased hard candies while you're trying to tear a passion to tatters. The most valuable resource any artist can have is a supportive community of collaborators and champions.

If you've identified dialogue as an important "why" of your work, as Epic has, then the next logical step is to focus on the "who." With which groups or communities do you want to converse? "Everyone" can be a tempting first answer to that question. "Everyone needs to see your play," said every theatre-maker's mother after every show always. Maternal enthusiasm aside, I've found this paradox to be true: the more specific you can be about who your play is for, the greater opportunity your work will have of reaching a larger and more passionate audience. An audience member that is deeply connected to the content of a particular play is more likely to see themselves in that play, find deeper meaning in that play, and in best scenarios, become a more active champion for that play and a future collaborator on others. Matt Gonzales is a brilliant education policy expert and one of Epic's great friends and partners.

MATT GONZALES, FOUNDER AND DIRECTOR OF THE INTEGRATION AND INNOVATION INITIATIVE (I3) AT NYU METROPOLITAN CENTER FOR RESEARCH ON EQUITY AND TRANSFORMATION OF SCHOOLS: I first

DOI: 10.4324/9781003079835-5

experienced Epic as a graduate student at Teachers College at Columbia. I was watching the performance of *10467* in 2015 and I was really blown away by the work and the research of the young people. At that point, I didn't know what my professional work was going to look like. I was just a graduate student writing about race, equity, and segregation, but I've always been committed to amplifying and elevating youth voice. So, when I got a job at New York Appleseed directing their advocacy and policy on school integration, I was like, "What's the name of that organization that did *10467*? I've got to figure out who they are because I want to collaborate with them." And literally the same day, Jim emailed to ask me for an interview for the show that ended up being *Laundry City*. I remember going in for the interview and after it was over I was like, "I love everything you do. I want to collaborate with you." That was the beginning of us commissioning work together and building relationships with all the students, and the whole team at Epic. It's been awesome. Each time I get an email or a call from Jim I know something dope is going to happen.

The plays created by Epic NEXT are all commissions from partner organizations. Because our focus has been placing student artists at the center of a conversation about educational justice, all these institutional allies share a common interest in reimagining how schools serve students, families, and communities. Our Commissioning Partners represent a diverse range of disciplines, which include social justice advocacy groups, university research centers, legal service agencies, and arts education organizations. Their constituents provide the stories, experiences, and perspectives at the center of the play.

Commissioning Partners also support the process through a number of key actions:

- Providing early project funding through their commission
- Suggesting the general topic of the play and a direction for the initial research
- Sharing insights into the most salient moral and ethical questions being dealt with by members of their field today
- Networking within their professional circles to help secure interview guests
- Giving feedback to the ensemble during script development
- Identifying venues and audiences for performances
- Promoting the project and performances throughout the tour

The relationship is a true collaboration. Commissioning Partners commit to making connections between the ensemble and social justice allies in their field. The ensemble honors that commitment by writing and presenting a work of art that communicates aspects of their organization's mission and working values to the world. Ideal community partners bring a passion for civic dialogue that includes youth voice, a willingness to collaborate on an artistic process, and access to diverse constituencies eager to engage in a conversation. For the artists, there's an authenticity and immediacy to this kind of work because you are making it with and for the audiences you most want to reach.

At Epic, we don't have a set formula or process for identifying Commissioning Partners. Mr. Rogers, in one of his most quoted observations, encouraged young people to respond to their fears by looking for the helpers. That's a great place from which to start your search for a partner. When you figure out the problem that you want your work to address, ask yourself: who are the professional helpers who have chosen to make solving this problem their life's work? Reach out to these folks and let them know that you'd like to collaborate with them to make art that is part of the solution. In the parlance of Mr. Rogers, you want to help the helpers. David Tipson from New York Appleseed has passionately supported partnerships with Epic on both *Laundry City* and *Nothing About Us*.

DAVID TIPSON, EXECUTIVE DIRECTOR, NEW YORK APPLESEED: The whole movement nationally had been struggling with how to communicate the need for school integration to the general public. You wouldn't know this from reading *The New York Times*, but there's a lot of ambivalence about integration in communities of color and it's totally legitimate. There were things that happened in the Twentieth Century that were not in the best interest of people that were supposed to be helped by integration programs. All of those feelings are legitimate. We live in a polarized world today. There has to be room for people to think and not just sign on to one side or the other. I haven't seen any communication strategy better than *Laundry City* for acknowledging these very legitimate concerns that parents of color and communities of color have. It does something that only art can do. It gets us away from these simplistic binaries and acknowledges and explores a lot of different perspectives at the same time. Every member of the audience can find somebody in that play that they can say, "Oh, I kind of identify with her way of looking at things."

MATT GONZALES: When I first started this work a few years ago, integration and desegregation were being talked about in so many different directions. There wasn't a common set of definitions or ideas. Part of the role that Epic played was helping to bring the conversation into communities that had not historically had these conversations. People in Bed-Stuy or in Harlem were experiencing segregation and gentrification but no one had ever said, "What do you think about this issue?" There's a difference between me as a policy nerd coming in and saying, "Hey let's talk about segregation" and having young people come and speak their truth from a place that's grounded in their own research, their own experiences, and their own expertise. *Laundry City* helped to build a more comprehensive

Figure 4.1 Matt Gonzales from NYU Metro Center with Epic NEXT students Jeremiah Green, Jr., Davion Osbourne, Olivia Dunbar, Kyora Wallace, and Randy Figueroa before a performance of *Laundry City* at the American Educational Research Association Annual Meeting in San Antonio, Texas.

Source: James Wallert/photo courtesy of Epic Theatre Ensemble.

narrative around the issue of school segregation and integration. It built public awareness in a way that I never could. It helped us center the public policy work in youth voices across the city.

DAVID TIPSON: We're not trying to tell you what to think. We're saying not only do we believe this, but we're going to put it right out in front of you and we're even going to put some perspectives out there that don't necessarily align with the ones that we have. I think that shows a certain amount of confidence in not only our work but also in the community's ability to help us solve these problems.

CLARO DE LOS REYES: Through partnering with social justice organizations you're getting folks who are sharing an analysis of the world. Whether you agree with it or disagree with it is beside the point. Anytime students are exposed to people who can articulate their analysis of the world, that's going to benefit them.

MICHELLE BECK: For a lot of students, these are the first adults they have met who are not there to tell them what to do or how to do it. They're not their parents, they're not their families, they're not their teachers, they're not their babysitters. They are talking to them like adults; they are treating them with respect and dignity. It's shocking how that is a new experience for them – particularly students of color.

LUAN TAVERAS: Working with these adults inspired me to think more about what I'm doing. What steps am I taking to be a better contributing member of my society? How does my work impact the world? How can I make change? We need a lot of change. We all have the responsibility to create a better world.

GODFREY L. SIMMONS, JR.: For young people, they begin to understand that their world – what they're going through and how they behave and their actions – have reverberations beyond their community. You need to live and act with intention at all times. Your community is larger than just the Bronx or East Harlem.

RON RUSSELL: You have to be serious about the professional relationship that you're building. In the Epic NEXT process, the students are watching the building of a relationship with the outside world. We're making a relationship with people who know more than we do about the topic. They see adults making a relationship with folks outside of the organization and saying, "We're going to learn from these people; they have expertise." One of the things that is frustrating is when a student is insistent that they're not going to listen to the interviews; they're going to make their own thing. They just want to be creative. The creativity is not actually what we're trying to teach. We're trying to teach listening to people that have expertise, learning from them, and then helping them amplify what they have to say to a different audience in a different mode so people can hear it who normally wouldn't hear it. TED Talks were revolutionary because they specifically asked people with incredible expertise who had to put it in a way so anyone could understand it. That's the goal: to spread the idea. Really think about how you want to get these ideas into other people's minds. That's really hard to do. I think it empowers the students' voices, but it empowers them to understand themselves as a crucial part of a community or team. They're sort of the communicators of the team's ideas, which is perhaps the most important part of all, so they feel a great sense of pride when they craft a message, deliver it, and it's received. That's a key Epic value that a lot of youth organizations don't share: we're not just interested in one student's empowerment in a vacuum. We're interested in growing the team.

5 How do we create a safe and Culturally Responsive space?

In 2019, The Southern Poverty Law Center released a report titled, "Hate at School." The researchers analyzed data gathered from K–12 educator surveys and news media reports and found a surge in incidents involving racial slurs and symbols, anti-LGBTQ language, bigotry, and the harassment of minority students. A total of 69 percent of these incidents occurred in spaces where adults were present. Most of the hate incidents witnessed by teachers went unaddressed by school leadership. Nine times out of ten, school administrators failed to denounce the bias or use the opportunity to reaffirm their school's values.[1]

The American education system and the American Theatre, like most institutions in the United States that predate the end of Jim Crow, weren't designed to be accessible for everyone. They were actually built to segregate. Until white people in positions of power within these institutions acknowledge this history and commit to dismantling or transforming any remaining structures of oppression, it's unlikely that they're going to be part of the solution.

As a straight white man running a youth development program that primarily serves students of color, it's my responsibility to self-reflect daily on how effectively inclusive and anti-racist my practice is. I have to think deeply and critically about the texts I use for teaching. It's vital that I'm aware of my privilege and provide space and time for the artists and students around me to challenge any aspect of my language, behavior, or curriculum that they find problematic.

Culturally responsive-sustaining framework

Culture and life experience play a huge role in the way people learn. For decades, school leaders have employed racist admissions policies, curriculum centered around white European cultural norms, standardized tests that embrace the narrowest methods to measure students, and severe discipline codes to punish and exclude Black and Brown students. It's the duty of thoughtful, anti-racist educators to foster a learning environment that acknowledges and celebrates the culture, knowledge, and experiences of everyone in the room; to embrace difference rather than punish it.

DOI: 10.4324/9781003079835-6

In 2019, our partners in the New York City Department of Education launched an educational strategy that embraces students' identities called Culturally Responsive-Sustaining Education (CR-SE). It is a way of seeing diversity as a source of knowledge. From their website: "With CR-SE, students use their own identity to get education. They learn using aspects of their race, social class, gender, language, sexual orientation, nationality, religion, or ability. Studies show that students learning with CR-SE are more active in class. They graduate more often, with better grades. Their self-esteem improves, and they become better citizens."[2]

The play *Default* is a theatrical exploration of CR-SE and the Ethnic Studies movement. For educators who might feel uncertain about how to begin to create an atmosphere of cultural responsiveness, the text of *Default* itself provides an excellent set of discussion questions to use on the first day of class to get a sense of who is in the room:

1   With what culture or cultures do you identify?
2   What's one thing that you know about your culture?
3   What's one thing that you'd like everyone else to know about your culture?

It should go without saying that if you're going to pose these questions, everyone in the room, both the students *and* the adults, should answer them. In my own practice as a teaching artist, I make it a point never to ask students to do anything I'm not comfortable doing myself. At Epic, the expectation is that every artist needs to be comfortable having open conversations about race, culture, and identity.

MICHELLE BECK: I can sense when a person, particularly a white person, feels uncomfortable having a conversation around race. It's this little trigger that goes off – it's like my Spidey-Sense. I just know that if that person is not comfortable speaking about race, I cannot fully be in the room with them. I can't fully be honest with them. I can't fully be present with them. I can't relax. I will always be on guard. That doesn't mean that person has to know everything or have all the answers. It just means that they need to be willing to have the conversation. That willingness makes all the difference in the world.

MATT GONZALES: I have no patience for any teacher who's like, "Oh, I'm uncomfortable talking about race." I don't care. In New York City classrooms, your kids are 70 percent Black and Brown. You need to learn how to talk about race. You need to learn how to create an inclusive space. I'm sorry. That's not acceptable to me. I refuse to allow that to exist in our schools because the violence – the intellectual violence that gets done to kids is damaging and it can break a kid. And it can turn their trajectory in a bad direction. There's training in implicit bias. There is training in anti-racism. There is training in culturally responsive education.

There's training in restorative justice. Being an anti-racist teacher is not rocket science. It takes a little bit of intention, a little practice. It requires the archeology of the self. You have to dig inside of yourself. You have to understand how you exist in power in a school. If we're not understanding our own biases, own investments in racism, misogyny, white supremacy, all these things then we're going to enact it on our young people. But it's also just like – be a human and don't be terrible.

SARIN MONAE WEST: Intentionally creating an environment in which every voice is welcome and equally valued is a necessary starting point, but also a curiosity for how to deepen that sense of equality and openness. It's not like, "OK, I'm anti-racist. I checked that box. I'm done." Our country and our industry have a muscle memory that needs to be retrained. It's not going to be fixed by one session at the gym. That's not how a body gets altered. It takes a recommitment everyday to a practice of equality, a practice of unlearning, and a practice of curiosity.

MICHELLE BECK: Having a curiosity about individual experience is useful. Even when you are talking about groups and communities, there is a lot of nuance. You don't have to think like every Black person thinks. You don't have to think like every Middle Eastern person thinks. Just because you are a part of a community doesn't mean that you ascribe to all the thoughts and values of that community.

CLARO DE LOS REYES: When we talk about bias and racism, how do we as professionals in the field of arts and culture and education normalize our consistent assessment of how we're doing? How do we create rubrics for our organizations? How racist was I being today? How much did my implicit bias actually impact my work? There is a need to consistently assess these things.

MICHELLE BECK: We are so conditioned to seeing white people in power. Having people of color in the room in positions of power communicates that this is a space that could value me.

NILAJA SUN: On that first day, I ask each student to say your name as if it's the most important name in the room. One of the reasons why I start with that is because your name is the one thing that is hanging out with you for the rest of your life. As someone who has a name that is not Jane or Mary, I had to learn how to say my name with each of its three syllables so that if you choose to not remember my name it's not because I didn't articulate it. So when we ask them to really honor their name, there is something powerful about that, especially when some students' names are constantly mispronounced by elders or authority figures. On that first day, they know that someone cares.

DALISSA DURAN: I always felt like I had two names. My name when I'm home is Dalissa (Da-lee-sa) and at school it was the English pronunciation (Da-li-sa). From Pre-K to High School, I just let everyone call me Dalissa (Da-li-sa). I used to say you can call me Dalissa (Da-li-sa) but I prefer Dalissa (Da-lee-sa). I should have just said, my name's Dalissa (Da-lee-sa). I had to constantly remind myself, you write plays, you've been to Scotland, you've done all this. All those Epic exercises telling me it's OK to be who I want to be – it made me more confident as a person. I should be able to respect myself enough to say my name is Dalissa (Da-lee-sa). It makes me feel comfortable in a room and I need to be comfortable. I'm so happy now being called Dalissa (Da-lee-sa). That's my name. That was a big transition for me. It shouldn't be on the students to feel like they need to show themselves and be like, "Oh this is my identity. Please be OK with it." Teachers have to know who's in the room and how to make everyone feel valued.

MARILYN TORRES: I think how I introduce myself to the group is key. A lot of times as educators, the system is set up for us to be thought of as the ones who have all the knowledge. I'm very big about identifying who's in the room. I'm going to teach you what I know but I also really want to know who you are. I love to go around the circle: what's your first and last name? What's the name you want to be called? What do you think about that's connected to social justice? What's something about yourself that's important for us to know?

AIMÉ DONNA KELLY: I can have an idea of where I'd like the group to go, but how we get there is something that has to be a dialogue between this particular group of artists and me. I always start with an open question: What's on your mind today? What's on your heart? What do you want to express?

Figure 5.1 Epic Associate Artist Devin E. Haqq and Epic student Davion Osbourne.

Source: David Naranjo/photo courtesy of Epic Theatre Ensemble.

MELISSA FRIEDMAN: It's always about the uniqueness of the ensemble. This ensemble is like this. Each ensemble is different.

JACOB MING-TRENT: In the theatre, there are a lot of doors. A lot of gate-keeping. A lot of, "we're here, you're out there." A lot of separation. A lot of it has to do with fear. We need to create spaces where we can challenge each other. We can question each other. We allow people in to question and challenge us.

Space

Transformation is at the center of our work. During the course of touring every year, we'll transform dozens of ordinary public and private spaces into theatrical venues. However, the relationship between art and environment is reciprocal. The rooms in which we choose to create have a profound impact on the artists and the plays they build. College readiness is a major goal of Epic's youth programming. A total of 70% of Epic NEXT students are first in their family to attend college so in order to start to acclimate them to college life, we often look to find space on a university campus.

RON RUSSELL: I grew up steps from Louisiana State University. I could ride my bike there. My parents were in no way affiliated with LSU. They didn't teach there. They didn't work there. But I can't tell you how many times I had a camp on the LSU campus or we had a field trip to a museum on the LSU campus. Unfortunately, for a lot of young people in New York, the local college resources are not well used by neighborhood high schools. As a result, these colleges often seem disconnected from their communities. Sections of the universities have walls around them. High school students aren't usually allowed to walk through college campuses. When Epic NEXT is on campus at NYU for five weeks, it helps the students to get excited about college beyond just the classes that they might take. They get a chance to feel what it's like to be a student on campus and they realize, "Oh college acts as a safe space where I can explore my burgeoning adulthood."

LUAN TAVERAS: On the first day, I walked in to NYU and it felt like I wasn't supposed to be there. But after several days, I built up my confidence. Just walking through that hallway with all the pictures of these NYU alums and the people that you look up to, the people that you've seen in TV and movies, the people that you wish to work with, walking past them on your way to make your own original work definitely had an impact on me. The idea that you're creating something that is bigger than yourself became very real for me in that space. Every day I made it a point to prove that I belonged there.

MEKHI TUDOR: At first it kind of intimidated me because you know people are going to be there who are on their way to the highest level cause it's friggin' NYU. So it's like, "Oh my god!" But it's also kind of cool that you're in the same space where Mahershala Ali honed his skills to be so great.

In New York City, everything revolves around real estate. Space is at a premium and finding a centrally-located venue with adequate amenities can be a huge logistical and budgetary challenge. It would certainly be less expensive and less complicated to house all of our activities at one of our partner schools, but we feel that investing in the space is a significant part of investing in the students.

MELISSA FRIEDMAN: Space means something to young people. We've chosen to partner with high schools that are under-resourced, often in buildings that lack good light, are over-heated, with poor ventilation, sometimes with no windows, spaces that are not always clean. So when we choose our space for our work in the summer, it's important to honor the students by giving them the space they need to grow. We're saying, "You're worth it. You deserve this."

We're looking for spaces large enough for the full ensemble to get in a circle, with breakout rooms for smaller group work. Striking a balance between a place that is quiet enough to do our work undisturbed, yet not so quiet as to stifle the natural sounds of teenagers making theatre can be a challenge.

NILAJA SUN: Every single year something different is happening in America. Every single year something different is happening in New York. Many years we're in different spaces in the city. Maybe one year we're surrounded by college kids in one place, maybe another year we're in an actual theatre. We're surrounded by heat in some places; air-conditioning in other places. Cacophonous sound or super quiet. And that informs how I facilitate the art. I always ask where will we be and how can we ensure that these young artists feel as comfortable as they can while making their art? It's best if the students are in a space where they are allowed to scream and yell and hoot and holler, and fully be themselves. If we're on a college campus where we have to be aware of summer classes around us and people constantly telling us to quiet down, that "police in the mind" mentality will show up in the plays that they ultimately create.

MICHELLE BECK: It has to be a place where students can be loud, especially for Black and Brown students. They are told to be quiet. That they are too much, that they need to tone down their behavior, their voices, their language, everything. So being in a space where they can make a lot of noise in the work but also so they can blow off steam on a break. That's not always possible. At NYU, there was a woman that was protective of the space and very anxious and difficult around students making any sort of noise, but we were in the East Village so at lunch the kids could go downstairs and scream on a loud New York City street which was helpful.

Bringing parents onboard

We ask a lot from the students, so their families need to be a committed part of the team. For the application process, we require a face-to-face meeting with a parent or guardian of each participant to review the schedule and requirements of the program. We make every effort to remove any barriers that might keep families from participating. This includes providing numerous opportunities to meet at different times and locations, designating separate space and supervision for younger siblings during the meeting, and arranging for an interpreter when needed.

RON RUSSELL: If we're going to train students over multiple years, if we're going to invest in them as the arts leaders of the future, if we're going to have a college access component to the work, if we're going to tour, if we're going to ask for a significant summer commitment, then we need to have parental buy-in from the beginning. It's a lot to ask, so it's important to actually meet the parents to find out what their concerns are and try to address them before we start.

MELISSA FRIEDMAN: The commitment is really big and they're young. As the parent of a 14-year-old kid, I cannot even imagine my child participating in a program of this kind of commitment without an opportunity for me to understand directly what was expected of them. It's imperative for us to introduce ourselves to our students' families. This opens up the lines of communication. I'm also trying to impress and excite them about the opportunity. In these parent meetings, we share who we are, we highlight our credentials and recognition and most importantly the commitment Epic is making to each student. I often show pictures of Epic mentors at college graduations. We see students all the way through to college graduation and entry into the workforce. We're interested in lifelong connections with the communities we serve.

We ask each parent to sign a consent form that stipulates the following:

In order for Epic to effectively provide one-on-one mentorship, artistic training, college prep, and performance opportunities to your child, you must agree to:

- Support and allow the Epic Next student to attend every session for the full duration of the program.
- No absences or lateness.
- Completely clear your child's schedule of babysitting, doctor/dentist appointments, and other family obligations during this time period.

It's a big ask and we acknowledge that. Many Epic NEXT students come from low-income families where they are the primary babysitter for younger siblings.

Over the years, we've had students dealing with incredible challenges like nego-tiating the foster care system, moving in and out of homeless shelters, managing physical or cognitive disabilities, and navigating America's immigration process. As arts educators and arts administrators, it's our responsibility to handle these issues with sensitivity and not make any assumptions. We work with individual students to make every appropriate accommodation, but it's critical that the lines of communication with parents and guardians are always open, honest, and clear.

DALISSA DURAN: You guys are very blunt and honest with parents about the commitment. These are the weeks your child needs to be here. Yes, you might need your child to cook, to clean, or to babysit, but you have to give your child the benefit of this time to benefit themselves. My mom saw the joy this gave me and the way that my drive was strengthened after that first year and she was like, "Yes! Epic, Epic, Epic!"

SADE OGUNJIMI: In my first summer, I was late to Epic every day, at least twenty minutes until one of y'all pulled me aside and said, "Listen, if you want to do this, you need to be here and you need to be on time." That was the first time that anybody had told me that being on time was important. In school, I used to miss my first period class all the time, I just wouldn't be there. At no time in my schooling up to that point had anyone been like, "You're late to school everyday. You need to be here on time."

LIZETTE PADUA: Those were some strict rules – you have to come every single day, you've got to be dedicated to this – which is understandable because this is a serious theatre company. That's what I really like about Epic. It's nothing to play around with.

Notes

1. https://www.splcenter.org/sites/default/files/tt_2019_hate_at_school_report_final_0.pdf
2. https://www.schools.nyc.gov/about-us/vision-and-mission/culturally-responsive-sustaining-education

6 How do we get started?

I know many artists who refer to the first rehearsal of a theatre production as their first day of school. I think the metaphor is apt. The first day of school is always an adventure. New relationships are being forged. Everybody's a little nervous. Everybody wants to make a good impression. Everybody wants to do well. At Epic, we spend quite a bit of time planning our projects so that we can take all of that delicious "first day of school" energy of potential and marshal it into a positive and productive environment for the days and weeks that follow.

Setting the tone

Authenticity is a key component of any arts-education initiative. The most successful teaching artists I know don't have a radically different set of behaviors or protocols for the classroom than they use for the rehearsal room. They're not trying to project a teaching persona that is different than who they are as a working arts professional in the field. Neither are they "dumbing down" their craft for young people. I think, too often, educators assign tasks to students that they think are manageable. Some students manage them; others don't; many in the room are bored including the teacher, who has likely been assigning and grading the same rote assignments for years. My pedagogical approach has always been to present students with the most difficult challenges I'm currently facing as an artist. I'm very transparent about my own struggles with the task and I ask them to tackle it with me over the course of the semester or residency or workshop. Rather than giving beginner students some bite-sized assignment to complete that is commensurate with my uninformed estimation of their ability, I find going in with a big, knotty challenge instantly creates an atmosphere of collegiality: "I'm not giving you the answers to something I already know; I have some tools I can share so we can work together to answer a tough question." It's also more engaging, both for the students and for me: I get bored very quickly in a classroom if I'm not learning something. Finally, by making the work genuinely rigorous, you're leveling the playing field for everyone in the room: "This stuff is hard for everybody, including me, so don't feel discouraged if you don't get it right

DOI: 10.4324/9781003079835-7

away. In fact, I've been working on this for years, so if you do get it right away, please keep it to yourself for a little while otherwise you're likely to hurt my feelings!" This approach requires the dismantling of some very old and seductive education mythology that positions teachers as the possessors of all the answers. It also requires educators to get comfortable being a little bit vulnerable in front of their students, but once you push through that, I think the classroom can become more productive, democratic, kind, and fun.

"Extreme collegiality" would describe the atmosphere I'm trying to create when I'm the one facilitating a room full of young artists, but the quality and tone of each arts experience will and should vary depending on the style and experience of the individual teaching artist.

GODFREY L. SIMMONS, JR.: I think it's important to be silly. Silliness is really important because permission to be silly is very hard to come by, particularly when you're dealing with Black and Brown students. Particularly boys. Little boys are taught by parents of color not to act silly because if they act silly they could get killed. Being able to provide a safe space for students to be silly without judgment is really important.

DALISSA DURAN: I was only able to do all of this work because I was pushed to be goofy. Epic puts students in a space where we all can be weirdos together. We all can make fools out of ourselves and cut loose.

AARON KROHN: We need to love the work. We need to love each other. Liking and loving are not the same. Liking is about my enjoyment of something or someone. Loving is about taking care and looking out for someone. We don't have to like someone to love them, but loving often breeds liking. Love is action. Like is passive. Love is throwing yourself in. If you don't know what that is, then throw your body in there and do it. The mind will follow the body.

BRANDT ADAMS: You should always make it a point to pursue your own joy in the room with the students.

MARK HARRIS: Always be positive. If you go negative with a group of students, you've lost. You've reduced yourself in their eyes.

MELISSA FRIEDMAN: You should never think that nurture and rigor are mutually exclusive. You will be asked again and again and again by the students, the teachers, and the administration to pick nurture or rigor. You will be asked. It will be insisted upon that you must choose. You have to be nice with no standards or you have to be mean and bloodless and rigorous. That is absolutely not true: you can marry nurture and rigor.

CLARO DE LOS REYES: It's not just the rigor of putting a show on, there's also an emotional and social rigor. Knowing that students are coming from all types of different backgrounds and situations – maybe disenfranchised or lower income. Different types of situations that might affect how they participate and how they are able to respect certain rules. Knowing that ahead of time will help you navigate your collaboration with them.

Company agreements

An important early act of collaboration that the ensemble can undertake is to work together to build a shared set of expectations for everyone in the room. It's a good idea to start these conversations early and write the company agreements down on something that can be posted in the room. There's no rush to codify the agreements by the end the first day. This should be a living document that can be referenced and amended throughout the course of the project.

CLARO DE LOS REYES: Giving students the opportunity to attain ownership and agency over a process is one of the best things that education can do.

AUBREY SAVERINO: First and foremost, it's important to start a dialogue with the students about what creates a safe space. What do you need from other students? What do you expect from yourself? At Epic, we embrace the idea of safe space/brave space: we can't take risks, we can't have fun, we can't make exciting bold choices if people don't feel safe first.

MELISSA FRIEDMAN: Safe space paves the way for brave space. In order to create a safe space a couple of things need to happen. We start with a circle: creating opportunities for us to be in a circle together. There is democracy in a circle. There is no one person at the head of a class. Everybody is on equal ground, equal footing. I lean on my philosophy of bringing truth, courage, and love into the room. Love for each other, caring for what each other has to say, love for the work. I don't bring in a piece of text that I don't love; I don't do an exercise that I don't love. I try to always treat people with love and respect. So when I see a moment of students teasing each other or even "fake teasing," I'm pretty strict about it. I will gently but firmly highlight that moment and talk about what that means, and how it is a common ritual amongst teens to "fake tease" and it may seem to be coming from a place of love in your mind, but I want to just look at the text and not the subtext. If the text is "You're stupid" then that's not creating a safe space. We're going to be extremely loving in all of our actions and all of our words. If students talk after "curtain" is called on a scene, then we start again. We get used to these protocols. I'm not reprimanding; I'm explaining: "This is why we're starting over again because I want you to feel like you can be brave and you can be glorious and you can step into your authentic truth. In order to do that you need to be heard. You need to feel heard. So we're going to take it back again, not because I'm shaming you but because that's what's necessary for you to feel safe."

CLARO DE LOS REYES: The role of the facilitator is making sure that the expectations are clear at all times, but it doesn't mean it's a punitive experience.

ANTHONY VAUGHN MERCHANT: If you say that anything is acceptable, you have to be OK with anything. You have to mean that shit. If you say "there are no wrong answers," you can't later say, "you're wrong."

Figure 6.1 Epic Associate Artist Anthony Vaughn Merchant with Epic NEXT students Dantae Duwhite, Lashanda Alvarez, and Davion Osbourne.

Source: David Naranjo/photo courtesy of Epic Theatre Ensemble.

MARILYN TORRES: The group is going to tell you what it needs rather than you telling it what it needs. That creates safety in the room. The teaching artist is the group's leader not their master. You're always giving them space to be who they are and develop their own leadership.

Assessment

Creating a positive culture of self-assessment and reflection is one of the best ways to nurture rigor and provide everyone in the ensemble with tools for growth. Prior to the start of the Epic NEXT Summer Intensive, the mentor artists gather to discuss the goals for each unit and what Social-Emotion Learnings are demonstrated in each activity. The overall list varies from project to project and ensemble to ensemble, but these are some examples of SELs that we've found to be present in the practice of theatre:

- Resilience
- Collaboration
- Courage/Risk-taking
- Focus
- Precision/Rigor
- Curiosity/Availability
- Authenticity
- Flexibility

It's important to note that on the first day, the mentor artists will offer up a list of SELs to the ensemble, but it's up to each ensemble to establish definitions for themselves. How a group chooses to define and measure Courage and Risk-taking, for example, will be unique to that particular group. Once the language is agreed upon, the mentors and students work together to create individualized assessment tools that the students use to track their own progress with respect to each of the SELs.

SARIN MONAE WEST: Establishing a 1 to 5 numerical rubric for reflection is helpful because it reinforces this idea that you don't have to be a 5 every time. "OK, I'm a 1 at this and these are practical things I can practice to get to a 3 next time. These are ways I'd like to challenge myself on a daily basis to help expand my sense of curiosity or courage or whatever."

CLARO DE LOS REYES: Nurturing dialogue is so important. Something I do quite often, even within the first activity or first series of activities, I'll ask, "What did you like? What didn't you like? Was that too hard? Why? What can improve the activity?" Sometimes there's a belief that questions can mess up the flow of a session, but once you normalize feedback and assessment right off the top, like asking – "What did you feel? You can disagree. What's your opinion? We value your opinion" – being that transparent in practice establishes that the teaching artist is a person who is down for a dialogue and down to collaborate and make adjustments, not someone who is like, "I know everything and I'm going to make you do this." Throughout the whole process, the students are assessing the situation, whether it's assessing themselves or assessing how you're doing as the facilitator. I think a lot of teaching artists are afraid to do that because it's exposing. Sometimes that's the last thing you want to do – I mean open up yourself to feedback to participants who may not obey the Liz Lerman style of giving feedback. There's definitely a vulnerability around it, but really I feel that the best way to serve the group in front of you is to ask them questions. And you have to think about how to best ask these questions, because the style and way you ask questions influences the type of feedback you get; how do you get honest feedback from the people you're serving?

ANTHONY VAUGHN MERCHANT: At the end of each day, I always ask each person to tell the other people in the group something that they saw them do well today. It gets them outside of themselves. It keeps the positivity up. It keeps them looking at other people and learning from other people.

NATALIE PAUL: I always find time for the students to journal. We're on our feet so much and collaborating so much, the journaling allows the students to be quiet with their thoughts for a little bit. With all the talking and all the collaborating, sometimes you just need a moment to talk to yourself.

SARIN MONAE WEST: I try to pose questions that allow the students to think critically about what felt good and what was good. What went well and why? If it was good what made it that way? Balancing that by asking the other group members what they noticed helps keep the catastrophizing at bay. It's really impactful to receive glowing feedback and honest criticism from your peers.

LUAN TAVERAS: At the end of each day, my mentor went down the list: how do you think your artistry improved? How do you think your courage improved? She was very honest with me and you have to be honest with yourself. There's no faking it with her. She constantly drove home the point that perfection doesn't exist, but you're more than enough. Everybody's on their own path. Everybody thinks differently. Everybody's going through the same things but in different ways. Sometimes you have to take a breath and be patient with yourself. You should always be patient with yourself and others.

AARON KROHN: Mantras are really important. "Turn your inner critic into positive ideas" so you go with "I have more to say" as opposed to "It's too short." The first step is, don't say your self–critique out loud. It becomes more real when you say it out loud. Saying out loud, "I know it wasn't very good" is worse than thinking "I know it wasn't very good" because you haven't offered it and you haven't apologized. If you think it wasn't very good, think of something you want to improve and say, "I'd like to do more of that."

Warm-ups

Warm-ups help prepare the ensemble for the day's activities. They can be used to build energy, focus, spontaneity, or awareness. We're always on the lookout for new theatre games and activities, but here are a few Epic standards.

Shay Shay Coolay

This call and response warm-up, based on a folk song from Ghana, is excellent for building energy and risk-taking. Begin by teaching the ensemble the words:

TEACHING ARTIST: Shay Shay Coolay
ENSEMBLE: Shay Shay Coolay
TEACHING ARTIST: Shay Covista
ENSEMBLE: Shay Covista
TEACHING ARTIST: Covista La La
ENSEMBLE: Covista La La
TEACHING ARTIST: La La key la la
ENSEMBLE: La La key la la
TEACHING ARTIST: Shay hayenday
ENSEMBLE: Shay hayenday
TEACHING ARTIST: Shay hayenday
ENSEMBLE: Shay hayenday
TEACHING ARTIST: One
ENSEMBLE: Two

Figure 6.2 The Epic NEXT ensemble warms up before a rehearsal.

Source: David Naranjo/photo courtesy of Epic Theatre Ensemble.

TEACHING ARTIST: Three
ENSEMBLE: Four
TEACHING ARTIST: Five
ENSEMBLE: Six
TEACHING ARTIST: Seven
ENSEMBLE: Eight

Then the Teaching artist adds a movement and emotion to each line. The group must repeat exactly what the Teaching artist does. Then ask for student volunteers to take over leading the next rounds of Shay Shay Coolay.

Sound around

This is an effective early exercise to engage the ensemble's sense of spontaneity. A student sends a clap to the person next to them and it gets sent around the circle. Then do it again with a vocal sound – letting it transform with each person. One at a time, each ensemble member initiates a new sound and movement and sends it around the circle.

Zip Zap Zop

The players stand in a circle. Each player prepares their "zapper" by placing their palms and extended fingers against each other. The first player points their zapper at another player, at the same time saying "Zip!" The receiving player points to another player, saying "Zap!" The third player then passes "Zop!" to a fourth player. Player number four then passes "Zip!" etc.

Counting to 21

This warm-up game nurtures a sense of focus within the ensemble. Standing in a circle, the entire group must count to 21 together. Only one person at a time may call out a number. If two or more people speak at once, the group must start at the beginning again. The Teaching artist should discourage solutions that make the problem easy to handle, such as raising your hand before talking or going in a pre-determined order. Hold on to the restrictions and the sense of fun will emerge automatically.

Brain scrambler

Students "mill and seethe" (moving around the space without pattern while balancing the space). When the Teaching artist says "Stop," the ensemble stops moving. When the Teaching artist says "Go," the ensemble resumes "milling and seething." Next, when the Teaching artist says "Jump," the ensemble jumps in place. When the Teaching artist says "Name," each person shouts out their name. Next, when the Teaching artist says "clap," the ensemble claps their hands together once and when the Teaching artist says "spin," the ensemble performs a 356 degree spin. NOW the directions are reversed, when Teaching artist says "stop" the ensemble goes and when the Teaching artist says "go" they stop. The ensemble says their name when the Teaching artist says "jump" and jumps when the Teaching artist says "name." The ensemble spins when the Teaching artist says "clap" and claps when the Teaching artist says "spin."

Captain's coming!

We were first made aware of Captain's Coming by our friends at Massive Theatre Company in New Zealand. It's a wildly fun game that requires a combination of energy and precision. The players start in the center of the room. One player is assigned to be the Captain. When the Captain calls out an order, the ensemble has to perform the accompanying action. Anyone unable to do the action or maintain it, is out.

Order: "Captain's Coming"
Action: Stand and salute
Order: "Swab the deck"
Action: Mime mopping the floor
Order: "Climb the rope"
Action: Mime climbing an endlessly long rope

Order: "Man overboard"

Action: Run to an edge of the space, stand on one foot, put a hand to your brow, and look out for the man overboard. Stay in this position until the next order.

Order: "Octopus"

Action: One player stands behind another player and both players wave their arms to look like a single octopus.

Order: "Treasure chest"

Action: Three players work together to form a treasure chest. Two players hold hands at arm's length to make the chest; a third player stands in between them to be the sparkling treasure.

Order: "Mermaid"

Action: Loudly sing a weird underwater opera of your own composition.

Order: "Beached whale"

Action: Lie on the ground and make sounds like a beached whale.

Order: "Pirates"

Action: Close one eye, make a hook with one finger, stand on one leg, and shout "Arghhh!"

Order: "Shark attack"

Action: The captain becomes a shark and tags the crew. If the shark tags you, you're out.

MELISSA FRIEDMAN: I often choose my warm-ups based on the time of day. If it's an early morning class, I'll anticipate that the students will need energy. If it's post-lunch and the room is crazy, they might need focus.

RON RUSSELL: For me, warm-ups are a diagnostic. I try out a couple of warm-ups early on to see what's working and where the challenges are with a particular group. If I walk in and the group is extremely lethargic, then I'll do a warm-up like Captain's Coming that is insanely active and precise. What is the feeling in the room right now and what do we need to do? Do we need to work on precision and focus? Do we need to work on energy? Do we need to just throw in some joy?

MARILYN TORRES: Warm-ups get people giggling. Laughter's a great unifier. It gets them out of their head. They're not thinking about their hair, their physical appearance, what someone is thinking about them. Warm-ups take them out of their heads and into their hearts.

MELISSA FRIEDMAN: I train teaching artists in backward-mapping. If at the end of this class, students need to learn a particular skill or reach a particular artistic benchmark, then we need to determine the warm-up activity that's going to begin to move us toward that goal. I'll often lead a warm-up activity that has the form of something I'm going to use later. For example, if I want the students to speak chorally in a shared speech later in the lesson, then I will start with a Counting to 21 warm-up exercise at the beginning of the class so that later I can say we're going to use the same structure of Counting to 21 but this time we're going to use the words of this text. If I have a call and response warm-up at the beginning, it might be because I want them to incorporate a call and response into a protest scene they're writing later in the day.

DEVIN E. HAQQ: The ritualistic aspect of it is key. Repeating the same exercises, activities, and warm-ups over and over has the practical effect of giving them the skills they need to perform, but it's also creating this sense of community in the room. We all know these tongue twisters. We all know this game. We all know these vocal warm-ups. And if you're consistent, at some point in the process anybody can lead them.

GODFREY L. SIMMONS, JR.: You should always find someone who wants a lot of attention to help lead things and you should always find someone who does not want a lot of attention to help lead things.

7 How do we create an essential question?

A question can start a group of people on a journey. An answer often ends that journey. As you can probably tell from the chapter titles in the first part of this book, I'm a big fan of questions. Our goal as Citizen Artists should be to pose simply stated, direct questions about the essential nature of humanity which engage nuanced thinking, empathy, and personal life experience to such an extent that an audience member could spend several lifetimes wrestling with them and never arrive at any definitive answers.

An essential question is the foundation of Epic Theatre. It will guide the research and encourage deep thinking and learning about the topic. The essential question is like a "clothesline" on which the ensemble can later hang ideas, characters, dialogue, transactions, emotions, images, satire, poetry, and music. The stronger the clothesline, the more material it can support.

Good essential questions should be:

Open-ended: It should not be a question that can be answered with a yes or a no. Neither should it be answerable with a single sentence.

Non-judgmental: For example, "Why is educational segregation bad?" contains within the question a judgment that educational segregation is bad. "With NYC Public Schools more segregated now than they were before Brown v. Board of Education, what does 'separate but equal' mean to us today?" invites the audience to decide how they feel about segregated schools.

Direct and concise: Deliverable with one sentence on one breath is a good rule of thumb.

Thought-provoking without guiding the direction or outcome of the thinking: The question shouldn't have just one or two clear answers. The ensemble needs to be open to ambiguity and seek out multiple viewpoints.

Supported and enriched by knowledge and research, but answerable by anyone: The best essential questions are ones that you can ask to scholars, specialists in the field, or regular audience members with no special expertise and everyone's answers can have equal import and validity.

DOI: 10.4324/9781003079835-8

> ***Relevant and resonant to the members of the ensemble and the audiences they want to reach:*** The best essential questions stimulate our emotions, our intellect, and our moral compass.

How does an ensemble write an essential question?

- Think about beginning your question with one of these key words or phrases: why, how, if, what impact, what effect.
- Try to use direct, simple language that makes sense to everyone in the group.
- Collaboration is not easy. When trying to come to consensus around the wording of your essential question, each member of the ensemble should embrace the ethos of the John Denver song, *"Hold on Tightly; Let Go Lightly."* Make a strong case for your idea, but when it becomes clear that the ensemble is moving in a different direction, be flexible enough to adapt to the will of the group without resentment.
- Don't rush this process. Take the time to craft a question that clearly articulates the focus of your investigation and truly excites the group. Also remember that you might need/want to modify your essential question as you learn more about the topic through the research process.

Here are examples of Essential Questions from the plays in this book:

Play: Default
Topic: Ethnic Studies and Culturally Responsive-Sustaining Education
Essential Question: What difference does it make to students if the curriculum reflects the history, experiences, and knowledge of their communities and families?
Play: Perfect Circle
Topic: Bullying
Essential Question: Why is bullying so pervasive when everyone says they're against it?
Play: Nothing About Us
Topic: Educational segregation
Essential Question: What does "separate but equal" mean today?
Play: Overdrive
Topic: Standardized testing and assessments
Essential Question: What impact does standardized testing have on teachers and students?

MICHELLE BECK: These questions are very complicated and complex. In school, so often, there is a right or a wrong answer. There aren't many gray areas. Life is a gray area. It helps students understand for the first time that there is so much complexity and nuance in the world.

Figure 7.1 Miladys Sanchez performs the opening lines of Default backed up by Shaena Gibson and Liana Morales. "What does culture mean to you?"

Source: Anjelic E. Owens/photo courtesy of NYU Metro Center.

MELISSA FRIEDMAN: Centering a project around a big question gets at truth. It gets students engaged in debate, nuance, and empathy. It lends itself to cohesiveness on the project.

RON RUSSELL: I think an essential question helps the student universalize the art and make it accessible to more people. A good essential question drives us toward systemic causes rather than surface eruptions.

8 How do we conduct interviews?

We began the Epic NEXT program during the summer of 2012. That same year Epic was developing a new play called *Dispatches from (A)mended America*. *Dispatches* began in 2008 as a conversation between Godfrey L. Simmons Jr., a 42-year-old Black man, and Brandt Adams, a 25-year-old white man. We've elected a Black man as President, so what do we do now? Is the "Race question" answered? In the month leading up to Barack Obama's 2009 Presidential Inauguration, Godfrey and Brandt traveled throughout the South conducting 100 interviews in an attempt to better understand the significance of the election of America's first African-American President. Their completed script wove together their own original writing with verbatim excerpts from the interview transcripts and called for an ensemble of six actors to play 36 different characters over the span of 90 minutes.

I was one of the actors working on *Dispatches* and it provided one of the most formidable and enjoyable acting challenges of my life. I was playing eight different characters, all based on real people. The show was staged in the round with the cast sitting among the audience. Entrances and exits were made by moving in and out of your chair. No costume changes. No props. No backstage. The bulk of the stagecraft was handled by actor transformation. As a selective extrovert/shameless on-stage show-off, I was in heaven, but I also felt an enormous responsibility. These were real people, any of whom might walk into the theatre on a particular night to see the show. Were that to happen, I would want each of them to see their truth fully represented onstage. Each "character" and their point of view deserved equal weight, nuance, and compassion. To differentiate all these characters required me to use every tool in my actor's tool kit while at the same time keeping my personal value judgments in check. Playing all these people successfully was plenty to keep me busy; no one needed to see or hear my evaluation of them anyway.

The *Dispatches* experience was a world-class workout of craft and empathy and I immediately wanted to jump back into further exploration of that kind of theatre-making. So when we were designing the curriculum for the first summer of Epic NEXT, we decided to hire the cast of *Dispatches* to be the mentor artists and culminate the project with a student-created play that incorporated elements of verbatim theatre. That's been the model for us ever since.

DOI: 10.4324/9781003079835-9

Figure 8.1 A post-show conversation from Epic's production of *Dispatches from (A)mended America* by Godfrey L. Simmons, Jr. and Brandt Adams.

Source: Robert Chelimsky/photo courtesy of Epic Theatre Ensemble.

Interview prep

Interviews are a huge part of our Tier 2 creation process. The ensemble talks to 30–40 stakeholders over five days and each interview typically lasts between 30–45 minutes. The more thought and preparation you put into the process, the better the material you're likely to get.

Come up with a specific set of three to four questions to lead off every interview. Included in this set should probably be some version of your essential question. By asking each person a set of the same questions, you'll be able to easily identify where there is agreement and where there's contrast. When it comes time to pull the script together, your material can be organized by those initial responses and you'll be able to easily create a kind of dialogue between the characters. Because Epic NEXT plays always deal with education, we frequently begin interviews with the question, "What is the purpose of school?"

GODFREY L. SIMMONS, JR.: I think every set of questions should include, "With what groups or communities do you identify?". That's probably best if that's the first question. You're getting the subject to interrogate it for themselves before they talk about the thing you're talking about.

It completely changes the way they talk about the thing you're talking about. You get them out of a canned answer and into being alive to who they are.

BRANDT ADAMS: When I'm asking someone who they are, I try to get something in at the top that gets them to tell a story. Like "Tell me the story of your name," gets them into a less fact-driven place. It's good for the questions to get at how somebody's life relates to the topic you're talking about.

Set up a recording device with a clear and easily readable timestamp (our device of preference is the GarageBand app on a MacBook). This will allow you to make notes about what specific quotes you want to capture and where/when your transcription team can look to find them. FaceTime or Zoom can work for remote interviews.

BRANDT ADAMS: I like to get to the space ahead of time and have everything set up so when guests arrive, it's seamless. Marc Maron is famous for always having the recording going when they walk in the room. I don't do that because I think it can make some people uneasy when they find out about it. But once the recorder is on, I leave it on. That can be some of the best stuff when you take a break or get up for a drink of water or you're just chatting. That stuff can be so rich. Stuff that I can actually turn into a thing that would be interesting on stage.

Try to make your interview guests feel comfortable

People frequently tell us, after the fact, that they felt nervous at the top of an interview. This makes sense. Everyone wants to feel eloquent and insightful and no one wants their words to become a source of contempt or the butt of a joke. If the interviewee is a guest in your space you should attempt to create as comfortable an atmosphere as possible. The interview team should be between two and five people. A larger group of interviewers can feel intimidating. Make sure all the ensemble members introduce themselves before you get started. You can either gather around a table or sit in a circle of chairs. Have a bottle of water ready for the guest. Take every opportunity to make the first few minutes feel more like a friendly conversation and less like a deposition.

GODFREY L. SIMMONS, JR.: Having more than one person there to interview is almost always better. It makes it feel like there's a team and that there are going to be different perspectives. The person talking will talk to different people for different reasons. It's really weird. They could be more comfortable talking to someone because of the person's gender or someone else because of the person's race or someone else because they think they have kind eyes.

SARIN MONAE WEST: Having a team there to interview provides the space for each student to be able to truly observe and not always have to come up with what question comes next. It allows them to observe physicality. It allows them to breathe in this other person in a way that makes the experience less about their own feelings of how it's going and more about this person's stories. It allows the stories to be extracted without judgment or outside influence.

DAVID TIPSON: We need to get away from this idea that one smart person can solve the problem. There's evidence that some of the most highly cited articles in scientific journals are the ones written by a very diverse team of scientists. The fact that people are coming from different ways of being, different ways of knowing, different ways of seeing the world is actually allowing them to probe deeper, to challenge each other, to get away from group think. We have a better opportunity to understand the issues and move forward if we acknowledge different perspectives and try to incorporate them into the ways we think about solving problems.

Before you begin the interview, tell your interview guest the topic you're investigating. Remind them that the recording isn't for broadcast, but rather to enable the ensemble to go back and capture their exact words in a transcript. Also, let them know that the interview transcripts are completely anonymous and that if any of their text is used in the play, they will not be identified by name. Make sure to thank them before and after the interview for taking the time to share their thoughts with you.

Interview techniques

During the interview, take thorough notes. This has several practical functions that have already been stated above, but it also demonstrates active listening which communicates to your interviewees that you are invested in their answers and that you value what they're saying enough to write it down.

Ask open-ended questions. Yes or no answers aren't likely to add much to the performance text or your understanding of the topic. If someone says something that seems confusing or odd, be prepared to ask follow-up questions. Some of the best responses come from personal stories, so if the guest's answers are more philosophical or theoretical, it's good to have follow ups prepared like, "Can you tell me a story about a time when you felt something like you're describing?" or "Have you had any personal experiences with that?"

BRANDT ADAMS: You should have a flexible plan. You have your list of questions but you need to show up willing to divert from them. Allow enough space for your interviewee to go where they want to go. Be present enough to pursue the thing that's happening in the room. It's like acting – you can have your plan but in the moment you have to deal with the actual person in front of you.

Ideally, the team shouldn't talk a lot during the interview. If your guest asks you a question, of course, you can answer, but the goal is not to have a back and forth conversation. If you are fortunate to have a guest who rambles on a bit, that's great. The longer people talk, the more comfortable they become, and the more likely they are to share their truths. Much of the material we end up using in Epic NEXT shows frequently comes from the last 5 to 10 minutes of a 45 minute interview.

LIZETTE PADUA: Some interviews, I'm not going to lie to you, they annoyed me. They weren't answering the questions. They were beating around the bush. It was a struggle.

Yes it was. In fact, the students' observations of how reluctant many adults were to talk frankly about racism and white supremacy inspired the "Beating Around the Bush" scene from *Nothing About Us*.

Be respectful, open, and generous to different points of view. The concept of safe space/brave space that the ensemble has been cultivating throughout their work, applies here too. Your interview guest may say something that conflicts with your own beliefs. That's OK. In this moment, and for the duration of this interview, it ain't about you. Capturing true diversity of opinions throughout this process leads to a richer and more nuanced play.

Here are the interview questions the student researchers created for each of the plays in this book:

Nothing About Us

1 What is the purpose of school?
2 Who benefits from educational segregation?
3 How did we get here?
4 What does diversity in education look like?
5 Can you describe your ideal school?

Default

1 What is the purpose of school?
2 Who should decide what our school curriculum will be?
3 Why does it matter what students learn in school?
4 What difference does it make to students if the curriculum reflects the history, experiences, and knowledge of their communities and families?
5 Should the teacher of an Ethnic Studies class reflect the ethnicity being studied? Why or why not?

Overdrive

1 What is the purpose of school?
2 How do standardized tests support that purpose?

3 What are physical, emotional, and psychological effects do standardized tests have on students?
4 How does standardized testing affect the relationship between teachers and students?
5 What is the relationship between standardized testing and educational segregation?

Perfect Circle

1 What is the purpose of school?
2 What are the essential rights of students in high schools?
3 How do you define bullying?
4 When does bullying turn into discrimination?
5 Why is bullying so pervasive when educators all say they're against it?

RON RUSSELL: Every interview starts badly for the students and gets better. Students are so used to seeing edited interviews on television, so they think that interviewing is going to be a simple exchange where they ask the questions and the ideas come out. What happens is, they have to become metacognitive. They have to be thinking while the interview is happening, "Is this the information that I really need? Not does it answer my question, but is it the right stuff?" And it creates an incredible pressure. It's great. They get so stressed out. That level of stress is really useful for a young person because it causes them to reflect, "How do I get better at this? Do I need to take better notes? Do I need to reorganize my questions? Where did I succeed?" Over time, I know this process teaches young people to feel more comfortable talking to adults that they don't know. A lot of students don't have a lot of opportunities to be around adults. Most teachers create so much professional distance in the classroom that it's more of a performance of a person. In the interviews, students are able to talk to real people.

LUAN TAVERAS: To me, it was a little bit intimidating during those first interviews. They're adults and you're this teenager asking them about this big topic and exploring these big ideas. At first, I was a little too careful. Over time, I learned to engage with them more and ask them more about their experiences and just more comfortable.

XAVIER PACHECO: It's crazy because I was 15 when we interviewed people who we incorporated into our original piece. Now eight years later, here I am at NYU Grad Acting and one of our classes is called Toolbox, where we go out and interview people and incorporate their identities into a performance for class.

MARILYN TORRES: I always tell students, "There are people who came before you who fought for you to be here" but it's usually from books or what you see on TV. When you interview someone who is actually in the fight, who is in the struggle, it makes it real and it validates you as a human being. These are real people who are actually doing the work and you've got to honor them and give them a voice.

SADE OGUNJIMI: During the interview process, there's an emphasis on being able to ask challenging and compelling questions. We learn that it's OK to make people a little uncomfortable. Having uncomfortable conversations is how we get a lot of things done. Conversations around a social issue can be uncomfortable for some people. Navigating those conversations at an early age prepares and equips you to enter college at a predominantly white institution without it defeating you. Because of those interviews we did, I was a lot more comfortable asserting my presence as a Black person, getting people to question their rhetoric, putting myself in other people's shoes while not allowing other people's opinions of me to stop my progress.

ABEL SANTIAGO: In school, it was always hard for me to ask questions, even when I was confused. If I was lost, I wouldn't raise my hand. I just stayed lost. Through our research and interview process, being able to exercise that act of asking questions was so important. And that carried over. Now in college classrooms, I'm able to ask questions about anything. When I'm at rehearsal, I've become the actor who asks all the questions. I learned that's what rehearsal is for: to ask questions.

XAVIER PACHECO: As a result of those interviews, we all felt supported by what we had learned. Listening to what they were saying: their lives, their experiences, their stories, and finding more value in that than we could have anticipated. We all thought we were doing these interviews to make a show. What we were really learning about was the incredible depth that every single person walks into a room with, regardless of what they've experienced in their life. It was eye-opening because it was a chance to approach story-telling through one of the most honest and direct forms of communication you can have.

9 What are enabling constraints?

It has been said that one of the most daunting things for a writer to contend with is the blank page. How do I start? Where do I start? It may seem paradoxical, but unlimited freedom can be paralyzing to creativity. Art thrives on restrictions. Sometimes writers need a set of constraints to enable collaboration, courage, and creativity. Here are some elements that we build into the requirements of every Epic NEXT play.

The play should be written to be performed by five actors

The plays are conceived, researched, and written by a group of 15–20 students, but designed and directed to be performed by an ensemble of five actors. From a practical standpoint, limiting the cast to five allows a producer to say "yes" more often, thus extending the reach of the work. By triple or quadruple casting each role, you can have more than one performance happening at the same time in different places. It also reduces the pressure on any one student's schedule. In our 2018–2019 season, there were 48 Epic NEXT performances, many of which took place during weekday mornings and afternoons and required an excused absence from school. This volume of work wouldn't have been possible with a single cast.

There are also aesthetic and community-building benefits to an acting quintet. Because the plays feature verbatim material pulled from interviews as well as original creative writing, the dramatis personae can range anywhere from 25 to 45 characters. Each actor has to physically and vocally bring life to a diverse group of people and perspectives. This virtuoso display of empathy models the thoughtful, respectful, bold, and inclusive mindset that we want our audiences to embrace in the conversations that follow the play.

The production may use five chairs

Preferably five identical chairs, these will allow the director to have some limited "set" options and to create levels. We have not yet come across a venue on tour that couldn't manage to find five chairs.

DOI: 10.4324/9781003079835-10

The production must utilize no more than one hand prop

These plays rely on actor transformation rather than parading a bunch of stuff around the stage. That said, a sign in big block letters that reads, "THE BUSH" can add a lot to a scene about white people "beating around the bush" while discussing the relationship between white supremacy and educational segregation. A clipboard, the universal symbol of authority and access, is indispensable when playing a psychometrician conducting a standardized test to see if tonight's crowd meets the qualifications of a good audience. You get one prop – make it count.

The play must be no longer than 30 minutes

Years ago, as a Masters student in a graduate acting program, I was required to write and perform a 15-minute solo play as part of my thesis. Somewhere between a first and second draft, my thesis advisor suggested to me that, "The only thing better than a fifteen minute solo play is a twelve minute solo play. The play hasn't been written that wouldn't benefit from some judicious cuts." If you've composed a compelling essential question and interviewed smart, eloquent people and written exciting scenes then you're going to end up with an abundance of material from which to build a play. You'll probably have enough material to build 10 plays. You're going to be tempted to stretch the running time to fit all of the great stuff. Resist that temptation. Art exercises a great deal of its impact by what it leaves out. It's the imagination and participation of the audience that completes the work of art – you have to leave room for them in what you're making. Try to limit your script to the material that most strongly frames and reflects your essential question. A play that is focused and concise is more likely to yield a post-show conversation that is focused and productive.

A 30-minute running time will also afford producers greater flexibility in terms of where and how the play can be presented. Because the plays of Epic NEXT deal with education policy, they resonate strongly with teachers, students, administrators, school district employees, education researchers, and lawmakers. A shorter play can fit neatly within a class period, a school assembly, a PTA gathering, a professional development session, an education conference, or a town hall meeting while still allowing time for post-show conversation.

The play must contain at least one moment of direct interaction with the audience

There's a popular phrase in entertainment: "Sit back, relax, and enjoy the show." The first two parts of that phrase don't apply here. We don't want audiences to sit back or relax. We want them fully engaged and actively

Figure 9.1 Epic NEXT student Luan Taveras leads the audience in the bachata during a performance of *Default* at New York University Metropolitan Center for Research on Equity and Transformation of Schools.

Source: Anjelic E. Owens/photo courtesy of NYU Metro Center.

wrestling with the questions of the play. We're all in the same room together and it's important for aspects of the staging and the script to acknowledge that fact. Whether it's asking the audience to stand for a bachata lesson or answer a pre-show question or participate in a call and response, the play should make it clear to the audience that their role is not that of a passive watcher, but rather an active doer.

The play must contain a bi-lingual moment

Language access is a key to engaging diverse audiences and creating an atmosphere that is inclusive and welcoming. Past ensembles have sometimes struggled to come up with plot-driven reasons why characters might sometimes speak in Spanish. If a clever multi-lingual conceit presents itself, that's great, but I don't think you need to spend much time worrying about that. The best reason to deliver parts of your play in Spanish, French, or Mandarin is simply because there are Spanish, French, or Mandarin speakers in the audiences you want the play to reach.

The play must contain a moment of music

Music can heighten a scene and appeal to an audience on an emotional level. This constraint is totally up to the interpretation of the ensemble based on the interests and talents of the group. It could be a hum, a whistle, a beat, a stomp, a rap, a live guitar solo (that guitar would then count as your prop), or a fully choreographed musical number.

The play must contain a moment of unison speech

This is another great way to add rhythm and musicality to the text.

Sometimes it's helpful to add additional elements depending on the topic and the nature of the ensemble. Here are a few more examples of enabling constraints that we've used in past projects:

- a frozen tableau must open or close the play
- a reconciliation
- a change of heart
- a discovery
- the sound of the wind
- a song of celebration
- 30 seconds of unison movement
- the sound of laughter
- 15 seconds of silence
- an unexpected entrance
- a moment of magic
- at least one instance of repetition (this can be physical or verbal or both)
- a sigh of relief
- a clear tempo change
- a moment of indecision
- a loss

Members of an ensemble may look at some of the more abstract constraints and ask, "What does 'a moment of magic' mean?". I think it's important for the teaching artist not to try to provide an answer more specific than, "I don't know. You tell me." Encouraging the students to approach these constraints with a spirit of creative rebellion can lead to some wonderfully unexpected and powerful results. These are the rules: you can't break them, but you can certainly bend them to your will for the good of the storytelling.

MELISSA FRIEDMAN: One of the wonderful things about being an artist is that you can go into flights of fancy, but you need a foundation that roots you into something. I think enabling constraints are really helpful for artists. The juiciness of an essential question together with enabling constraints allows you to get to work and creatively flourish.

Figure 9.2 Chrisaury Guzman, Luan Taveras, Shaena Gibson, Esmirna Matos, and Miladys Sanchez perform *Nothing About Us* for The National Coalition on School Diversity in Oakland, California.

Source: James Wallert/photo courtesy of Epic Theatre Ensemble.

MEKHI TUDOR: I like using enabling constraints because it helps me focus. They give me a place to start. My mind is everywhere so when you give me constraints I know I can't go too far off track. It keeps me grounded.

MICHELLE BECK: Setting parameters doesn't make the work right or wrong. It just cocoons you. It makes you feel a little safer. Because instead of having to write about everything in the world that's ever happened, you have a boundary. Then if you have an impulse to break that boundary or go outside of it, that's great because you've identified an impulse within you. That's what we're trying to do – to get kids to trust their impulses, to trust their intuition, to trust their own curiosity.

RON RUSSELL: I like things to be unmanageable. That's how I like to start creative processes. Like "That seems impossible. How in the hell are you going to put all those things together?" Then you come up with the enabling constraints that provide the guide and the boilerplate for how we're going to get there.

LIZETTE PADUA: At first it was like how are we going to tell a story without props? You have to tell the story with your body, with your movement, with your characters.

LUAN TAVERAS: It makes you ask yourself: why this prop? Why can't it be this or this? What's the key artifact that truly contributes to the story?

MARK HARRIS: You need to cast the audience in a role. They need to know who they are in your piece so they know how to behave in that piece.

VERN THIESSEN: I had a young student who wrote a play and in her script, it said a character was reading something from the Koran. And I said, "What is she reading?" And she said, "Well it's in Arabic so, you know, it's not going to matter." And I turned to the actress and I said "Do you speak Arabic?" And she said, "Yes." And I said "Do you know any verses from the Koran?" And she said, "Yes." And so suddenly there was this multi-lingual aspect of the play and the writer, this 16 year old kid who was an immigrant from Pakistan, saw that it was possible to see her world reflected on the stage.

10 How do we populate the world of the play?

Once you've finished your research, you'll want the ensemble to identify potential characters who could appear in the play. These are characters that we're all going to spend weeks developing and that we're asking audiences to invest in deeply so we should be intentional about each and every one of them. Who do you want to spend all that time with? Which characters have the potential for the richness and complexity that we need to keep our audience with us throughout the journey of play? Does your cast of characters represent all perspectives on the topic? Begin by asking the students to think about all of the people connected to the essential question, starting with those stakeholders who are impacted the most. Some of their interview guests might inspire ideas for characters. You can collate their thoughts with a graphic organizer that uses a series of concentric circles like Figure 10.1.

Figure 10.2 shows a specific example of the stakeholder/character brainstorm that the students generated for DEFAULT.

Once they've identified who might be in the world, ask the ensemble to consider what kinds of relationships, transactions, and conflicts they're interested in exploring between some of those people. These don't have to be fully fleshed out ideas for stories or scenes. Right now we're just collecting impulses.

Some examples, again, from the brainstorming process that led to the play *Default*:

- A struggling student of color going to her white U.S. History teacher to ask for help in the class.
- A teacher of color being pressured by a principal to get her students to pass a state's standardized exam.
- A parent talking to a child about the importance of knowing about their family's culture
- Students code-switching when speaking to different adults.
- Two teachers discussing how to make their curriculum more culturally responsive.
- An Ethnic Studies instructor teaching a class.
- A mixed-race kid trying to figure out how to answer the ethnicity survey question on the PSAT exam.

DOI: 10.4324/9781003079835-11

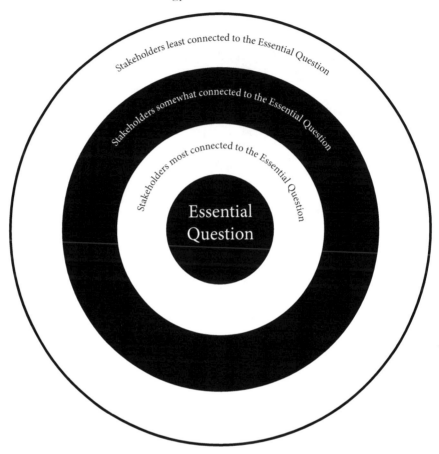

Figure 10.1 Graphic organizer template for brainstorming essential questions stakeholders.

- A white college counselor advising a student of color.
- A moment of tension between a Haitian–American student and a Dominican–American student.
- A white Assistant Principal organizing a series of superficial, and possibly offensive, multi-cultural day activities.
- Student voices at a protest.
- A superintendent leading a town hall discussion with many of the stakeholders.
- A Dominican–American student teaching other students how to dance the bachata.

JACOB-MING TRENT: We've got to get them to question their own lives; to get them to really investigate their day-to-day lives, as boring as they may think it is at the outset. I'll ask students, "How often do you go to

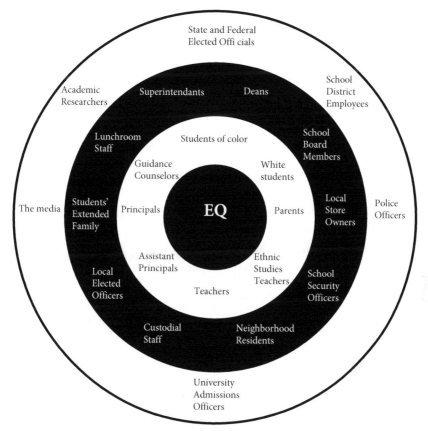

Essential Question: What difference does it make to students if their school's curriculum reflects the history, experiences, and knowledge of their communities and families?

Figure 10.2 Graphic organizer stakeholders example from *Default*.

the bodega or the corner store? How often are you there?" They tell me they're there everyday. So I'll say, "What's the name of the person working behind the counter? How much do you know about that person?" I do this to get them to start learning about the world around them and questioning what they're seeing. Why do we do things this way? When they become more inquisitive, the work generates itself.

LUAN TAVERAS: These touring shows wouldn't work if it was just one point of view. We'd just be exploring one side of the problem, but then once we get in the talkback, there's this other side of the room. If we represent everyone, then everyone in the audience can say, "You know what, I feel reflected and I also have this to share." We might not agree with it, but at least we're talking about the problem. The problem is being discussed and we're getting closer to an answer that might benefit everyone.

VERN THIESSEN: Plays can help students to identify the central ethical dilemma of their lives. What are the difficult decisions that you're facing in your life that are impossible to solve?

MARILYN TORRES: I love going to the source: the artist's well. What's in your well that you think about, that you feel passionate about, that angers you, that inspires you, that makes you move in the world? I ask a lot of questions. What do you think about connected to social justice? What inspires you? What's the thing that you could talk about forever? That's the material that a young person is going to plug into that they then can create a whole world around.

AARON KROHN: This whole idea of being creative and imaginative we think means that there's this right answer, but imaginative means just being open to what's already there. The more obvious, the more universal.

NATALIE PAUL: There are no mistakes. When students believe in this idea that there are no mistakes, it means that creativity is constant. It means that you can bring your whole self to your writing process. Who you are is not a hurdle you have to get over in order to be an artist. It's your fuel.

MELISSA FRIEDMAN: There's sometimes a little excavating that we have to do as artists because on top of the students' truth and lived experiences is a layer of what they've been told by the media, by television, by the internet. So there's a regurgitation that happens within the first few ideas: "I have an idea! Let's do this TV show that I watch" or "I have an idea! We should do this thing from Tik Tok." The first couple of ideas are often really derivative. One of the skill sets is reflecting back and asking them, "Where does this idea come from? Does it come from your truth or does it come from something you're regurgitating back?"

ANTHONY VAUGHN MERCHANT: Last summer, I was leading a group of young women. And I said, "OK, let's talk about shit that you hear as young women." And we just brainstormed a list of shit you've been told. Not shit you've been told you're told. Not like, "as women people are going to tell you blah, blah, blah," but shit that you have heard. And because everyone put in on that list of shit they've been told and everything got the echo/nod from everyone in the group, we've all agreed that these are real, now we're working from a shared common experience and building scenes and characters based on ideas that we have in common.

MARILYN TORRES: I put everything on the wall. What's the theme that keeps popping up? What characters are coming out?

MARK HARRIS: The exercise I call "Living Museum" helps break them out of a narrative mindset. That's an exercise where they break their script into characters and you put the characters on pedestals around the room and you can ask them what their stories are. You walk around the room and hear monologues from each character. I think that helped to free them up from thinking it has to be a "play."

AIMÉ DONNA KELLY: I love the idea of writing on your feet so I'll start with improvisation work. I don't want it to get too cerebral. I want students to get in the body of their characters.

AARON KROHN: In improv, we say yes and then we add something. The first thing is planting that "Yes, and…" quality. That I think is very important. I remember very distinctly, with the first group I had I said to them, "In this writers' room, let's say yes to everything."

MELISSA FRIEDMAN: I do a lot of training in "Yes, and." How do you build on an idea? We're going to take one person's idea and we're going to "Yes, and" it. We're not going to say, "No. No." We're going to "Yes, and" it. That doesn't mean that we're going to go with it. We're just going to "Yes, and" it. Then we're going to take somebody else's idea and we're going to "Yes, and" it. Then as a group, we'll look at all these ideas generated by one and developed by the full and we'll look at them separately, not competitively.

11 How do we come to consensus?

Getting two collaborators to come to agreement around an artistic vision can be challenging. Achieving consensus between 10, 20, or 35 arts collaborators is daunting at best. When it's time to make decisions in terms of overarching concepts or conceits for the script, we try to employ principles of democracy with a spirit of extreme generosity and empathy.

It's important to make clear to everyone in the room that the Teaching artists are there to help facilitate the decision-making process. They are not there to decide anything or to make summary judgments on the quality of student ideas. Before I go into any consensus-building moment, I make it a point to reference the John Denver ditty, *"Hold On Tightly; Let Go Lightly"*: It's great to strongly advocate for your personal artistic vision, but if in the course of conversation it becomes clear that your idea doesn't resonate with the rest of the ensemble, then you have to be prepared to cede to the will of the group without resentment.

Here are some exercises that can be helpful to employ when trying to help a group find consensus.

The elevator pitch

Pose this scenario to the students: you're an aspiring screenwriter who can't get a meeting with a movie executive to tell her about your amazing new screenplay. You know if she hears your idea, she's going to love it. So you wait in the lobby of the 20 story studio building. When the movie exec gets on the elevator to travel to her 20th-floor office, you jump on with her. Now with a captive audience, you have the time it takes to get to the 20th floor (about 45 seconds) to pitch her your movie. You have to decide, in advance, which plot points to share. Who are the key characters? What are the most unique, exciting, and funny moments? What word choices will be most persuasive?

An elevator pitch can help students to boil down an idea to its most essential elements. What is it about your idea that you love? When a teaching artist is looking for avenues of compromise, this kind of clarity can save lots of time and hurt feelings. If a student's idea is to set the play on a space station, but during their elevator pitch they spend most of their time talking about

DOI: 10.4324/9781003079835-12

Figure 11.1 Epic NEXT student Daniel Bland listens to his colleague Davion Osbourne give an Elevator Pitch.

Source: David Naranjo/photo courtesy of Epic Theatre Ensemble.

this dynamic engineer character named Leon, it may be that what they love most is the engineer Leon character and it's possible to adapt and translate that character and their dynamic qualities into a non-space station setting. It may turn out that what they love most is just the name Leon and if you call another character Leon, they're good!

The caucus

The caucus, a form of democracy that takes place out in the open, is character-ized by participants showing their preference through "voting with their feet." Ideally, you want to use the caucus when there are three or four distinct ideas with strong support. The initial generator of each idea moves to a different corner of the room. The ensemble then votes with their feet by moving to the corner with the idea that they like best. A count is taken. In these groups, students can refine their ideas and present possible scenes to the whole group. After these presentations, students have the opportunity to walk to a different idea if they were persuaded by what they saw and heard from another group. A new count is taken. The idea with the fewest votes is removed from consid-eration and those ensemble members move back to the center. They are now the undecided voters. The undecideds are given the opportunity to talk about what elements are important to them and what they would like to see in the three remaining concepts to get their votes. The three remaining groups create new presentations (which could include characters, dialogue, scenes, and/or stage descriptions) and try to incorporate the undecideds' ideas. After the second round of presentations, the undecideds (and anyone else who would like to change positions) pick a new corner. The caucus continues until there are no more undecided students and we've built consensus around a single concept. Ideally, the ideas expand to become more inclusive of everyone's suggestions.

Sometimes what sounds like an interesting concept for a play doesn't lend itself to a group of writers easily generating interesting dramatic material. Because the caucus requires students to give their concept a "test drive" by quickly cranking out rough drafts of potential scenes, the ensemble can see which concepts yield promising early results.

RON RUSSELL: Consensus takes an enormous amount of time. More homogenous teams get work done faster. More diverse teams get work done better. You're going to end up with a better product if you take the time to get everyone to come to consensus. A lot of facilitators practice a negative view of consensus which is about eliminating things that stick out of the dead center. Cutting off the edges of the thing until we get down to something we can agree on because we're all pretty much unhappy with it. So consensus has gotten a really bad name. I think of consensus as building a big unmanageable glob of a mess with everyone's ideas represented. When you tell everybody that their core thoughts are going to make it in. No one's shit is going to get cut, but you are going to have to be adaptable in looking at the core of your idea, not at the surface expression. So if the surface expression of your idea is a dragon and we're not in the medieval world anymore, you're going to have to think, what's a dragon in the projects in 1987? What is the dragon now? What is it about the dragon that originally appealed to you? Your idea is going to make the group better and you don't have to lose it. You just have to make sure you understand what it is and how it fits.

DALISSA DURAN: What makes it Epic is the collaborative process. All those hands and minds in one pot. You have all these teenagers that come from underfunded schools, thirty kids who all want something. I have this idea so it has to be in the play. I wrote this monologue so it has to be in the play. It's ridiculous!

MARK HARRIS: It helps students understand how to make a case for an idea in a positive way and how to keep the end goal in mind. Giving up a part of your idea might better serve the end goal.

DEVIN E. HAQQ: You have to know the kids you're dealing with. If someone's idea gets lost, especially if it's one of your group's strong personalities, that person can check out. You have to make sure that everyone's voice is present somehow. Sometimes it's in the way things are delegated. "OK we didn't pick your idea for our concept, but can you be in charge of writing this crucial scene and can you use an element of that concept you had for the conflict in this scene?"

MELISSA FRIEDMAN: When there's passion around an idea there can be hurt feelings. It can feel bad, but you can also open up your vision and see that the very nature of collaboration means that everyone is giving a little and getting a little.

MICHELLE BECK: What you say is valued. Even if the ensemble goes in a different direction, what you said was considered. It was brought to the table. It was part of the conversation.

MELISSA FRIEDMAN: I think it's really important to acknowledge that they can write on their own. I've gone so far as to hand a notebook to a student who lost out on a concept and say, "I think you should write this."

NILAJA SUN: As older theatre makers we can ask, "How does this idea serve the greater community? How does this scene serve the audiences we want to reach? How does this line serve the artists in this room?"

SARIN MONAE WEST: The needs of the group outweigh individual ideas but everyone's ideas are super important. If a student is invested in the bigger picture of the story that we're telling as a team, there are always opportunities to contribute and participate. It requires flexibility on the part of a student to be able to actually respond in the moment to what the story is now and how it's changing.

NILAJA SUN: It really has a lot to do with how you as the leader structure your lesson plan and your schedule. Don't try to rush to consensus in one day. Maybe you have it separated by a weekend so the students can dream about their ideas so that when they come in on Monday they're like, "Oh I had this idea…"

MELISSA FRIEDMAN: One of the most powerful tools is the undeniability of the "Ummm." When the "Ummm" happens in the room, we have to obey. When the whole room goes, "Ummm" it means the group was moved emotionally by the concept together. All at once. Everyone. I'm not talking about three "Ummm"'s, but a group "Ummm". That is undeniable.

RON RUSSELL: I chafe at the idea that young people should make something that is clean and perfect. I think the messiness is really good. I don't think an emphasis on cleanliness and perfection yields a good product – and even if it does it can yield it at the expense of the team.

12 How do we write scenes?

The touring scripts don't usually feature the typical linear plot structure of a "well-made play." These plays rarely adhere to Aristotle's unities of time, place, and action. The essential question is the unifying force that binds everything together with each scene in the play serving as a unique response or reaction to that question. I'll return to the metaphor of a well-written essential question as a sturdy clothesline: if you build a good one, you can use it to support all kinds of characters, dialogue, transactions, emotions, images, ideas, satire, poetry, and music.

Once the students have identified the characters that make up the world of the play and the kinds of transactions that they're interested in exploring, they can start developing scenes.

Here are a few elements of basic dramatic structure to consider when setting up any scene.

Objectives, tactics, and obstacles

A conflict should be at the core of every scene. A writer can create a framework to build in a clear conflict by identifying objectives, tactics, and obstacles for each character.

> Objective: What a character wants in the scene.
> Tactics: How a character pursues what they want in the scene.
> Obstacles: What prevents a character from getting what they want in the scene.

The tactics and the obstacles should be connected to another character in the scene. Epic uses a specific written format to ensure that every objective, tactic, and obstacle are aligned for maximum impact.

Avoid the win/win at all costs

When stating character objectives in a two character scene use this sentence framework:

[Character A] **is trying to convince** *[Character B]* *[to take a specific action].*

DOI: 10.4324/9781003079835-13

To guarantee that the conflict is clear, Character B's objective should be in *direct opposition*:

[*Character B*] **is trying to convince** [*Character A*] [*to take the exact opposite specific action*].

Imagine that you are setting up a scene between a mother and a daughter. The subject of their conversation is the daughter's desire to borrow the family car. Using our framework you might state their objectives like this:

Daughter wants to convince Mother that she should be allowed to borrow the car.
Mother wants to convince Daughter that she should not be allowed to borrow the car.

Because the conflict is clear and in direct opposition, the audience will know at the end of the scene who "won" or at least who is "winning." If the writer doesn't state an opposing conflict, the scene could get muddled. For example:

Daughter wants to convince Mother that she should be allowed to borrow the car.
Mother wants to convince Daughter that she should clean her room.

These objectives aren't the best because it's possible for both things to occur. The daughter could borrow the car and clean her room: a win/win! Win/win outcomes are great for real people in real life but they tend to be bad for real audiences watching scripted drama. Establishing objectives that are in direct opposition to each other is the key to creating clear conflict with a win/lose outcome.

Using tactics: avoiding stereotypes

A playwright can vary the tactics a character uses which can increase the dynamism in the scene. Following a character's path in pursuit of their objective is often what audiences find most enjoyable and engaging about watching a play.

When charting out character tactics, I prefer to use the verb infinitive form:

To [*verb*]. For example:
To accuse
To calm
To mock
To inspire
To destroy

Changing tactics will have a major impact on the dialogue. If we start to create some dialogue for our mother/daughter car borrowing scenario using the tactics list above, you can start to get a sense of how dramatic that impact can be:

(To accuse) DAUGHTER: You never let me do anything, Mom!

(To calm) MOTHER: OK, honey, let's just take a breath here.

(To mock) DAUGHTER: "Let's just take a breath"! Do you have idea how silly you sound?

(To inspire) MOTHER: I just want you to experience the amazing feeling of earning something you worked for.

(To destroy) DAUGHTER: I HATE YOU!!!

You don't always want to have characters shift tactics every line. A character should try a tactic, until it's clear it won't work and then switch to another one. Figure 12.1 provides a list of tactics you can consult.

It's true for playwrights as well as actors: thinking of characters in terms of the objectives and the tactics they employ will steer you away from generalizations and stereotypes. No human being is always nice, mean, hateful, loving, happy, or sad all the time. There are no purely good or evil people. Well-written characters represent complex people who have needs they are trying to fulfill through the means that are available to them.

"...but I love him!"

There are two kinds of obstacles to track in a scene:

> A character's *External obstacle* is the other character (and their opposing objective) in the scene. This is easy to figure out and easy to notate.

A character's *Internal obstacle* is some thought, feeling, or belief that makes it more difficult for them to pursue their objective. An internal obstacle should immediately follow the objective in the sentence and it will almost always start with the word "but." Some examples of objectives with internal obstacles (in bold) could include:

> I want to convince Mekhi to leave town tonight, **but I love him and can't bear the thought of losing him.**
>
> I want to convince Professor Dunbar to give me an A in the class, **but I know I really didn't earn that grade.**
>
> I want to convince Esmirna to break up with her boyfriend, **but I can't tell her the reason why.**
>
> I want to convince my son to clean the living room, **but I feel guilty about making him do it because it's really my mess.**
>
> I want to convince the School Superintendent to change the school district's admissions policy to be more fair to everyone, **but I still want my child to go to the best school.**

LIST OF TACTICS (ACTION VERBS)

To accuse	To destroy	To infuriate	To seduce
To alarm	To distract	To interrogate	To shock
To amaze	To distress	To intimidate	To sicken
To amuse	To educate	To irritate	To silence
To befriend	To electrify	To lure	To slap
To blame	To empower	To make guilty	To soothe
To beg	To enchant	To massage	To startle
To boss	To energize	To mesmerize	To stun
To belittle	To enliven	To mock	To tame
To bully	To enrage	To mother	To taunt
To calm	To entertain	To mystify	To tease
To challenge	To entice	To nag	To tempt
To charm	To enlighten	To needle	To test
To coax	To excite	To overwhelm	To tickle
To comfort	To flatter	To pamper	To threaten
To command	To fluster	To panic	To thrill
To confront	To frighten	To pester	To torment
To crush	To harass	To plead	To warn
To dare	To horrify	To praise	To welcome
To dazzle	To humiliate	To ridicule	To wound
To deify	To hurry	To rouse	To wake up
To delight	To hypnotize	To scare	
To demand	To impress	To scold	

Figure 12.1 Chart of tactics.

A well-written character in a well-written scene has at least two things to contend with: the other person in the scene and their own self-doubt about the correctness of their objective. A character's internal obstacle often goes unspoken for at least awhile (sometimes it's never explicitly stated in the play)

Figure 12.2 Epic NEXT students Christina Liberus, Hailey Petrus, and Kyarrah Ebanks
work on writing a scene together.

Source: David Naranjo/photo courtesy of Epic Theatre Ensemble.

and audiences may not immediately be aware of it, but if a writer is clear and
has articulated it for themselves, it can provide some amazing fuel for compelling dialogue.

Environment, Relationship, Conflict, and Resolution (ERCR)

I recommend trying to establish these four elements before sitting down (or
standing up in a devising process) to write a scene.

Environment: Where and when does this scene take place? The more
specific the time and place, the easier it will be to write the scene. "A
house" doesn't give a writer much to work with. Breakfast time at
the kitchen table in a small studio apartment in the Grand Concourse
neighborhood of the Bronx is more evocative.

Relationship: Who are the characters in the scene and what is their
relationship to each other? "Friends" doesn't tell you much. The
more clear, rich, and complicated you make the relationships as
you're planning out the scene, the less you'll have to worry about
figuring out those dynamics later, which will allow you to just focus
on creating authentic and sparkling dialogue, which I think is the
most fun part of writing a play.

Conflict: What is the clear problem or issue between these characters?

Resolution: At the end of the scene it should be clear who "won" or at least who is "winning." Did "Character A" convince "Character B" or not? Was ground gained or given up on either side?

Once you've charted out the environment, relationship, conflict, and resolution (ERCR), it makes it easier to make adjustments. For example, if you're struggling to generate compelling dialogue for the car borrowing scene between the mother and the daughter, you can make an adjustment to one element of the ERCR and see of that helps. If the scene was originally set in a living room, you can try keeping the relationship, conflict, and resolution the same but setting it at the main reading room of the New York Public Library instead and see how that affects the characters' dialogue and tactics. The fact that a library is a quiet space may provide some interesting new obstacles for each of the characters. Play with adjusting those ERCR elements until you find a scenario that seems to write itself!

Dialogue warm-ups: first line/last line

Some quick and easy writing warm-ups are a great way to get students in the right (write?) frame of mind to generate dialogue. Ask the ensemble to take out something to write with and copy this down:

A:

B:

A:

B:

A:

B:

A:

B:

Ask for a suggestion for a first line from the ensemble (Perhaps someone suggests, "What are you doing here?". Everyone writes down this first line for Character A. Now ask for a suggestion for a last line (Perhaps someone suggests, "I'm pregnant."). Everyone writes down this last line for Character B. So in this example, everyone's page should now look like this:

A: What are you doing here?

B:

A:

B:

A:

B:

A:

B: I'm pregnant.

Each student in the ensemble has 60 seconds to finish the scene on their own. This is a writing warm-up so don't think too much about it. Just write whatever comes to mind. Let it flow. It doesn't have to be good. It doesn't have to make sense. It just has to get done! Share out the scenes. Try additional warm-ups with First Line/Second Line, Sixth Line/Last Line, etc.

Get in late; Get out early

This is a phrase I learned from playwright Vern Thiessen. Conflict is the most engaging aspect of any scene. You should maximize the amount of stage time for conflicts and reduce the amount of stage time given to anything else. For example, a young writer will often think that they need to start a scene with two characters walking into a room and greeting one another like this:

DAVE: Hi Chrissy.
CHRISSY: Hi Dave. Is mom up yet?
DAVE: Not yet.
CHRISSY: So are you making breakfast?
DAVE: Yes.
CHRISSY: Cool.
DAVE: You know, you really hurt my feelings yesterday.
CHRISSY: I did? How?
DAVE: That joke you told.

Zzzzzzzzz… A more experienced writer will realize that the audience doesn't necessarily want or need to see the greeting and the build up to the conflict, and they will choose to start the scene in progress and bring the audience into the conflict at a point nearer its peak:

CHRISSY: Oh why don't you shut up, get a sense of humor, and make the breakfast! It was just a joke, Dave!
DAVE: Did you see me laughing yesterday, Chrissy?!
CHRISSY: Shhh! You'll wake up mom!

Exposition sucks. It's best to get to the good stuff, and the conflict is usually the good stuff. You can look to find ways to embed all the same expositional information in your dialogue (Brother/sister, breakfast time, joke went wrong) but begin the scene at what is likely a more interesting entry point for an audience. Similarly, you probably don't need to see every character say their goodbyes and leave the room. Once it's clear that one of the characters has won the scene, type "Curtain," and move on to the next scene and the next conflict. It's rarely a good thing for an audience to feel like they are ahead of the story. Start your scenes late, end them early, and let your audience have fun catching up.

Sensory prompts

Using sensory prompts can be a great way to unlock poetic language and imagery around an abstract concept. For example, if you wanted to explore the concept of freedom, you might ask the students to finish the following sentences:

- Freedom looks like…
- Freedom sounds like…
- Freedom smells like…
- Freedom tastes like…
- Freedom feels like…

VERN THIESSEN: Most of the time, when you come into a classroom of high school students, and say, "We're going to write a play" they may not know what a play is because they haven't recognized that plays are existing all around them all the time. So the first thing to do is to say, "Just because you may not have gone to a theatre and sat in a seat and watched someone on a stage act, that doesn't mean that you haven't seen a play." There are plays happening in your house every single day. It might be a fight between you and your parents or it might be on the bus on the way to school or it might be the drama that is happening in your classroom. There are drama and plays all around. They initially believe that plays are really hard to write and they think of Shakespeare as an example. They need to know that plays are not mystical. They are things that you can build, like just like you can build a model or paint, like a paint by number. There is an easy set of tools that you can use to release the play from the paper.

MELISSA FRIEDMAN: This is something you already have. Just reinforcing, you already have a point of view, you already inherently understand what status is, you already know what a want and a need is, you already use tactics in your everyday life, you already recognize what is unfair and unjust. You already have these things. Now let's build some skills so you can make a choice about what you put out into the world. So this idea of, "I'm not a writer" has to get dispelled right away.

CLARO DE LOS REYES: Students are actually generating tons of writing and dialogue in their text messages with their friends. The tricky thing with writing a play is that it does mimic a school setting a lot of the time – sitting down and writing. Even that broad physical experience of sitting down and writing is the epitome of what they think an academic does. So how do you get around that? I've encouraged young writers sometimes to use dictation on a smartphone. They can audio record themselves speaking, but then they have to transcribe it. The act of transcribing can then itself be an interesting process because the act of writing can bring with it an editing process, like "I want to change this line to sound more like that." So already they're creating a second draft in a way. That's something I've been experimenting with a lot lately. How do we still generate the material that's not pen to paper at the top? How do you not let the writing process stymie someone's thoughts? Some rappers write – someone like Nas or Eminem writes in pages. Jay-Z just freestyles and he remembers it. Those are completely different processes and no one is saying one is better than the other, right? Some folks need to craft on paper and others don't. That's an unexplored territory in teaching playwriting. You're still teaching how to create dramatic text, character voice, setting, but how can generating material be even more diverse? How do we overlay the concept of multiple intelligences on generating work?

13 How do we organize our material into a first draft?

Another way to approach the creation process is through an analysis of style. The scenes that students begin to craft for their plays tend to fall into one of four categories:

"The real" An exploration of how the essential question impacts ordinary people in everyday situations; the heart and soul of the play.

"The absurd" An exploration of the essential question through metaphor or satire; decoding/translating; If this is true what else is true?

"The research" An exploration of the essential question through verbatim reports from the field.

"The poetic" An exploration of the essential question through music, movement, poetry. The hook.

All of these scene structures can illuminate the essential question in different ways and it's a good idea to make sure that the play is made up of scenes from each of the four. I think the best way to examine these structures is to look at some examples from Epic NEXT plays.

"The Real"

Bertolt Brecht defined the concept of realism through a political lens. For Brecht to be real in drama is to show the show cause and effect relationship between the dominators (bolstered by society's dominant viewpoints) and the dominated. "The Real" is that which shows the nuances of humanity's most intractable problems and gives voice to bold and broad solutions.[1]

In 2016, the students were researching educational segregation. They quickly learned that the subject is extremely complex and tied to numerous other issues such as gentrification and housing policy, resource equity, systemic and internalized racism, the white savior complex, and a set of specialized terminology with nuanced differences like desegregation, integration, busing, rezoning, charters, magnets, specialized, independent, screened, and non-screened schools. The NYC Department of Education is the largest school system in the country with 1.2 million students, 300,000 full-time employees, and a

DOI: 10.4324/9781003079835-14

labyrinthine administrative apparatus that can be dizzying for students and parents to try to navigate. In speaking to their own families, several members of the ensemble could see clearly the confusion that a parent can feel just trying to understand all the complex, inter-connected dynamics of segregation. In their play *Laundry City*, the students created this soliloquy for Mrs. Malavé, the parent of a student attending a school going through a rezoning process (It was commissioning partner, Matt Gonzales who first suggested translating this monologue into Spanish, which we did for later performances).

MRS. MALAVÉ: What does this mean? What does this mean? White people moving in? Here? Of all the places? We're quiet. We don't even get news coverage whenever a little boy is shot out here. What will they bring? Higher rent, more and more white people. I'm gonna get kicked out. I can't. This is the only place I know. I grew up here – been here my whole life. Mami and Papi are gone, God rest their souls, so I can't even ask them for advice. What am I gonna do? How will this affect Jeylin? Her school? Maybe the government will finally help them. Is that who takes care of the schools? But... it's morally wrong to use children as a means to better a whole school. They're not tools, they're people. But, Jeylin. Her school needs that attention. SHE needs that help and attention. This is good. More white people means more money. Even if I get kicked out after Jeylin is in college, at least she'll get to go. *(sigh)* C'mon, little blanquitos. Bring some help.

Figure 13.1 Melysa Hierro performs a monologue as Mrs. Malavé for a performance of *Laundry City* at Teachers College, Columbia University.

Source: David Naranjo/photo courtesy of Epic Theatre Ensemble.

The play *Building Blocks: Colorful Minds* looked at the impact that racism and sexism have on diversity in STEM fields. The students spoke to a number of women employed in computer science and engineering who talked about the challenges of working in fields that have been historically dominated by men. In this excerpt, Ms. Davis, a high school Chemistry teacher, has just witnessed a male colleague take credit for an education program that she developed.

MS. DAVIS: What the hell? What. the. hell, just happened? No... he did not just give credit to himself and his son! Not for my work... no... NO! I won't take it! I've worked my ass off doing the thing I love, and for what? To be seen as just a gender? I am more than that! These kids are able to enjoy chemistry because of me! They'd still be struggling on the Periodic Table if it weren't for me and my teaching methods! I do so much for these kids and the school and I get nothing! Nothing. So, Mr. Housner, you won't get the last laugh at all, because I SWEAR TO YOU ON ANYTHING THAT "MY TIME OF MONTH" WILL BE THE LAST SMART REMARK YOU SAY TO ME OR ELSE I'LL-
(MIA enters and interrupts MS. DAVIS's monologue.)
MIA: Ms. Davis?
MS. DAVIS: Yes, Mia?
MIA: You're like a scientist right?
MS. DAVIS: Yes.
MIA: But you're also like a mom, right?
MS. DAVIS: Yeah.
MIA: But you also go on field trips, like you climb and you run, and you're involved in lots of activities?
MS. DAVIS: Yeah.
MIA: So I could do what you're doing too, right?
MS. DAVIS: Absolutely.

Other examples of what I'd classify as "the real" include Shaena's lesson from *Default* and the "Mr. Alecander" scene from *Perfect Circle*.

AARON KROHN: A good play is a specific story about everything. It's a particular group of people going through something important to all of us. It asks and wonders about an experience that reverberates with all of us.
GODFREY L. SIMMONS, JR.: This work is political and it's ancestral. When you walk on a stage your ancestors are with you. That shit goes at least seven generations back. There are so many layers to how you got here in this moment to tell these stories and someone with your bloodline has been through this exact thing. Somebody's dealt with it. It's there. It's in you. It's your responsibility to bring all of this stuff from ancestors to bear on this story that hopefully is going to be universal and span the ages. That's your responsibility as someone who is telling stories. Connecting them to the political ramifications of what they're choosing to do and

Figure 13.2 Kyarrah Ebanks, Nashali Perez, Jhadia Edwards, Miguel Delacruz, and Sandia Reyes perform a scene from *Building Blocks: Colorful Minds.*

Source: David Naranjo/photo courtesy of Epic Theatre Ensemble.

connecting those political ramifications to the deeply personal that goes further than who they are, but connects to their ancestral birthright to tell their stories. We all have that birthright to tell our stories. Our ancestors gave up something for it.

The absurd

The physicist Neils Bohr noted, "Some subjects are so serious, they can only be joked about."[2] Humor is fundamental to creativity and imagination and it can be an extremely effective tool to engage an audience: it wakes them up, challenges their expectations, and provides them an opportunity through laughter to re-consider established schools of thought.

Epic NEXT students receive intensive improv training. There is a principle of improvisation: ***"If this is true, what else is true?"*** It's a form of logical creativity an artist can employ to highlight the absurdity of commonly accepted norms.

In 2015, while researching educational inequities in New York's education system, a group of student artist/researchers came across this passage in the state's constitution regarding students' rights:

Children are entitled to ***minimally adequate*** physical facilities and classrooms which provide enough light, space, heat, and air to permit children to learn. Children should have access to **minimally adequate** instrumentalities of learning such as desks, chairs, pencils, and **reasonably** current textbooks. Children are also entitled to **minimally adequate** teaching of **reasonably** up to-date basic curricula such as reading, writing, mathematics, science, and social studies, by **sufficient** personnel **adequately** trained to teach those subject areas.[3]

This repeated refrain of "minimally adequate" struck them as very odd. What does "minimally adequate" teaching look like? How does minimally adequate teaching differ from terrible teaching? Should minimally adequate be the bar that's set for any aspect of education and child development? With an intentional *"If this is true what else is true?"* mindset, the ensemble started to riff on what "minimally adequate" might look like in other areas of art and life. Here is an excerpt from their play *10467*:

VOICE OVER: The Minimally Adequate Players present: A Minimally Adequate Poem

ALEX: How now.

ROBERT: Brown cow.

ABEL: The end.

(ALL BOW)

VOICE OVER: The Minimally Adequate Players present: A Minimally Adequate Children's Story

ALEX: Once upon a time, a dog went outside.

ROBERT: He died.

ABEL: The end.

(ALL BOW)

VOICE OVER: The Minimally Adequate Players present: A Minimally Adequate Love Song

ROBERT, ALEX, AND ABEL: Girl!

(ALL BOW)

VOICE OVER: The Minimally Adequate Players present: A Minimally Adequate Fire Safety Lesson

ROBERT: Fire!

(ALEX throws a cup of water on ABEL)

ABEL: The end.

VOICE OVER: The Minimally Adequate Players present: A Minimally Adequate Love Scene

ROBERT: Do you love me?

ALEX: Sure.

ABEL: The end.

(ALL BOW)

ABEL SANTIAGO: We were doing research one day and we came across that paper that talked about "Minimally adequate." I remember me and Robert looked at each other like, "Minimally adequate air? Wow." At

Figure 13.3 Abel Santiago, Robert Simmons, and Alex Britvan as the Minimally Adequate
Players in *10467* at National Black Theatre in Harlem.

Source: Melissa Friedman/photo courtesy of Epic Theatre Ensemble.

that moment, I knew we found something we could play with. Literally.
And we got up on our feet and started playing. What would minimally
adequate football look like? What would a minimally adequate motiva-
tional speaker sound like? It started with the research but very quickly we
were able to get out our heads and into our bodies to create.

For additional examples of "Is this is true, what else is true?" look at the
opening "audience assessment" scene from *Overdrive* and the "Bully-Free
Zone" scenes from *Perfect Circle*.

MEKHI TUDOR: We started talking about a Bully Free Zone sign that somehow just magically stops bullying. How big is a Bully-Free Zone? How
far does it stretch? I wrote a few things and we started doing some
improv. It was a really fun game that we started playing. In improvisation, it's always about playing the game. *Perfect Circle* isn't a light
play, so it gives the audience a break from the grit of a heavy topic like
bullying.

Another pathway to the absurd is through ***decoding or translating*** – actively
analyzing people's subtext and exposing what uncomfortable truths they are
trying to hide through euphemisms and clichés.

In 2016, while interviewing professional educators about segregation, the ensemble became frustrated with what they perceived as evasiveness and an unwillingness to talk directly about the issues in terms of race and class. They created the duo of a nervous Public School Principal and his subtext translator, "Keeping it 100":

MR. MADISON: Good morning students and faculty.

KEEPING IT 100: Good morning worthless subjects.

MR. MADISON: We have much to talk about

KEEPING IT 100: I'm talking so shut up.

MR. MADISON: Soon we will be admitting new students to our school.

KEEPING IT 100: White students are a-comin'.

MR. MADISON: Don't worry this is a good thing

KEEPING IT 100: Calm your asses down, this shit is good.

MR. MADISON: Nothing will change.

KEEPING IT 100: Everything's changing.

MR. MADISON: This is happening because of the rezoning going on in Brooklyn.

KEEPING IT 100: This is happening because white people are colonizing Brooklyn.

MR. MADISON: This is a great opportunity to make our school great again!

KEEPING IT 100: This is a great opportunity to snatch that white money.

MR. MADISON: We will be getting supplies!

KEEPING IT 100: We getting shit.

MR. MADISON: New textbooks

KEEPING IT 100: New shit.

MR. MADISON: New lockers

KEEPING IT 100: New places to put your shit.

MR. MADISON: And a brand new gym that you students will be able to have and use.

KEEPING IT 100: Shit…we're getting lots of brand new shit.

MR. MADISON: We will show them our school spirit.

KEEPING IT 100: We will show them how white we can be.

GODFREY L. SIMMONS, JR.: As Black or Brown people, there is a certain kind of acquired genius that happens because we have to operate on three different levels every minute of the day. In the United States, we're either operating on the level of what I'll characterize as "country," or urbanity, or bullshit Queen's English. These are these different three levels that you're operating on – there are probably more. How we speak, how we interact with people, how we interact with the world. When you enter the world you have to ask, which world are you in, within your own group? Because there are all of these different ways in which we operate dependent on class and education. Then when we get into the "halls of power" that are largely white and largely male spaces, there's a whole other level of shifting you have to do. And I wish people knew how brilliant every single person who is Black or Brown is at navigating it. I wish

Figure 13.4 Davion Osbourne and Randy Figueroa perform a scene from *Laundry City* at National Black Theatre in Harlem.

Source: David Naranjo/photo courtesy of Epic Theatre Ensemble.

that people understood the genius that is developed over time, regardless of what they do with their lives. It has very little to do with models of success but every single Black or Brown person develops a particular genius at being able to navigate that. A lot of people have no clue and would not be able to even touch that kind of genius.

For more examples of decoding/translating, look at the "Beating around the Bush" scene in *Nothing About Us*.

ANTHONY VAUGHN MERCHANT: We were talking about a sketch from A Black Lady Sketch Show and I asked, "What's the funny thing about this?". I was ready to break it all down and say, "Look how they heighten it. Look how it rests." All of that. So I asked "What's funny about this?" and Nay (a student) said, "Cause it be like that sometimes." And I was like... there it is. That's the secret sauce. The shared experience. I threw out my curriculum and said, "Let's just call it the 'It be like that sometimes' factor." Let's just roll with that. What is the thing that everyone will go, "Yeah, for real though"? What is the thing that makes us all go, "Mmm–hmmm"?

JACOB-MING TRENT: For me, writing is a way of asking, "What if...?" That's what I do. What if these events occurred? What if this thing we do everyday, we didn't do and let this other thing happen?

AARON KROHN: Conscious contradiction – You might think if Mother Courage is poor and moving around she should have less stuff with her. Maybe not. Maybe she should have more stuff with her because she's stealing stuff. Have fun with that conscious contradiction because usually what you expect the character to be doing or to be like, the contradiction often is a great idea that works with the character.

The research

We allot a large percentage of time in our development process for the interviews. The students interview between 30–40 people who are either directly impacted by the essential question or who have chosen to devote their professional lives to addressing it. The interviews provide vital context and information for creation but they often can be a source of exciting and even poetic text. We encourage the students to use the research to drive their story-telling.

Here is an excerpt of a Town Hall scene from *Laundry City* that was constructed by collating a series of answers to interview questions.

MR. MADISON: What do you think is the solution to New York City's school segregation problem?

WELLS: I think – Hold on, hold on. Let me think about that.

PHILLIP: We need to get more Black men as teachers, more Black men as school administrators, but no one is talking about why aren't they there.

SARAH: There are the "three R's" that we need to address: 1. Racial enrollment – How do you choose my school and how do I make sure I select fairly? 2. Resources – how do you make sure every single school has the same resources? 3. The last piece is relationships – Once we're all in the building, if y'all haven't met each other and there's racism in the building, you're not going to talk to each other or learn how to work together. How do you fund teachers to help them build clubs that establish relationships across racial lines?

JOE: I think where we get confused is conflating the quest for adequate educational opportunities with a quest for integration. The theory of action was if you import basically white middle class students, they would then advocate for all of the students in the school, they had more social and political capital and they would essentially serve as the saviors for the Black and Latino students in the school. I think that's racist. I think it's classist. I don't believe in the savior complex – that you need to have folks swoop in and save the poor Black and Latino children. I believe that Black and Latino folks have agency and have power that has been untapped.

SARAH: For me, it's not that certain communities are less powerful; it's that certain communities haven't been given the floor. How do we give people the floor? Segregation was intentional. Integration has to be intentional. Segregation was forced. Integration has to be forced.

WELLS: What do *you* think is the solution?

MR. MADISON: Do you think that there should be some sort of revolution that needs to occur in order for our voices to be heard?

ERNEST: I think there needs to be a national movement.

TANYA: A revolution is eminent. That's just going to happen. Trump? It's going to happen. Trump has risen the sleeping dog. The south has awakened.

JOE: I acknowledge that in history violent uprisings sometimes have made a difference, sometimes on the side of justice and equality. I don't believe that we need that in order to achieve a high quality education for people of color. I shy away from calling it a revolution or even using the term radical because I think it alienates a lot of people who agree in principle, but people get scared when you use words like revolution or radical.

ABDUL: We need integration. It doesn't have to come from a revolution, it just has to come.

PHILLIP: Who says the goal is integration? I think for me the goal is about having high quality schools.

MELYSA: Were you born yesterday? INTEGRATE for god sakes!

TANYA: If integration made money somehow, then America would do it. Integration is not the goal.

Figure 13.5 Davion Osbourne, Olivia Dunbar, and Rodwell Masquitta in *Laundry City* at NYU.

Source: David Naranjo/photo courtesy of Epic Theatre Ensemble.

Sometimes ensembles create structures to provide a dramatic context for the interview material, like a town hall or a protest, but often an ensemble will decide to create stand-alone choral pieces like this excerpt from *Building Blocks: Colorful Minds*.

MAN 5: James Damore, Google Employee. Last August: "Women don't make up 50% of the company's tech and leadership positions not because of sexism but because of differences in their preferences and abilities. Women have more 'neuroticism', higher anxiety, lower stress tolerance."

WOMAN 1: You know, in most STEM fields especially in Silicon Valley it's super "Bro-y" right?. And some people might think, "Oh I don't want to go into a room where nobody looks like me and so I'm not going to go into a STEM field." I sometimes look around and like wow literally nobody here looks like me right?

MAN 5: Lawrence H. Summers, Harvard President in 2005 suggested men outperform women in math and science because of innate biological differences.

WOMAN 2: They're not used to females being out there. Those words have been said to me.

MAN 5: Maybe you should be sitting on a beach and hanging out with your friends instead of working. Why don't you find a rich man to take care of you?

WOMAN 1: And it's not just me.

WOMAN 4: Every girl that works here has gone out to a field and heard that.

MAN 5: Dr. Paul Topinard, French Phrenologist. 1911. "Men bear all of the responsibility and the cares of tomorrow."

WOMAN 2: I'm not even kidding. I sat down at the table and then one of my bosses says to me:

MAN 5 AND WOMAN 2: Oh Elaine, you're allowed to sit at the big kids table with all of the boys?

WOMAN 2: and I'm like – I just – I can't believe this is happening – I didn't know what to say.

MAN 5: "The sedentary women, lacking any interior occupations, whose role is to raise children, love and be passive."

WOMAN 3: There's a lot of sexism, right? We might meet somebody who has an attitude of

WOMAN 3 AND MAN 5: Oh boys might be better suited to science

WOMAN 4: And

MAN 5 AND WOMAN 3: Oh you might just want to have kids or get married or something.

WOMAN 3: We constantly hear this whole topic of "work-life" balance.

WOMEN 1–4: Really?

WOMAN 3: And it's always focused on women too.

MAN 5: Charles Darwin. 1871. "The average of mental power in man must be above that of woman."

Figure 13.6 Casandra Gilbes, Davion Osbourne, Dondrea Wynter, Christina Liberus, and Joham Palma in *Building Blocks: Colorful Minds.*

Source: James Wallert/photo courtesy of Epic Theatre Ensemble.

WOMEN 1–4: REALLY?

LUAN TAVERAS: Those four true stories that make up "You Become the System" from *Default*. It took a certain courage for them to go there and share their experiences and it makes it special every time we perform them. These are real people. These are their stories. You have this responsibility to tell their stories well, to truly drive their points home, to truly be in the moment. You want Joey, Natasha, Shino, and Mike to live in those spaces to tell their stories. You want to do them justice.

The poetic

Some truths can't be fully represented by a simple recitation of the facts. Poetry is the language of revolution. It stirs our passions and elevates our consciousness. It creates new pathways between our intellect, our emotions, and our sense of morality. In this excerpt from *Laundry City*, the character Adande presents different points of view on integration:

ADANDE: Yes! Our schools need integration.
　　Nothing benefits from school segregation.
　　Diversity is growth & ya have to be aware
　　That separate but equal is never gonna be fair.
　　If schools are integrated then we socially advance
　　But we're still separate therefore limiting the chance
　　For greatness to truly emerge from the nation
　　So how do we prevent that? Desegregation.

ADANDE: No! Nothing will come from integration,
　　All we really need is equal education.
　　If the white kids flood our school, that is not mixing up – that is
　　gentrification.
　　We need to bring up the law and demand academics we desperately need.
　　We can't let them hold us down. We have to rise up, demand, evolve,
　　and succeed.

ADANDE: Ladies and gentlemen we are gathered here today
　　To discuss a serious topic happening everyday.
　　A problem first addressed way back in the 50's
　　In a case known as Brown versus Board of E.
　　But, the issue still stands.
　　We need to learn together we need to join hands.
　　With all the benefits that come with integration
　　Why are we still dealing with school segregation?

This rap kicked off the play *10467*:

TYRONE: Bureaucrats turned to politricksters.
　　Pulling the same trick.
　　How much money we gonna make
　　off these fools Is what they think.
　　Doing everything they can to make

Figure 13.7 Davion Osbourne in *Laundry City* at NYU.

Source: David Naranjo/photo courtesy of Epic Theatre Ensemble.

sure that they stay on top
I pray to god that these dudes don't
ever step foot on my block.
You don't know how good we should have it.
these ain't luxuries we should have.
Don't put it into the back burner.
They wanna make us broke and stupid,
so we can't make it out
whether its making it to college
or taking a bus route
But I promise you I won't let Inequity get the best of me
brothers are Killings brothers and living just for a check you see.
We all live, we sleep and die in the same class
It's kinda like Hinduism
A class system turned to a caste system what's the issue.
We focused on building buildings instead of building our Future,
It's us. We stay silent – it's us.

The raps in *Nothing About Us* and *Default* are great examples of poetic responses to their respective essential questions.

MICHELLE BECK: There is a natural inclination in a lot of students to write poetry. I don't think that's an impulse that needs too much encouragement, especially if you've invited their feelings into the room. They have a lot of feelings at that age.

MELISSA FRIEDMAN: Emotion is quite powerfully embodied in an effective teaching artist. We're often taught in school to not feel anything. Connecting education to your heart is such an important part of humanity. Feeling emotion isn't a sign of weakness. Your vulnerability is you revealing your humanity. I think this idea that in the classroom we're supposed to pretend that we never feel sad or scared or angry but only on task is dangerous. For young people? We're working with teenagers and we're supposed to pretend that there are no feelings?

Some scenes might fall under multiple categories: these tend to be extremely effective storytelling moments. The Liana/Shaena/Alyssa choral scene from *Default* is very much the real combined with the poetic. Matt's "White Lips to White Ears" monologue features the real, the absurd, and the research. The rap from *Overdrive* is a great example of the convergence of the real, the absurd, and the poetic.

Notes

1. Bertolt Brecht, "The Popular and the Realistic," in *Brecht on Theatre*, ed. and trans. by John Willett, New York: Hill & Wang, 1964, pp. 108–110
2. Pais, Abraham. *The Genius of Science: A Portrait Gallery*. Oxford University Press. 2000, p. 24.
3. *Campaign for Fiscal Equity, Inc. v. State*, 86 N.Y. 2d at 317, 1995.

14 How do we revise scenes?

With a 30-minute time limit, sometimes the ensemble has to make some difficult decisions about editing material. Revision can be challenging for any writer. Here are some concepts that we employ to make the process less painful.

Subtext

Subtext is what's underneath the words. It's a concept that all students are familiar with, although they often don't know it by that term. "Throwing subs" (implying something negative about someone online without explicitly naming them.) is a popular bit of contemporary slang. Emojis are an attempt to communicate unspoken intentions in text-only formats.

In life, people don't always come right out and state their objectives: sometimes it's out of a fear of rejection ("I just like her as a friend") or an attempt to spare someone's feelings ("No, I never would have guessed that's a hairpiece.") or to manipulate a situation for personal gain ("I think Cassio's an honest man"). Why might a character in a play speak in subtext? If their external or internal obstacle is formidable enough, plainly stating their objective might be too dangerous.

To experiment with how subtext can impact language, select a character from one of your scenes. Write a line of dialogue that communicates the following lines of subtext without using the exact words:

- I'm not sure who you are, although I think I'm supposed to.
- I'm deeply in love with you.
- You smell really odd.
- Your boyfriend is cheating on you.
- I've never felt more lonely than I do right now. Please don't leave.

Be specific about how this particular character might express this thought without coming right out and saying it. How subtle can they be? Can they mask their intention from the other person while at the same time making it clear to the audience what's really going on? Read these sentences aloud. The rest of the ensemble can try to guess which subtexts are being communicated.

DOI: 10.4324/9781003079835-15

Figure 14.1 Epic NEXT students Casandra Gilbes, Esmirna Matos, and Lizette Padua review a scene with Epic Associate Artist Marilyn Torres.

Source: James Wallert/photo courtesy of Epic Theatre Ensemble.

Now take a look at your scene: where is this character plainly stating their objective? Is there an internal or external obstacle that might prevent them from coming right out and saying it? If not, maybe you need to provide a stronger obstacle. Under duress, what might they say instead?

I am...

I don't know that you can teach originality, but I think you can identify what truly original writing looks like and encourage writers to explore their own creative possibilities. I look to bring in pieces of text with language or imagery that seems totally unique, so much so that you can't imagine anyone having put those particular words together in that particular order before. "Jabberwocky" by Lewis Carroll features the lines:

> One, two! One, two! And through and through
> The vorpal blade went snicker-snack!
> He left it dead, and with its head
> He went galumphing back.

I challenge anyone to tell me they've previously encountered those words in casual conversation. They're totally unique and they evoke quite an image!

We'll look at work from other artists like Langston Hughes, Tom Waits, Maya Angelou, or Kendrick Lamar. What "pops" for you in this text? What feels strange and new? What sounds totally original? I encourage the students to write down words or phrases in these works that they've never heard before. We analyze the use of metaphor and imagery. Are there words here that the writer just invented? Shakespeare invented over 1700 now common words by changing nouns into verbs, changing verbs into adjectives, connecting words never before used together, adding prefixes and suffixes, and devising wholly original words.

After we've broken down some of these texts, I'll give students a challenge: you have 10 minutes to attempt to write 20 absolutely original sentences that I, Jim, have never heard before that begins with the sentence starter, "I am…." Think of using metaphor, simile, imagery, and even inventing new words. Can you stump me? There's always at least one student that's tempted to go down the route of pasting together a stream of curse words, so in order to discourage that I make sure to mention in my instructions that I possess an encyclopedic knowledge of profanity.

In 2004, Christina Gonzalez, a 14-year-old student in a North Bronx classroom responded to this "I am…" prompt with the sentence, "I am as lonely as a math teacher in the Museum of Natural History on Valentine's Day." A remarkably evocative image coupled with what I believe to be a totally original turn of phrase. That is a very particular kind of lonely! I realized that prior to this book, I had never actually written that sentence down so that I might remember it later; I never needed to. Who could forget that sentence? I've kept in close touch with Christina over the years: she worked for Epic as an alumni Producing Associate and I am pleased and proud that she's chosen to continue her career in arts education.

Once the students have completed this "I am…" exercise, I encourage them to take a look at their first drafts. Are there opportunities to revise lines of dialogue along this vein? How can your text sing with originality?

No small parts

When Stanislavski said, "There are no small parts, only small actors.", he had obviously never encountered some of the parts written into our students' first drafts. Sometimes young writers will populate a script with characters whose only functions are to provide exposition or advance a plot point. If you come across ANGRY PARENT #4 or KID #7, it's likely that the script might benefit from a deeper exploration and investment in some of those characters.

Encourage the writers to select a character from their scene that they feel they know the least. On a sheet of paper have them answer the following questions:

1   What is your character's name?
2   What are your character's pronouns?
3   Is your character in a relationship?
4   Does your character have children?
5   What is your character's occupation?
6   Describe where your character lives and who else lives there.
7   Describe your character's relationship with money.
8   Describe your character's relationship with politics.
9   Describe your character's relationship with religion.
10 Describe your character's relationship with their mother.
11 Describe your character's greatest fear.
12 Your character has a secret: what is it?

Now revisit your scene and see if you can incorporate some of these discoveries into the text. How might these details impact the scene?

Meeting of the minds

This is a variation of a protocol pioneered by The Lark, a theatre laboratory in New York City dedicated to supporting playwrights. The writer is given total control over the sharing process: they choose a piece of writing to share aloud with the group, select readers, and provide whatever pre-reading context they wish. After the piece is read aloud, the writer then gets a pre-determined amount of time to field thoughts from the group. Potential questions they might put to the group include:

- What do you think?
- What words or phrases "pop" for you?
- What do you wonder about these characters?
- What do you find interesting about this scene?
- What questions does this scene raise for you?
- What other opportunities for conflict do you see in this scene?
- What do you predict will happen next?
- No questions. Thanks for listening!

It's important that the writer has complete agency over the discussion. The rest of the group should only respond to direct questions from the writer and no unsolicited feedback or questions should be accepted. In fact, it's totally fine if the writer determines that they don't need or want any additional feedback.

VERN THIESSEN: Time limits are a big thing for me. As soon as you put a time limit on something, it short circuits thinking. Try to work in a way in which people can only respond from their instincts because if they think too much they will destroy the passion and the real drama that is happening. For the most part, young artists do way too much thinking. Sometimes, I will give the students a very short period of time to cut their scene in half. That usually means cutting out all stage directions; cutting out all junk words. So if a character is saying, "I really think that you should get out of here," then you may need to cut it down to "Get out of here." Getting down to the power words. What are the essential words that you need in this scene?

LIZETTE PADUA: Hearing it out loud is one of the things that really helps me revise. In your head, what you're writing might make sense to you, but when it's read out loud you can hear what you need to fix.

LUAN TAVERAS: You put so much effort into your first draft. You want this first draft to be great. You want people to love it, but you have to take into account that it's a *first* draft. There's always more work to be done. You're always fine tuning.

MEKHI TUDOR: You can't be afraid to write what you think is garbage. That's where art dies. There were a lot of times where I would write something and I wouldn't like it, but people would hear it and tell me that it sounds good. I'm my own worst critic, so sometimes I need other people's opinions to help figure out when something is working.

DEVIN E. HAQQ: Even as a professional, I'm writing something now and it's terrible. It's terrible and I don't want to continue but I know this is part of the process. I just have to get this all out as a first draft and then I'll have a screenplay and I can go back and make it something passable.

15 How do we rehearse our play?

Here are some core principles, techniques, and protocols that young directors and performers can use to establish and nurture a rehearsal environment that is fun, safe, efficient, creative, respectful, anti-racist, inclusive, and democratic.

Casting

In 2018, as part of our Off-Broadway season, Epic produced a play, I wrote, called *The Winning Side*. Based on the true story of Wernher von Braun, Chief Rocket Engineer of the Third Reich and one of the fathers of the U.S. space program, *The Winning Side* explores some of the hidden history behind the Apollo 11 moon landing. The cast of the production featured three Black men and one white woman. We had a post-show conversation with our audience after every performance, many of which were led by me. Many evenings after I wrapped up the "official" post-show talk, and the audience was leaving the theatre I would be approached by a sheepish white audience member (it was never a person of color) who would start a covert dialogue with me that usually went something like this:

WHITE AUDIENCE MEMBER: You're the playwright, yes?
JIM: Yes!
WHITE AUDIENCE MEMBER: I loved the play.
JIM: Thanks!
WHITE AUDIENCE MEMBER: I was wondering about the casting…
JIM: Yes?
WHITE AUDIENCE MEMBER: Well… there were characters in the play like Wernher von Braun, Lyndon Johnson, John F. Kennedy, Neil Armstrong…
JIM: Yes.
WHITE AUDIENCE MEMBER: The actors playing those characters were… Black.
JIM: Yes.
WHITE AUDIENCE MEMBER: Weren't they?

DOI: 10.4324/9781003079835-16

JIM: Yes.

WHITE AUDIENCE MEMBER: But … in real life… those men were… white.

JIM: Yes.

WHITE AUDIENCE MEMBER: Weren't they?

JIM: Yes.

WHITE AUDIENCE MEMBER: So why did you…?

JIM: Yes?

(*Long Pause.*)

WHITE AUDIENCE MEMBER: Why…?

I made it a point to never finish a white audience member's sentences in the middle of one of these awkward post-show inquiries. I'm always happy to answer the question, but it only seems fair for them to at least have to ask it.

The question they were desperately trying not to ask me was, "Why would you cast actors of color to play white historical figures?" In the case of *The Winning Side*, the simplest answer was because those actors kick ass and they were the best possible actors to play the roles. As a larger company value, Epic wants to ensure that the actors on our stages represent the diversity of our city. When you employ principles of color-conscious casting, it invites audiences to reflect on their own notions about the construct of race. This kind of reflection is something that most white people in America aren't asked to do it on a regular basis, and I think our country would be so much better for it if they did.

Epic partners with high schools whose student populations are predominantly Black and Brown. In eight years, we've never had a white student-artist in Epic NEXT so by necessity our shows require students of color to play white characters. I think the act of having Black and Latinx teenagers portray adult white characters with empathy and nuance invites the audience to consider how race and racism inform the issues around how we educate our children.

In terms of casting specific roles in an Epic NEXT show, I try to allow the students to have as much ownership over the process as possible. As we're conducting interviews, I encourage students to talk about the interviewees to which they feel the most connected so they start to claim those characters. As they are developing original material, I encourage the writers to keep the ensemble in mind so they are writing material for specific actors. In this way, the bulk of the casting emerges organically and the only decisions left to make are small adjustments for balance. Everyone is playing a minimum of five characters so there are no small roles!

Another unique aspect of our casting process is the fact that each of the five roles in a show is triple, quadruple, or quintuple cast. We may perform a play as many as 60 times during the year, with many of those performances taking place during school hours. So in order to not place too much of a burden on any one student actor, every role is shared. I've found that this sharing is actually great for our rehearsal process. A small team of actors working

Figure 15.1 Epic Executive Director Ron Russell and Jolan Nagi, Director of Youth
          Support Services for the New York City Department of Education with Epic
          NEXT students Kayla Villanueva, Marasia Coates-Peña, and Mekhi Tudor
          in the rehearsal room for *Perfect Circle*.

Source: Sade Ogunjimi/photo courtesy of Epic Theatre Ensemble.

together to develop a single role can help each other learn lines, give each
other ideas for interesting character choices, and serve as cheerleaders for each
other throughout rehearsals and beyond.

Open rehearsal policy

Back in 2004, during a conversation with the drama critic John Heilpern,
we were reminded that Peter Brook ran a number of his rehearsals in Public
School classrooms. Since part of our mission was to build bridges between
the professional theatre and Public School students, that seemed like a logical
choice for Epic as well. For the last 16 years, we have set aside between 3 and
5 days on every production calendar to rehearse in front of high school students in New York City Public School classrooms.

These are real rehearsals. Stage management tapes out the floor and sees
that we stay on schedule with normal rehearsal breaks all in compliance with
Equity's union rules. The only difference is that for these rehearsals, we have
20–30 assistant directors in the room. As they're directing, Melissa or Ron
will tell the students what the goals are for a particular scene we're working
on and turn to them for feedback. They can offer suggestions for staging,

transactions, pauses, or tactic shifts. The actors try out different choices and get immediate responses from our in-class collaborators.

We suspected that this would be a cool experience for the students, and it definitely is, but we never imagined what an impact this way of working would have on our art and artists. For playwrights working on new work, they get immediate detailed feedback from an audience on specific scenes and moments – a kinder, gentler version of a "focus group." For directors and actors, the students can help shake up a scene with a new set of choices to explore that might not otherwise have presented themselves in an isolated rehearsal room.

We've brought this open rehearsal policy into our work with Epic NEXT. We extend and open invitation to commissioning partners and their colleagues to sit in on rehearsals at any point in our process. As we're building the shows, this direct feedback from the communities they're attempting to reach is invaluable to the student/artists. Several guests to our rehearsal room have gone on to host a later performance and in a couple of cases, these visits have led to the commissioning of a new piece.

JACOB MING-TRENT: There's something about the hierarchy of the theatre that we need to move away from. I think we need to set up spaces where people can be invited in to watch the rehearsal process. We need to do more communicating with people that are affected by the issues that we're discussing in the room. We need to create more of a sense of community around each production that we're doing.

Verbatim theatre technique

After casting is finalized, we make the audio recordings of the interviews available to the ensemble. We ask each actor to listen to the recording of their first character. What information can you gather just from the sound of their voice?

Volume: Does this person generally speak loudly or quietly during the interview?

Vocal pitch: Does this person generally have a high or low pitch to their voice?

Vocal inflections: Can you notice any patterns or musicality in their speech? Does the pitch tend to go up or down at the end of sentences?

Vocal rhythm: Does this person tend to speak quickly or slowly? Are there many pauses in the middle of sentences or before they speak?.

Vocal tics: Are there repeated sounds, words, or phrases that punctuate this person's speech? Common examples of vocal tics are sounds like, "Um," "Ah" words like, "Like" or "Yeah," and phrases like, "you know" or "do you know what I mean."

Figure 15.2 Epic Associate Artist Michelle Beck rehearses a scene with Epic NEXT students Jerson Guevara, Raiana Torres, and Shannon Goodman.

Source: Melissa Friedman/photo courtesy of Epic Theatre Ensemble.

> ***Regional accents or dialects:*** Take note of any consonant or vowel substitutions that might be the result of where someone was born or raised.

After the analysis is complete, the actor begins the process of building a voice for their character. To be clear, the goal of this process is not pure imitation. It's a kind of artistic dialogue between the voice of the artist and the voice of the interview guest. What we end up with is an original character based on a real life person. We've also found that this kind of deep text and vocal analysis can also aid in memorization – something we don't provide a ton of time for students to do during the summer!

Once you've completed this work of building a unique voice for each character, you may need to do some recalibrating for clarity. If two of the people you interviewed have similar vocal qualities, it's possible that two of your characters might sound too much alike for an audience to easily distinguish them. You can slightly adjust your characters' volume, pitch, or inflections to build greater contrast.

GODFREY L. SIMMONS, JR.: I think about character and I think about the idea of doing a deep dive into different aspects of character. Voice. Having them listen to recordings together. Picking up things about character. How does that character walk? How does that character move through the world? What can you tell just from their voice given the story they just told?

Figure 15.3 Epic NEXT student Shaena Gibson performs a monologue from *Default.*

Source: Anjelic E. Owens/photo courtesy of NYU Metro Center.

Character physicality

You can further distinguish your characters by creating a clear physical vocabulary for each person. The ensemble members who conducted each interview can share any general impressions of the interview guests' physicality that might be helpful. Once again the goal is not imitation, but rather to use these observations to inspire the creation of an original character. Here are some aspects of physicality to consider:

Gaze: Where does your character generally place their eyes? Do they tend to look to the ceiling, straight out in front of them, or to the floor?

Posture and stance: How does this person take up space in the room? What do they do with their feet? Do you they have a wide or a narrow stance? Would you describe their posture as open and expansive or closed and guarded? Do they stand up straight or slouch?

Movement centers: What parts of the body lead this person through space? During rehearsal, you can experiment with different movement centers. Someone who leads with their nose has a very different gate than someone who leads with their chest, or hips, or chin. Try on several different centers and see what feels right.

Speed: Does this character tend to move quickly or slowly through space?

> *Floor pattern:* Another way to analyze physicality is to imagine look-
> ing at a character's path of movement from a bird's eye view. What
> would that path look like? Do they make longer or shorter moves
> across the space? Do they make sharp turns or more gradual curves?
> Do they use the entire space or stick to a "home base"?
>
> *Gesture:* Is there a key gesture that might distinguish one character
> from another? Some people have subtle physical tendencies that can
> be useful to employ in creating and communicating a character.
> Maybe one of your characters touches their face when they speak or
> crosses their arms or aggressively "talks with their hands."

The ensemble should approach all of this physical and vocal character work
with empathy, kindness, and sensitivity. You want to honor your interview
guests and their right to express themselves. You certainly don't want to
mock anyone or highlight any physical disabilities or speech impediments.
Whoever suggested that imitation is the sincerest form of flattery has never
had their essence dissected and mimicked by a teenager with an axe to grind
so please be nice!

SARIN MONAE WEST: It's really valuable as an actor but also as a human being
    to have a deep sense of curiosity and empathy for people who think, act,
    and look differently than I do. I think it's more of a challenge to accu-
    rately represent people who experience the world differently than we do.

LUAN TAVERAS: That's the thing about this work. Having empathy for oth-
    ers. Even if you disagree with them, you're going to have to play them.
    You're going to have to drive their point, no matter how much you dis-
    agree. No matter how much you may hate saying that. You have to find
    something in yourself that might have been within them when they said
    these things. You have to imagine the circumstances that may have led
    them to say these things.

SARIN MONAE WEST: It connects to trusting an audience to not need my per-
    sonal influence over this character and trusting that this person exists in
    the world and has a right to exist in the world and can and should share
    their experiences. The actor in that instance just becomes a vessel for
    information. It's not about how good an actor I am; it's just about sharing
    this person as they were.

Thoughts on directing young artists

There are a number of challenges that can arise when training young artists
how to rehearse. Convincing students of the value of repetition can be tough
if they're coming from classrooms with a culture that values completion over
refinement. Memorizing lines will be new to many of them. It's easy for
veteran actors to forget how they learned to remember lines and channel
nervous backstage energy into a dynamic onstage performance. Once again,

Figure 15.4 Epic Co-Artistic Director Melissa Friedman rehearses a scene with Epic NEXT students Christina Liberus, Lizette Padua, and Liana Morales.

Source: Sade Ogunjimi/photo courtesy of Epic Theatre Ensemble.

I believe authenticity and transparency are the keys: you have to be clear about your own process for navigating rehearsal and find the simplest way to communicate it clearly in order to guide young people toward performances.

You also have to know the skills of the artists in the room. Sometimes we have a group of young people with terrific collaborative instincts, exceptional spatial awareness, and no fear whatsoever about delivering their material directly to an audience. In those instances, my role looks less like that of a traditional theatre director and more like a hands-off producer occasionally offering some thoughts. Some groups might need a little more guidance in one or more areas and so I'll take on a bit more leadership in terms of the staging. Every ensemble is unique so every rehearsal process will require the adults in the room to assess when and how they can best assist. Knowing when not to jump in is a highly underrated pedagogical skill!

MARILYN TORRES: I love rehearsal – there's something about beautiful chaos. Some teaching artists run from that, but you have to know that the chaos leads to the great work.

MELISSA FRIEDMAN: I try to use language like, "what do you *love* about that?" rather than "what do you *like* about that?" I keep coming back to truth, courage, love. Is there a way we can be more courageous in this moment? Can we get at the truth of this scene more? How can we love this moment more? These are the values of the room: truth, courage, love. Is the work embodying our values at every turn?

AARON KROHN: There's something about the posture of "play" that is critical to rehearsal. When you were five and you played a scene between this dinosaur and this baby doll you did not care how well it went. You didn't care about being watched. You were there.

VERN THIESSEN: It's about striving for excellence not perfection. Kids understand excellence. They understand that Kobe Bryant was an excellent ball player. He was not always perfect.

CLARO DE LOS REYES: What parallels can I draw with significant people in their lives? Is it that Mamba's mentality, like Kobe practicing free throws when no one is watching? Do you talk about Black Thought in The Roots who does vocal exercises before he raps? People are like, "What? he does that?" Yeah, just like a Shakespearean actor would do vocal exercises. Black Thought does exercises to have dexterity in his mouth. I guess it's cool to look like you just rolled out of bed and you can do these highly skilled things, but I like to make spotlight examples of individuals who put a lot of work for hours and hours and hours to perfect their craft, when no one is looking.

NILAJA SUN: The voice work: amplification. It's easy for us as professional performers to reach the back row, but it's very hard to rush amplification and articulation with young people. This is really deep for African-American communities or communities where your parents and you have come from somewhere else to get to America and you are told not to speak up – for your own good, for your own safety. Just do your work, be super quiet, and get that American Dream somehow. That is something that is always going to be prevalent and I can understand that. This world tends to see exuberance in Black and brown teens and think of it as an assault. So, we as theatre educators have to work against that.

DEVIN E. HAQQ: I like doing run-throughs early. I like to see other people's work. That motivates me. You always have one or two stars who know their lines and are driving their scenes and being leaders. The other people in the group need to see that, so they know, "Oh, I've got work to do." It's game time.

SARIN MONAE WEST: I've experienced a hierarchy in professional rehearsal rooms that can put the actor in a position of powerlessness. Identifying those power structures is a huge step. Creating an environment where the students and the teachers are considered equals is really valuable. "I've dedicated my life to this, but there are going to be things that you will see that I will miss and there will be things that I will see that you will miss. It takes all of us to tell this story. Your own experience of the piece is just as valuable as my observations." It keeps all the students invested when they have the opportunity to share what they think about the work.

BRANDT ADAMS: The most important thing is to show up and model being the kind of collaborator that you want them to be.

NILAJA SUN: Affirmations. Affirmations. Affirmations. Even when you're feeling like everything is going to hell, you have to remember that the theatre angels are going to bring this all together. You too have to believe in the process. You too have to believe that the students have these innate gifts that you may or may not be seeing in rehearsal but that will emerge in the performance. You have to see all of it as great or moving in the direction toward greatness. That's when you kind of become this Ra–Ra–Ra, Vince Lombardi character where you're just coming up with every affirmative monologue about getting there together. I hope Vince Lombardi wasn't the one who was a pedophile. He wasn't, was he?

16 How do we perform our play?

The director Peter Brook coined the phrase "Rough Theatre" and distinguished it by its absence of style. Brook's Rough Theatre isn't an art form for light entertainment. It's raw, aggressive, and revolutionary. Theatre in the rough requires the artists and audiences to reimagine everything and anything the actors take up in their hands can be used as a weapon against complacency and oppression.[1]

When we began touring with Epic NEXT in 2015, the first show we took on the road was *10467*, which dealt with educational inequity and featured a cast of 17 actors, a full theatrical lighting plot, costumes, sound, props, and projections with a running time of 85 minutes. For reasons of practicality, mobility, audience engagement, and aesthetics, we have chosen to limit the production values of our touring shows to five actors who all wear a uniform Epic T-Shirt, one prop, no special lighting cues (when we do perform in theatre spaces, we leave the house lights up in the audience), and some limited sound design controlled by a laptop and run through a portable (8″×3″×3″) speaker: Nothing that can't fit comfortably in my backpack!

Spatial awareness

The plays are staged in a way that is flexible enough to work in a variety of spaces, with an emphasis on keeping the actors as close to the audience as possible. There is no designated backstage area and the actors are always visible. Much of the action of these plays takes place in, around, behind, and through the audience. Our ensemble has performed the same play for a gathering as small as 4 people and a crowd as large as 3,000. The actors have to calibrate their performances to the demands of every space.

RON RUSSELL: Spatial relationships are very much how I see plays. When I read a play, I start to see it in space. I don't just read the words as literary, no matter who the writer is. Even Shakespeare. What are these characters doing? For instance, in this scene, this person has to be upstage of the other person. That's the relationship that matters. If you don't have much depth in the space then you're quite close and if you're in a giant

DOI: 10.4324/9781003079835-17

Figure 16.1 Epic Co-Artistic Director James Wallert with Nashali Perez, Jeremiah Green, Jr., Olivia Dunbar, Davion Osborne, and Randy Figueroa before a performance of *Laundry City* at PS 15 Roberto Clemente School in New York City.

Source: David Naranjo/photo courtesy of Epic Theatre Ensemble.

auditorium, you're as far away as possible. So the idea is there's a spatial skeleton to the play that we're contracting or expanding depending on the space. Once young people get it, they can start to kinesthetically do it on their own. I also think that there are benchmarks throughout the play that are moments of silence or of things landing. Maybe there are four of them in a 30-minute piece, but those four things have got to land. Landing it is something that you as an artist have to determine where you can do that best. It might be that in order to land a particular moment I'm going to have to walk around the back of the audience and make them turn around and look at me because we're in too tight of a space. I need space around me for this moment. It's good acting and it's also about group mind and kinesthetic response.

BRANDT ADAMS: I had a teacher who used to say to me, "I don't ever hear bad line readings. I just hear actors who don't know where they are in space."

LUAN TAVERAS: You can't neglect the space. You have to accept it for what it is. For me, it's about tracking. When you get to the space you have to take the time to track where you should be for every moment. I go here. Esmirna walks through here. But sometimes you have to take a risk. If you always stay connected to the other people in the show, you can take the risks together and know you're going to get where you need to be. All our exercises and warm-ups play into that group awareness.

Figure 16.2 Miguel Delacruz, Davion Osbourne, Olivia Dunbar, Nashali Perez, and Rodwell Masquitta before a performance of *Laundry City*.

Source: James Wallert/photo courtesy of Epic Theatre Ensemble.

I got your back

This pre-show ritual comes from the improv world: right before curtain, every member of the ensemble checks in with every other member, pats them on the back, and says, "I got your back." We've been pleased to learn that alums of the Epic NEXT program, often carry this catch phrase with them into their college theatre departments and sometimes beyond.

LUAN TAVERAS: That's why it's so successful, the students who have been through this program go into other spaces with different ideologies but still carry the same mindset that we're only here to see ourselves and others grow, not to diminish anyone or cut their growth short.

ABEL SANTIAGO: The idea of ensemble starts with all of us struggling together. During those improv games was when we really started to form a real trust as a family. You don't know what you're going to say, but the whole super objective of the game is to trust the person you're on stage with and support them. That's where, "I got your back... I got your back... I got your back..." came from. That whole, "I got your back" thing is so special. I thought it was weird at first, but by the time we went through the whole summer together – through all the writing, and rehearsing – at the end by the time we were getting ready to go onstage, I knew when we said, "I got your back," we all meant it. It allowed us to take care of each other even though we were all nervous.

MEKHI TUDOR: I can be anxious a lot and it calms me down. When I hear someone say, "I got your back" it calms me down knowing that I can look at this person and know that I got them and they got me. It isn't just my show. It's our show.

On the road

Touring their own work around the country and internationally is huge in terms of youth development. For many student artists, the tour is their first opportunity to leave New York City.

ABEL SANTIAGO: Coming from low income communities, touring was such a huge thing for us. We never got the chance to leave the Bronx, leave Harlem, leave Brooklyn, leave our neighborhoods. So when you guys were like, "We're going to Albany," I was like, "Albany?! What are we

Figure 16.3 Epic Co-Artistic Directors Melissa Friedman and James Wallert with Epic NEXT students Xavier Pacheco, Kayla Bennett, Jordan Mayo, and Divine Garland in Edinburgh, Scotland.

Source: Ron Russell/photo courtesy of Epic Theatre Ensemble.

talking about?" And then to go to Scotland was incredible. I had never been on a plane ever so I was like, "Oh my god. What is happening?" We were performing for all these higher ups in education. We were performing something we cared about for people who could change things. So the tour was overwhelming but filled with joy.

MEKHI TUDOR: Staying in hotels was cool because I never really had that experience. It made me want to strive for more in my life. Epic had me experience a quality of life that I really like. Going to a fancy hotel in Washington DC I was like, "I like this. A lot!" I felt amazing. It made me want to reach for certain heights so I'm able to experience that again.

LUAN TAVERAS: You feel very independent. It's like, "Damn, I'm actually doing this! I packed my things and I'm an actor going somewhere to present this piece! I got this!" Just that feeling of independence is very cool.

Note

1. Brook, Peter. *The Empty Space*. Touchtone. 1968, p. 66.

17 How do we lead a meaningful post-show discussion?

Epic's mission is to place theatre at the center of civic dialogue. To that end, we host a post-show discussion after everything we produce. The conversations after performances of the Epic NEXT touring shows are facilitated solely by the student writers/performers themselves. A number of really excellent youth organizations and student-centered educators sometimes get very uncomfortable about leaving high school students onstage alone to lead a discussion about the questions and themes in their work. Some feel the need to have an adult ally onstage to facilitate the discussion or to address any problematic comments from audience members. We made a decision very early on that if we trusted the students to research, write, and perform a provocative and thoughtful work of investigative theatre then we should trust the students to talk about that work without an adult spokesperson. If the research process has been rigorous and complete then the students possess an expertise in the material and their own lived experience that should allow them to address most reasonable questions that may come up. I believe increased student agency and autonomy are key metrics for the success of a multi-year youth development program. The more completely the students can take over the mechanics of an Epic NEXT production, the more successful I feel as a producer. When we're on tour, I know it's really working when I'm just the roadie: my job is to drive the van, run sound, and sell T-Shirts.

One of the first pieces of advice I give students is that it is completely normal to feel nervous facilitating a post-show talk. Leading a discussion for a play you wrote and just performed can make anyone feel a little vulnerable. I didn't approach anything resembling comfort with it until well into my forties! You should remove any pressure on yourself to "say something smart" during the post-show or to be an expert on anything other than your experience as a student, an artist, and a citizen. I also try to make it clear to student facilitators that "I don't know" is a perfectly valid response, *especially when it's true*. Even better, "I don't know, what do you think?" is a trusty discussion aid that's been employed by college professors for generations. It's not dodging: it's ensuring equal time. The five of you have just talked for 30 minutes: now it's the audience's turn.

DOI: 10.4324/9781003079835-18

Here are a few post-show discussion protocols that Epic regularly uses to kick off the conversation.

The standard

Because, we've been using this opening prompt for conversations since the founding of the company, students and artists sometimes refer to it as the "Epic Question":

> **Opening prompt:** Imagine that two weeks from now, you will wake up one morning and you find yourself thinking about the production you saw here today. What is it that you'll be thinking about? It could be a word, a line, a phrase, an image, or a moment. What do you think will resonate with you over time?

We've found this to be a very effective way to begin a dialogue for several reasons. The audience can ease into the discussion without feeling that they need to explain why they were struck by that word, line, phrase, image, or moment. It also provides a palette for the discussion moving forward. If most of the initial responses are about a particular scene or theme from the play, it's a good idea to focus your next question on that scene or theme.

Here are a few standard follow-up questions that can apply to most Epic NEXT plays:

- Why is this performance meaningful/relevant today? What questions or issues does it bring up for you?
- What social actions could you take to tackle the issues at the center of this play?
- If any of you have any questions for the artists about our process of creating this play, you can feel free to ask us.
- Any final thoughts or lingering questions?

Audience interviews

Interviews serve as the foundation of our research and creation process, but they can also be a great way to connect people, stimulate deep thinking about the theme, and provide opportunities for a more intimate and free-flowing exchange of ideas.

> **Opening prompt:** Today you saw a play that was created using a series of interviews. We'd like to begin the post-show discussion with an

Figure 17.1 The cast of *Nothing About Us* leads a post-show conversation at a Professional Development session for teachers and staff of PS 3 in New York City.

Source: James Wallert/photo courtesy of Epic Theatre Ensemble.

interview. Please find someone in the room who you don't know or don't know well. You have eight minutes to ask each other at least three of the following questions.

Questions can be tailored to the audience or the event. They can be the same questions posed to interview guests in the play or more focused on a particular theme or content area. Some sample audience interview questions include:

1 With what groups or communities do you identify?
2 Tell me a time from your childhood when an adult helped you find your voice.
3 Tell me about a recent accomplishment that made you feel proud.
4 What's a rule or law that you find unfair?
5 Tell me about a time when you spoke truth to power.
6 Tell me about a frustrating experience you've had dealing with technology.
7 Tell me about a positive experience you've had dealing with government.
8 What is the purpose of school?

Figure 17.2 Epic NEXT student Luan Taveras taking part in a post-show audience interview session for the Chancellor's Cabinet meeting at the headquarters for the
New York City Department of Education.

Source: Sade Ogunjimi/photo courtesy of Epic Theatre Ensemble.

Once these interviews are completed, you can bring the audience back
together for a standard discussion or move into Human Barometer.

Human barometer

Place three signs at three points in the room: "AGREE," "DISAGREE,"
"NOT SURE." Ask participants to choose to stand by one of these signs as
a starting place. The leader will read provocative statements and participants
will stand by one of these signs to signify their opinion. It is a silent exercise
until the leader opens up discussion. If someone hears a persuasive argument
made, they can move to a different sign.

Statements should be tailored to the play. Sample Human Barometer statements include:

- Money causes as many problems as it solves.
- Mostly, you should mind your own business.
- Ignoring enemies is the best way to fight.
- Presentation is as important as content.
- In order for a rule to be effective, rule-breakers have to be punished.
- "Good people do not need laws to act responsibly." – Plato
- The purpose of school is to keep or pull students out of poverty. – from

Nothing About Us

- Standardized tests are the best way to measure student learning. – from *Overdrive*
- It's OK for a white person to teach an Ethnic Studies course. – from *Default*
- Bullies don't operate outside of a school's norms. Bullies are the enforcers of a school's norms. – from *Perfect Circle*

There are several aspects of this protocol that I love: it allows someone to fully participate in the conversation and express an opinion, even if they don't feel comfortable speaking. Schools frequently reward quick decision-making. By placing a NOT SURE sign into the mix, you're honoring uncertainty and nuance. You're affirming that in a discussion of complex ideas, NOT SURE is a perfectly acceptable place to hang out for a while. It also gives participants the opportunity to change their minds during the discussion and for everyone to see those changes taking place in front of them.

JACOB MING-TRENT: Epic doesn't hide. You don't send somebody else up there to run the talkback so you're not going to get chastised. You guys are there.

MICHELLE BECK: The talkbacks are a crucial part of the development of the students. They have a space where they're holding space. They have the opportunity to speak in their own words. They have everyone in the room listening to them. They have everyone in the room respecting them.

LUAN TAVERAS: Our goal is to prove that young people deserve to be in the room where decisions are being made, so we have to show that we've done the work, we've interviewed all these people, we've displayed these different points of view.

DAVID TIPSON: We need to listen a lot more. The play shows deep listening by the students in the way they did their research, in the way they portray the people they interviewed, and in the post-play discussion.

SARIN MONAE WEST: In a world that is so polarized, especially on social media, it's really important to find a way to communicate with people that might disagree with you and work toward a future that includes all of us.

DALISSA DURAN: I'm always nervous, but I remind myself that this isn't about me. It's never about the person leading the post-show discussion. It's you giving the audience and the cast a way to connect. You're the connection point. It's your job to keep everyone on track. I get hyped. I feel ultimate bad-ass-ness. Look at me go!

MEKHI TUDOR: It was daunting as hell at first but after I did a few it became kind of fun. Because you're just having a conversation and these five people you're on stage with are your homies and you're going back and forth and bouncing off the people in the audience. It's like a crazy game of ping-pong.

XAVIER PACHECO: I think one of the things that I've gained from leading post-show discussions is a confidence in the essence of community. There's no script. There's no way to handle the process in advance, even if you know a lot of the people in the house. It's scary. I've learned that the most important thing in those instances is to be the expert. It's not about being an expert in theatre or acting or plays, but to be an expert on conversation. To be an expert on give and take. It's not going to be perfect every time, but it does give you a sense of moving forward when you think that way which is a key to dialogue – move it forward.

LIZETTE PADUA: We were at UCONN and after we performed, there was this girl and she was crying. She told us what she was going through when it came to standardized testing and that watching the play she said she had this feeling of, "Dang, you understand me." During the talk back we heard from other people and it was like, yeah a lot of people go through this. That's what these plays show: there are people out there who understand you. That's when I knew this play could really touch somebody's heart.

18 How do we pay for all of this?

In the first chapter, I outlined how the prevailing economic attitude of the theatre in this country has led to the establishment of a perpetual patrician-artist class. If you truly want to diversify the arts, you have to find a way to consistently pay Black and Brown artists and start paying them young. A lot of youth organizations claim to value art but don't fairly compensate young artists or early-career arts instructors for their work. How you define the specifics of fair compensation for your project can vary depending on your particular community, but if you're looking to establish a positive culture of valuing student work, a good way to start would be to look at adopting the minimum wage standards for your city or state.

Here are some strategies to fundraise for the projects and sell the shows.

- Your commissioning partner should provide some initial project funding as well as advice about where to look for other potential funding sources and possible venues for paid performances. They should have an idea of where to find the most passionate audiences for the work.
- It's important to ask schools, government agencies, community organizations, and conferences interested in hosting a performance to pay a fee to cover stipends paid to the student performers, as well as any travel or lodging expenses.
- This kind of process absolutely promotes workforce readiness. A number of city and state agencies as well as a few private foundations offer support for companies providing job training and paid internship opportunities for high school and college students. The New York City Department of Youth & Community Development, Ladders for Leaders, and Exploring the Arts Foundation are three such programs in the New York City area.
- For overnight trips, it's a good idea to connect with local colleges and universities. Many colleges already have the infrastructure in place to provide housing and meals for prospective students on their campuses and they may also be able to pay for a performance or two through student activities funds.
- You should research local, state, and national grant opportunities to apply for direct project support from foundation and corporate funders.

DOI: 10.4324/9781003079835-19

Figure 18.1 The cast celebrates after a performance of *Default* at New York University
Metropolitan Center for Research on Equity and Transformation of Schools.

Source: Anjelic E. Owens/photo courtesy of NYU Metro Center.

- As mentioned in the previous chapter, part of my job at these shows is to sell T-Shirts after the post-show discussion. It's relatively small in terms of a revenue stream, but I think it's an easy and immediate way for audiences to support the work. It's also great fun for any of us who happen to run into an audience member on the subway wearing their "I am Epic" shirt!

MELISSA FRIEDMAN: We're putting our money where our mouth is. We say that we are developing the future leaders in this country in the arts and beyond. If that's true, we have to prioritize that as an organization. When you work with young people who are typically placed at the margins of society, you have to place them at the center of your work and the center of your programming and the center of your budget. It is my great hope that Epic will be run by alums in the future.

DEBRA MORRIS: For the vast majority of our students, Epic is their first introduction to any sort of employment. So I feel it's my responsibility to steward them into understanding not only the language of employment, like tax forms or deductions, but also understanding that your employer needs you as much as you need them. Your compensation is not a gift. You provide a service and we pay you for that service. I feel a responsibility to teach them how to proactively communicate with an employer.

If you get your check and you don't understand why that number is what it is, you have every right to ask questions and clarify things. With artistic work, young people often feel like it's a bother to ask questions and that they shouldn't feel any ownership over the transaction. I want to empower them to expect clear communication and equal footing when interacting with arts institutions. You belong in these conversations. If something isn't what you expect it to be, don't assume that your employer will advocate for you. Speak up.

DAVID TIPSON: There's always the danger of reproducing the systems we're attacking. We can't say we want students to have opportunities and we want students to be treated fairly and then not pay them.

RON RUSSELL: There is a great value in communicating ideas. That is artists' job and they should be paid to do it. No one should ever not get paid to communicate ideas. When someone is communicating a message and sculpting that message that is a professionally authentic model and they should be compensated in a professionally authentic way. The students are doing a job. They're ciphering something to a new audience. The students need to understand that it is a job and people who are bringing them into perform need to understand that it is a job and that they need to be compensated. It raises the consciousness around the idea that theatre making is a profession that is viable. There is no truth in the concept that workforce readiness has to look a certain way and can't include the arts. In today's world, working in the arts and learning how to think in a collaborative fashion, how to be flexible, how to take in new information, and apply it is probably more valuable in the average workplace than any set of content or skills.

Part II

The Citizen Artist curriculum

19 Newspaper theatre

Here are a series of foundational skill-building exercises and activities to support the creation and revision process. I'm presenting these using Epic's standard lesson plan format with each lesson timed at 43 minutes to allow them to fit within the confines of most standard class periods.

Each lesson plan identifies four goals for each session: artistic, academic, social, and civic. We use the following instructional outline:

Introduction: What do students need to know at the beginning of the lesson?

Question and Answer: What do the students already know about the content of the lesson?

Warm-up Activity: How are you going to get the ensemble prepared for the activities of the day? Remember to plan this last and to ask yourself why you are leading this activity.

Opening Activity: These activities build on students' prior knowledge and help build a bridge to the main activities. Remember to plan this after the main activity is established.

Main Activity: These activities are challenging and build essential skills required in the project. If it's possible to do it without a warm-up or opening activity, it's either not a proper main activity or not challenging enough.

Closure: It's essential to reflect after each activity about how this is connected to the artistic process. It is also essential to reflect at the end of the lesson on what skills were learned and what was accomplished.

DEVIN E. HAQQ: You should always have a lesson plan that is about active student engagement. You should never go into a room and talk for 30 minutes about acting or theatre or whatever. I've seen people do that and the students go straight for their phones. You've got to engage them right away. You've got to hook them. You've got to take them on a journey. You should craft your lesson plan like a story with a clear inciting incident, beginning, middle, and end.

DOI: 10.4324/9781003079835-20

Artistic goal: To find artistic inspiration from a journalistic account of a current or historical event.

Academic goal: To engage in creative writing.

Social goals: To collaborate on a full group brainstorming activity. To practice respectful and supportive audience behavior.

Civic goal: To identify stakeholders in a community and explore the personal consequences of a public event.

Instructional outline

Introduction (1 minute): The Teaching artist explains that today we will explore a process for generating creative writing inspired by a newspaper article.

Question and Answer (2 minutes): The Teaching artist outlines the task for the day: "By the end of the session each of you will have written and performed a short monologue inspired by a news event. I would never ask you all to do anything I wouldn't do myself, so I have written a sixty second monologue based on a newspaper article. See if you can guess who the character I'm playing is, who the character is speaking to, what do I want from that other person, what's keeping me from getting what I want, and where are we? As always, live performance is fed by positive audience interaction so the more focus, positive intention, and sincere laughter you share with me the better my performance."

Warm-up Activity (7 minutes): The Teaching artist performs a monologue inspired by the article "German Parents Offer Baby on eBay"[1] (I've included my monologue here for reference but it's preferable for the Teaching artist or instructor to write one of their own.)

THE DOCTOR sits in a chair with a small flip-chart on his lap. He speaks to a patient sitting directly in front of him.

THE DOCTOR: OK, so now I'd just like you to take a look at each inkblot and tell me the first thing that comes to your mind.
(He flips a page.) Pizza. *(Takes some notes.)* Good.
(He flips another page.) Lollipop. *(Takes more notes.)*
(He flips another page.) Volkswagon. *(Takes more notes.)* Hm.
Oh no. No wrong answers here. How about this? *(He flips another page.)* Your stupid ass husband's stupid ass face. *(Pause.)*
OK, I think we should move on. *(He puts the chart away.)* Now, Maria: Let's talk about the incident. Now I understand that you felt this was only a joke. Certainly finding humor is a valuable habit of mind. But I hope by now you understand that many, many people, including the police and child services, didn't find it funny.
No, I didn't find it funny, either.
Well I happen to think I have an excellent sense of humor.

You know, Maria, I think you're missing the point.

No, I don't know exactly where your son is right now. Child Services has him in protective care – I'm sure he's fine.

Well, I'm sorry, that's not my decision.

No, I simply administer the tests and make a recommendation to the court. How am I leaning? *(Pause.)*

I think we should move on.

(End of scene.)

"What assumptions can you make about the character, the place, the situation, the environment, the person to whom the character is speaking, the status relationship, the objective, or the conflict?" The teaching artist hands out copies of the article and calls on volunteers to read the New York Times article aloud changing readers every couple of paragraphs. The teaching

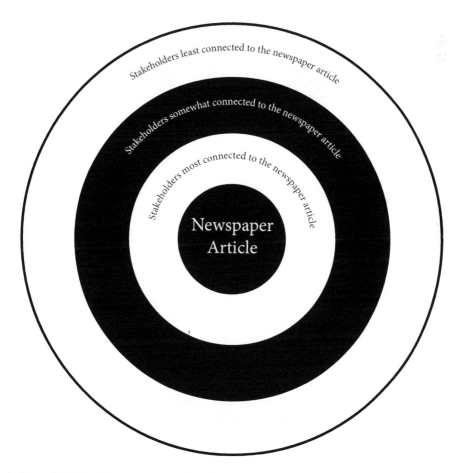

Figure 19.1 Graphic organizer template for brainstorming newspaper article stakeholders.

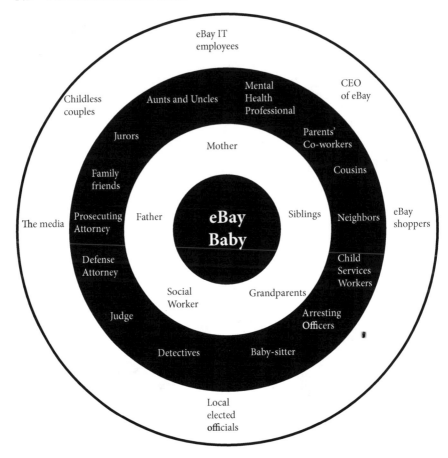

Figure 19.2 Graphic organizer stakeholders example from "eBay baby article."

artist answers any clarifying questions the group has about the situation then explains, "I read the article and was intrigued by the mention of psychological tests being administered and decided to write a monologue from the perspective of the mental health professional giving that exam. Who are some of the other people (or characters) who might be connected to this event?"

> *Opening Activity (10 minutes):* On a sheet of chart paper, the Teaching artist writes down all of the possible characters that could be connected to this story (Mother, father, baby, other relatives, police, psychologist, judge, CEO of eBay, childless couple hoping to bid, etc.) Organize your chart according to the depth of their connection to the story (see an example of the template in Figure 19.1).

Figure 19.2 is an example of a group's possible character brainstorm.

Main activity (18 minutes): Once the chart is filled out, pick a character and write a monologue from this person's point of view. Before you begin writing make sure you are able to answer the following five questions:

- Who am I (character)?
- Who am I talking to (relationship)?
- What do I want from this person (objective)?
- What is keeping me from getting what I want (obstacle)?
- Where am I (environment)?

You have ten minutes to write your monologue.

Share out: Find a partner and take turns sharing your monologues. Were the five questions answered by the text of the monologue? If not, make a few quick revisions for clarity. Time permitting, a few students can volunteer to perform their pieces for the whole group.

Closure (5 minutes): Why do you think playwrights choose to use historical research to create characters and dialogue?

Additional information

Materials Needed: Chart Paper and markers; Copies of NYT article; notebooks and pens.

Potential Challenges: Time.

Note

1. "German Parents Offer Baby on eBay." New York Times, May 25 2008. http://www.nytimes.com/2008/05/25/world/europe/25ebayby.html

20 Objectives and tactics

Artistic goal: To introduce the concepts of objectives and tactics.

Academic goal: To provide students with another tool for close reading of a literary text.

Social goal: To get the students working on their feet in pairs and in whole group activities. To introduce actor/audience relationship and protocols.

Civic goal: To explore societal power dynamics through the lens of objectives and tactics.

Instructional outline

Introduction (1 minute): The Teaching artist poses these questions: What is an objective? What is a tactic?

Question & Answer (2 minutes): The Teaching artist explains the theatrical definitions. An objective is what a character wants in a scene. Tactics are how that character chooses to pursue what they want in a scene.

Warm-up Activity – THE CHAIR EXERCISE (5 minutes): Break into pairs. Decide who's an A and who's a B. This scene needs one chair. The B's sit and the A's stand next to the chair. The A's have 1 minute to convince the B's to give them the chair. The B's do not want to give up the chair. There are three rules: The A's cannot physically touch the B's. The A's cannot touch the chair. The A's cannot hurl any objects at the B's. (Forget to tell the students these rules at your own peril!) After a minute has passed, switch – A's sit and B's stand. Same game; same rules. Share some of them. Discuss what worked.

- An objective is what a character wants from another character.
- A tactic is how they try to achieve that objective. Tactics are verbs.
- In most well-written two person scenes, Character A wants one thing and Character B wants *the direct opposite*. In the chair exercise, A wants to convince B to give up the chair. B wants to convince A that they should keep the chair. You know who wins at the end of the scene by whoever is sitting in the chair.

DOI: 10.4324/9781003079835-21

Put examples of tactics on the board based on the chair exercise. Tactics should be written in verb infinitive form. For example:

- to threaten
- to charm
- to demand
- to mock
- to inspire
- to beg
- to make guilty
- to wake up
- to warn
- to inspire
- to shock
- to distract
- to wound

Hand out copies of the Tactics List (Figure 20.1)

Opening Activity – TACTICS CIRCLE (10 minutes): Gather everyone into a standing circle. One at a time, each student should go down the list reading a tactic and performing it to the person standing to their right in the spirit of that tactic. For example, when delivering the phrase "To accuse," the student should accuse the person standing to their right. Go around the circle quickly until you've exhausted all the tactics on the list. How can a choice of tactic affect your voice, your facial expressions, your gestures, your posture?

Main Activity (20 minutes): Write the following four lines on the board. (If there is a different or longer two-person scene from another text that you are working on that you would rather use – go for it.)

A: Hi.
B: Hello.
A: Been waiting long?
B: Ages.

Ask two volunteers to read the scene aloud. What do you think might be the relationship between these two characters? Where do you think the scene could take place? Identify an objective for each character. Assign a tactic to each line. Now perform the scene again with the assigned tactics. Try the scene again with a completely different set of tactics. How did the scene change? Now with your partner from the chair exercise, rehearse the four-line scene. Decide where the scene takes place, what their relationship is, and what the objectives are for each character. Assign a tactic for each line. Play the scene several times trying different tactics until you find a sequence you like. Time permitting, you may provide the students with a short scene from an extant play and have them assign objectives and tactics to the scene for performance.

Share out the scenes. The class tries to guess which tactics were being played. Make sure that the audience gives the actors total focus while they

LIST OF TACTICS (ACTION VERBS)

To accuse	To destroy	To infuriate	To seduce
To alarm	To distract	To interrogate	To shock
To amaze	To distress	To intimidate	To sicken
To amuse	To educate	To irritate	To silence
To befriend	To electrify	To lure	To slap
To blame	To empower	To make guilty	To soothe
To beg	To enchant	To massage	To startle
To boss	To energize	To mesmerize	To stun
To belittle	To enliven	To mock	To tame
To bully	To enrage	To mother	To taunt
To calm	To entertain	To mystify	To tease
To challenge	To entice	To nag	To tempt
To charm	To enlighten	To needle	To test
To coax	To excite	To overwhelm	To tickle
To comfort	To flatter	To pamper	To threaten
To command	To fluster	To panic	To thrill
To confront	To frighten	To pester	To torment
To crush	To harass	To plead	To warn
To dare	To horrify	To praise	To welcome
To dazzle	To humiliate	To ridicule	To wound
To deify	To hurry	To rouse	To wake up
To delight	To hypnotize	To scare	
To demand	To impress	To scold	

Figure 20.1 Chart of tactics.

are performing and a round of applause when they are finished. The feedback should be trying to guess the tactics, not trying to criticize the performances.

Closure (3 minutes): How do tactics change the performance of a scene? How do you use tactics in your everyday life to pursue your own objectives?

Additional information

Materials Needed: Copies of Tactics list

21 Fundamentals of dramatic structure

Inspired by the work of Vern Thiessen

Artistic goal: To craft a plot that connects to a historical event.
Academic goal: To explore different ways of telling the same essential story.
Social goal: To collaborate together on developing a plot.
Civic goal: To set the stage for adapting essential political questions into drama.

Instructional outline

Introduction (1 minute): The Teaching artist introduces the goal of the day: "Today we're going to explore the fundamentals of dramatic structure! I sometimes refer to this lesson as, 'Learn how to make more than 650 million dollars in 43 minutes'. Interested? Great! Let's proceed!"
Question & Answer (2 minutes): What are the necessary elements of a play?

- Plot – What happens
- Character – Who makes it happen
- Setting – Where/When it happens
- Theme – Why it happens
- Dialogue – How it happens

Warm-up Activity (15 minutes): What's the difference between story and plot? In order to illuminate their relationship, we're going to analyze the historical events surrounding the 1912 sinking of the British passenger liner Titanic and the plot of the 1997 James Cameron film *Titanic*. What are the five basic story points for the actual events surrounding the real-life Titanic?

Story points

1 Ship sets sail.
2 Ship hits iceberg.
3 Ship sinks.
4 Most people die.
5 Some people live.

DOI: 10.4324/9781003079835-22

Now consider the movie *Titanic*. How would you describe the genre, characters of that film?

> GENRE: Romance/Drama
> CHARACTERS: Rich girl, Poor boy
> TITLE: Titanic

What are the five basic plot points of the film?

Plot points

1   People from different classes get on the ship.
2   Poor boy meets rich girl.
3   They fall in love.
4   Poor boy dies.
5   Rich girl lives to tell her story.

Notice (via the arrows in Figure 21.1) how James Cameron's plot connects to the story (or history).

Titanic had domestic revenue in the United States of over 650 million dollars. Now it's time for us to get some of that Titanic money. As a group, let's come up with a plot for our own version of Titanic. We have to:

*   Keep the same five story points.
*   Assign a different genre to your version (some possibilities include action, comedy, sci-fi, horror, thriller, children's story, noir).

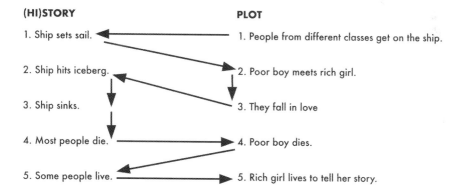

(HI)STORY

1. Ship sets sail.

2. Ship hits iceberg.

3. Ship sinks.

4. Most people die.

5. Some people live.

PLOT

1. People from different classes get on the ship.

2. Poor boy meets rich girl.

3. They fall in love

4. Poor boy dies.

5. Rich girl lives to tell her story.

GENRE: Romance/Drama
CHARACTERS: Rich girl, Poor boy
TITLE: Titanic

Figure 21.1 Story/Plot flowchart for *Titanic*.

- Use two new main characters (for example, captain, cook, engineer, detective, serial killer, vampire, alien invader).
- Give our play a title.
- Write five new plot points that connect to all five story points above.

Using the principles of "Yes, and..." we'll build the plot together and see how we do!

Main Activity *(20 minutes)*: Now you'll each work independently. On a separate sheet of paper, take seven minutes to come up with a plot for your own version of Titanic.

- Keep the same five story points.
- Assign a different genre to your version.
- Use two new main characters.
- Give your play a title.
- Write five new plot points that connect to all five story points above.

Share out a few new Titanic plots.

Closure (5 minutes): How did these different plots shed light on the same basic story? Why do we tell the same stories in different ways?

Materials needed: Chart paper

22 Ethical dilemma

Artistic goal: To examine how ethical dilemma can create drama.
Academic goal: To engage in a close analysis of a dramatic text.
Social goal: To work together in groups and in a whole class activity.
Civic goal: To explore the concept of situational ethics.

Instructional outline

Introduction (1 minute): The Teaching artist asks the students to define ethical dilemma.

Question and Answer (5 minutes): Have you ever been presented with a choice between something that you knew was *right* and something that you knew was *wrong*? What about this: Have you ever been presented with a choice between something that you knew was *wrong* and something you knew was *wrong* – and you had to decide which you believed to be less wrong? That's an ethical dilemma. Today, we will explore ethical dilemma in drama.

Warm-up Activity (15 minutes): THE ANGEL/DEVIL EXERCISE

The Teaching artist asks the students to think of a time when they were faced with an ethical dilemma that didn't have a clear "right" or "wrong" solution. Ask a volunteer to share the situation with the class, but not to reveal their ultimate decision. (If the students don't have an appropriate dilemma, the Teaching artist will have a situation at the ready). The student with the dilemma gets up in front of the class and is flanked by two other student volunteers who will each be responsible for defending a particular course of action. Each student has one minute to argue for their side with a 15-second follow-up. After each side has made its case, the person in the middle makes their decision based on the arguments presented. The student can then tell us what they actually did in the situation. Time permitting: another group of volunteers can play the Angel/Devil exercise or the entire class can play the game simultaneously in groups of three.

Main Activity (20 minutes): VALLEY OF PUBLIC OPINION

DOI: 10.4324/9781003079835-23

Read the Antigone/Ismene scene from Epic's adaptation of Sophocles' *Antigone*. (If there is a different or longer two-person scene from another text that you are working on that you would rather use – go for it.):

ANTIGONE: Ismene?
> Let me see your face. Do you not know?

ISMENE: I have heard nothing, sister,
> since our two brothers united in death,
> each killed by the other's hand.
> I know nothing further:
> whether I will prosper or suffer.

ANTIGONE: It's the burial. It's our brothers. Creon.
> Deifying one body and defiling the other.
> Eteocles will be buried with just use of justice.
> Polynices, who also died for his beliefs…
> the citizens will be instructed to leave his corpse unburied,
> not to cover him
> not to cry for him
> but leave him for the crows.
> That's the good news Creon brings for you,
> as he comes here now to proclaim his will,
> and set the punishment for any offender:
> not merely murder, but public stoning.
> Now you know our predicament.
> Now our noble birth must help us overcome it.

ISMENE: What can my weak hands do
> to loosen such a knot?

ANTIGONE: They're strong enough to help me lift a corpse.

ISMENE: You would break the law and bury him?

ANTIGONE: You would betray our brother?

ISMENE: You dare to defy Creon?

ANTIGONE: He cannot stand between me and my own.

ISMENE: We are only women, Antigone,
> we were not born to war with men.
> We are weak; we hear and we obey.
> To fight, and die, is senseless.

ANTIGONE: Well, I certainly wouldn't want you to be "senseless."
> You must be as you believe.
> I will bury my brother.
> If I die for my devotion, so be it.
> I will not dishonor the principles of the gods.

ISMENE: I am not dishonoring the gods
> by not standing against my country!

ANTIGONE: Just don't expect your country
   to stand for you against the gods.
   I'm going.

Discuss. What is Ismene's ethical dilemma? What would you do in this situation? Would you help your sister to bury Polynices or would you refuse and obey the law? After identifying the ethical dilemma, the student who read Ismene gets up. The ensemble divides into two lines facing each other – each representing the two main sides of this dilemma. As Ismene walks down the valley of public opinion, the students from each side of the dilemma (bury brother/obey the law) try to convince her to join their side. At the end of the valley, the Ismene physically chooses a side.

   Closure (2 minutes): How do playwrights use ethical dilemma to fuel their writing?

Additional information

Materials Needed: Copies of Antigone scene
   Potential Challenges: Time.

23 Subtext

Artistic goal: To introduce some techniques for writing and revising dialogue.

Academic goal: To introduce the concept of subtext.

Social goal: To work together on a whole class and small group activities.

Civic goal: To explore instances of subtext in the world today.

Instructional outline

Introduction (1 minute): Today we'll look at a technique to consider when writing dialogue.

Question and Answer (2 minutes): Do you know the expression "Throwing Subs?" What does it mean? "Subs" is short for subtext. What is subtext? It's what's underneath the words.

Warm-up Activity (7 minutes): FIRST LINE/LAST LINE

Students write this down:

A
B
A
B
A
B
A
B

Ask for a suggestion for a first line from the ensemble. Write down a first line for Character A. Ask for a suggestion for a last line from the ensemble. Write down a last line spoken by Character B. Give everyone 60 seconds to finish the scene (The teaching artist should do it too). This is a writing warm-up so don't think too much about it or try too hard to compose! Just write whatever comes to mind and write it quickly! It doesn't have to be good. It doesn't even

DOI: 10.4324/9781003079835-24

have to make sense. It just has to get done! Share out the scenes. Dialogue changes completely once you say it aloud.

FIRST LINE/SECOND LINE

Same as FIRST LINE/LAST LINE, but with first and second lines taken from the ensemble.

SIXTH LINE/LAST LINE

Same as FIRST LINE/LAST LINE, but with sixth and last lines taken from the ensemble.

Opening Activity (12 minutes): SUBTEXT: ONE WORD MONOLOGUES

Hand out index cards with the word "OH" on one side and a subtext written on the other. Each card should have a different subtext. After each performance of the word "Oh," the ensemble tries to guess the subtext.

Some examples:

* You just received a gift you hate from someone you love.
* You just received a much better grade on a test than you expected.
* You just walked into a party and saw someone wearing the exact same outfit.
* You were just asked out on a date by someone you find very attractive.
* You just walked in on your grandparents having sex.

How does that subtext change the meaning of the word?

Main Activity (18 minutes): SUBTEXT: IN DIALOGUE

On a sheet of paper, write a line of dialogue that communicates each of the following lines of subtext without using the exact words:

1 I'm not sure who you are, although I think I'm supposed to.
2 I'm deeply in love with you.
3 You smell really odd.
4 Your boyfriend is cheating on you.
5 I've never felt more lonely than I do right now. Please don't leave.

Each writer selects one of their sentences and reads it aloud. The ensemble tries to guess which subtext is being expressed. They state their guesses by holding up one, two, three, four, or five fingers.

Closure (3 minutes): How can different subtexts change the meaning of dialogue? What are some ways you see subtext used in the world?

24 Environment, relationship, conflict, resolution (ERCR)

Artistic goal: To introduce some techniques for writing and revising dialogue.

Academic goal: To introduce four elements of dramatic structure: environment, character relationship, conflict, and resolution.

Social goal: To work together in small group and whole class activities; to practice constructive peer feedback.

Civic goal: To explore the effect of rhetoric in modern communication.

Instructional outline

Introduction (1 minute): Today we'll look at four elements of dramatic structure: environment, relationship, conflict, and resolution (ERCR). Our goal today is to write scenes that illuminate each of these elements through dialogue. Show not tell!

Warm-up Activity (7 minutes): FIRST LINE/LAST LINE

Students write this down:

A
B
A
B
A
B
A
B

Ask for a suggestion for a first line from the ensemble. Write down a first line for Character A. Ask for a suggestion for a last line from the ensemble. Write down a last line spoken by Character B. Give everyone 60 seconds to finish the scene (The Teaching artist should do it too). This is a writing warm-up so don't think too much about it or try too hard to compose! Just write whatever comes to mind and write it quickly! It doesn't have to be good. It doesn't even

DOI: 10.4324/9781003079835-25

have to make sense. It just has to get done! Share out the scenes. Dialogue changes completely once you say it aloud.

First line/second line

Same as FIRST LINE/LAST LINE, but with first and second lines taken from the class.

Sixth line/last line

Same as FIRST LINE/LAST LINE, but with sixth and last lines taken from the class.

Opening Activity (15 minutes): ENVIRONMENT, RELATIONSHIP, CONFLICT, RESOLUTION

ENVIRONMENT: Where does the scene take place? The more specific the setting the easier it will be to write the scene.

For example: "Hey, what's up?" doesn't provide any information about place. It could anywhere. Try to craft a first line that provides at least some information about a possible location.

A: "Wow, the tide looks really high today! Look at those waves!" could indicate that the scene takes place at the beach.
A: "Welcome to McDonald's. How can I help you?" could indicate that the scene takes place at a fast food restaurant.
A: "Do you know if this train is going local or express?" could indicate that the scene takes place on the subway.

Students take turns writing and sharing one line of dialogue that indicates place. The rest of the class tries to guess the location.

RELATIONSHIP: Who are these characters to one another? The more specific the relationship, the easier it is to write dialogue for the scene.

For example: "Hey, what's up?" doesn't provide much information about relationship (other than perhaps these two people know one another because of how informal the greeting is). Try to craft a first line that provides at least some information about a possible relationship.

A: "Mom, you said if I cleaned my room, I could go to the party!"
A: "Sir, do you have any idea how fast you were driving? I'm going to need to see your license and registration, please."
A: "I want a divorce."

Students take turns writing and sharing one line of dialogue that establishes relationship. The rest of the class tries to guess the location.

CONFLICT: Conflict is at the center of all comedy and drama. The strongest two person scenes are often set up with one character wanting something and the other character wanting the exact opposite. At the end of the scene, you should be able to tell who won (or at least who is winning at the moment). If we look at the previous three sentences, how might we establish a clear and opposite conflict with the second line?

A: Mom, you said if I cleaned my room, I could go to the party!
B: I changed my mind. You're not leaving!
A: Sir, do you have any idea how fast you were driving? I'm going to need to see your license and registration, please.
B: I couldn't have been going faster than forty, officer.
A: I want a divorce.
B: I'm not giving up on this marriage and neither are you!

Students take turns writing one line of dialogue in response to a previous line, that establishes conflict.

Main activity (19 minutes): ERCR scenes

Select four student volunteers for an improv activity. Each student is responsible for one element of an improvised scene. The first student must establish an environment; the second must establish a relationship; the third must establish a conflict and the fourth actor must resolve the conflict and find a way to get everyone off stage.

Closure (1 minute): How do the elements of ERCR make it easier to create dialogue?

25 Caucus

Artistic goal: To collaborate on the creation of an artistic concept.
Academic goal: To identify the connections between form and content.
Social goal: To work in small group and whole group activities. To
practice the collaborative mantra, "Hold on tightly, let go lightly."
Civic goal: To come to consensus around a single idea using a demo-
cratic model of decision-making.

Instructional outline

Introduction (1 minute): Today we're going to begin a democratic process
of coming to consensus around a single idea.

Question and Answer (2 minutes): What forms of voting are you familiar with?
Today we're going to use a democratic form known as a caucus.

Warm-up Activity (8 minutes): COUNTING TO 21

The entire group must count to 21 together. Only one person at a time may
call out a number. If two or more people speak at once, the group must start
at the beginning again.

Opening Activity (12 minutes): ELEVATOR PITCH

One at a time, students volunteer to share out their concepts in 45 second
pitches. What are the most important elements to each pitch?

Main Activity (18 minutes): CAUCUS

Let's look at the three or four ideas that have garnered the most interest from
the ensemble. Each one of the concept creators moves to a different corner of
the room. The ensemble votes with their feet by moving to the concept that
they like best. In these groups, students refine their ideas and propose possible
characters/scenes to the whole group. The caucus continues until there are
no more undecided students and we've built consensus around a single concept. Be prepared for the consensus process to take several sessions.

Closure (2 minutes): How can we continue to work democratically and
practice the collaborative mantra, "Hold on tightly, let go lightly"?

DOI: 10.4324/9781003079835-26

Part III
The Citizen Artist plays

26 Default

Commissioned by Amy Stuart Wells and The Public Good at Teachers College, Columbia University
 Researched and written by Alyssa Duskin, Shaena Gibson, Miladys Sanchez, Liana Morales, and Luan Taveras

(Miladys performs her rap over a beat created by the ensemble.)

MILADYS: What does culture mean to me?
 Years of my ancestors going through slavery.
 What does culture mean to me?
 Days where my people died from going hungry.
 What does culture mean to me?
 Days of my people never being what they could be.
 What does culture mean to me?
 Times where there was happiness instead of misery.
 What does culture mean to you?
 What does culture mean to you?
 What does culture mean to you?
 (The beat cuts out.)
 Explain how dark you want to go.
 (A long tone proceeds a Principal's announcement over a loudspeaker. Shaena stands at the front of a classroom and listens to the announcement with a pained expression.)

PRINCIPAL HICKS (V.O.): Good morning students of Oliver R. White High School, this is your Principal Michael Hicks with an important announcement. This Wednesday we'll be celebrating Thanksgiving. The cafeteria will be serving turkey sandwiches with mayo on white bread. We'll have face-painting available for all students. BYOF – Bring your own feathers. The after-school gaming club will be playing Sorry. They'll be a special assembly re-enacting the first Thanksgiving with a joint presentation by the social studies and drama clubs. Those clubs will come together just like the Pilgrims and the Indians. Have a great day and remember: Education is the key to Knowledge!

DOI: 10.4324/9781003079835-27

Shaena's lesson

(Shaena begins a chant and encourages her class/the audience to join in.)

SHAENA: NO HISTORY, NO SELF; KNOW HISTORY KNOW SELF.
NO HISTORY, NO SELF; KNOW HISTORY KNOW SELF.
NO HISTORY, NO SELF; KNOW HISTORY KNOW SELF.

So that's a tradition given to me by my history teacher way back in my day. Before starting anything, we would say that chant as a reminder on the reason why we have classes such as this one. I'm Shaena, your new ethnic studies teacher.

Alright so the first lesson we'll discuss is our cultural independence. For example where my family is from; the Caribbeans; more specifically Barbados and Trinidad. Similar to America we had slavery, and similar to Native American history we were "discovered" and basically colonized by the British. But we eventually gained independence in 1962 and 1966. And over the next month we'll learn about each other's independence and the battles our people fought to take back our voice from others.

And I just wanna be honest with you guys. This will be fun, and different from your other classes. We'll get to learn more about one another and who we are, and who we want to be in the world. But sometimes it will be uncomfortable, we'll have hard conversations and we'll be angry at times. But I'll teach you how to take that anger and drive it into passion, art, and collaborative projects you can use to spread a message of hope and liberation! You already have a voice in you, and as a whole we'll teach one another ways in which we can use that voice to help instead of harm, to give back instead of taking, and to learn from the past so we don't repeat history.

So take out a pencil and something to write with; the first writing prompt is: Do you consider yourself free? Is independence something that can be given?

(School bell rings. Three young women stand facing the audience.)

ALYSSA: Mommy
LIANA: Dad
SHAENA: Mom
ALL: You always taught me.
ALYSSA: Taught me to be myself.
SHAENA: Taught me to work hard.
LIANA: Taught me to be proud of where I come from.
LIANA AND ALYSSA: To stay true to my culture.
ALYSSA: To have pride in it and love my Blackness.
SHAENA AND ALYSSA: To acknowledge its limitations and work.
SHAENA: Work hard to make it out of here.
LIANA: Work hard until sweat begins to run down your face.
ALYSSA: Work hard until you can't feel your fingertips anymore.
LIANA: Work hard until you've reached your best potential.

ALL: Work 3 times harder. 4 times harder. 5 times harder.

LIANA: Than everyone else.

ALYSSA: Because you have to be the best and prove everyone wrong.

LIANA: You have to be the best and represent your people.

SHAENA: You have to be the best because your ancestors couldn't.

ALL: And I get why you do it,

SHAENA: But do you know what that does to a kid? Feeling like I gotta run away from my past, leave it all behind. Like where I am surrounded by my people, my home, my family, my hood isn't somewhere I should settle. Like my ancestors lives are still impacting my own.

LIANA AND SHAENA: Like-

LIANA: I'm somehow responsible for representing all of my people. How can I represent them when you don't even do it yourself? Like you expect me to know things I was never taught. By you, by my teachers, by anyone.

LIANA AND ALYSSA: Like-

ALYSSA: I'm supposed to hide who I am. Hey mom, I may not look it, but I swear, I'm Chinese. You expect me to suppress The Lunar New Year, lanterns, Dim Sum, rice cakes, bright colors, stories, and savory smells. You make it seem like because I love that I can't love Rap, R&B, soul food, thick long beautiful locks, and everyone smelling like some version of coconut oil or Shea butter or cocoa butter. I can and I will love every aspect of all of my cultures.

LIANA: I can and I will continue to represent all of my cultures, even if you won't.

SHAENA: I can and I will succeed in my own way and on my own terms.

ALL: Do you even understand?

SHAENA: Of course you don't.

ALYSSA: Why would you?

LIANA: You never do.

SHAENA: Mom

LIANA: Dad

ALYSSA: Mommy

ALL: Nevermind

ALYSSA: It doesn't matter.

SHAENA: You're not listening anyways.

LIANA: You're never gonna change.

(A long tone proceeds a Principal's announcement over a loudspeaker. Luan stands at the front of a classroom and listens to the announcement with a pained expression.)

PRINCIPAL HICKS (V.O.): Good morning students of Oliver R. White High School, this is your Principal Michael Hicks with an important announcement. This Tuesday we'll be celebrating Pearl Harbor Day. The cafeteria will be serving bento boxes and pocky. The after-school gaming club will be playing Battleship. They'll be a special assembly featuring the American Pride Chorus singing Celine Dion's "My Heart Will Go On." Have a great day and remember: Education is Knowledge!

Luan's lesson

LUAN: Buenos dias mis estudiantes! Como estan, bien? Well throughout the year we are going to explore the Latinx culture, but for the first 3 weeks of school we'll have a focus on the Dominican culture. Quien aqui es Dominicano? Excellente, this is not going to be a typical class como la matematica, literatura, ciencias, o historia. My goal is to encourage student growth within each of every one of you. We are going to learn some of the history behind the Dominican Republic. After the death of Rafael Trujillo, whose 30-year dictatorship changed the entirety of things within the island. It poisoned and brutalized many things and left long lasting effects between two ethnicities. He was trained by U.S marines. After the liberation from his dictatorship, Jose Manuel Calderon recorded the first bachata song, "Borracho de amor" in 1962.

(The song "Borracho de amor" plays.)

Now I know what you are thinking, how are we supposed to dance to that? I get it, bachata is something that has evolved drastically over the years. Let's play something more modern.

(Borracho de amor cuts out.)

Now it's time to dance. Se pueden parar? C'mon don't be shy – stand up everyone. It's time to move our hips. You'll take three steps to the left and tap then three steps to the right and tap.

(Dile al amor by Aventura plays as Luan and the ensemble leads the audience in the basic steps of the bachata.)

And that's bachata. A dance that expresses freedom from higher powers, and that's exactly what you are going to feel through the year. Take your seats and open up your notebooks.

(School bell rings.)

Student/teacher twister

(A teacher sits typing her lesson plan into a computer. Behind her a three member chorus stands in a neutral position. A student enters.)

STUDENT: Ma'am? Can we talk?
TEACHER: Can you come another time? I need to work on today's lesson plan
STUDENT: I've been trying really hard in your U.S. History class and I'm still getting C's.
TEACHER: You don't turn in as much work as other students.

STUDENT: I've been talking to the other students, and we agree that this curriculum doesn't tell the whole story.

(The Chorus makes a physical shift to become three high school students.)

CHORUS 1: Do you get any of this?

ALL: Boring!

CHORUS 2: Like I'm going to remember this in two years.

CHORUS 3: I'm just here to get the credit.

STUDENT: Um; I've been going to tutoring.

(The Chorus makes a physical shift to become three high school teachers.)

CHORUS 1: Don't forget to study!

CHORUS 2: Everything will be on the test!

CHORUS 3: Use your head!

ALL CHORUS: Use your head!

TEACHER: I understand where you're coming from. I used to struggle in school just like you. During PD the teachers and I have been discussing the curriculum.

CHORUS 1: Just throw out the curriculum.

CHORUS 2: We just need to get them a 65 on the Regents.

CHORUS 3: Kids these days – all they do is complain!

ALL CHORUS: Fill their heads with lies!

TEACHER: Maybe if you apply yourself more you'll get better results.

STUDENT: How can I apply myself more than I have already been doing? We can't connect to any of this. Why won't you change the curriculum? Don't you care at all?

TEACHER: Changing the curriculum is more complicated than it seems.

(The Chorus makes a physical shift to become three high school principals.)

CHORUS 1: American History is their history.

CHORUS 2: Find a way to teach the curriculum and get these kids to pass or your fired.

CHORUS 3: Have them listen to Hamilton. *(Calmly)* Kids Like Rap.

ALL CHORUS: *(Frantically)* KIDS LIKE RAP!

STUDENT: We're all gonna fail. Don't you care at all?

ALL CHORUS: *(To teacher)* Don't you care at all?

TEACHER: Maybe you should talk to the guidance counselor about your feelings.

(The Chorus makes a physical shift to become three high school guidance counselors.)

CHORUS 1: Believe in yourself!

ALL: Trust me!

CHORUS 2: You don't want to end up a cashier at McDonald's do you?

CHORUS 3: Work hard, and you could be the manager!

STUDENT: Miss I'm just so tired. I'm tired of learning the same thing every-day about the same people.

TEACHER: What does your mom have to say about all of this?

(The Chorus makes a physical shift to become three mothers.)

CHORUS 1: ¿Por qué estás fallando en la clase de historia? If you don't develop a stronger work ethic, then you're gonna get stuck here.

CHORUS 2: What's the reason of me risking everything and leaving my family behind if you are not going to try your best at school?!

CHORUS 3: I just don't get it. Explain to me how do you go to school every single day, but come home with these grades?

ALL CHORUS: What are you doing all day?

TEACHER: Oh, um, I mean, education is the key to knowledge. It prepares you for the world. It prepares you for college.

(The Chorus makes a physical shift back to become three high school guidance counselors.)

CHORUS 1: Maybe you should consider something more your speed. Like a nice community college.

CHORUS 2: I'm sorry. I really am but you have to understand that this is the real world. Life is unfair and most times your dreams don't come true.

CHORUS 3: Sometimes we dream big, but the future is small, sweetie.

ALL CHORUS: The future is small.

STUDENT: This class is just teaching white history to a bunch of Black, and Brown kids. We're never gonna use this information again after this so what's the use?

(The Chorus makes a physical shift back to become three high school students.)

ALL CHORUS: What's the use?

(Student exits.)

TEACHER: I have 170 students, five classes of about 34 students each, and a stifling curriculum that limits my student's potential. So what am I supposed to do?

(The Chorus shifts back to neutral and considers the teacher's question. They have no answer. A long tone proceeds a Principal's announcement over a loudspeaker. Miladys stands at the front of a classroom and listens to the announcement with a pained expression.)

PRINCIPAL HICKS (V.O.): Good morning students of Oliver R. White High School, this is your Principal Michael Hicks with an important announcement. Ni Hao, This Thursday we'll be celebrating Chinese New Year. The cafeteria will be serving Lo Mein and Octopus. The after-school gaming club will be playing Chinese Checkers. They'll be a special assembly featuring the American Pride Chorus singing the music of BTS. Have a great day and remember: Education is Key!

Miladys' lesson

MILADYS: Hi, my name is Miladys Sanchez and I'm your multicultural ethnic studies teacher. Before we start today's lesson, I'm going to ask you all a few questions. Now, the first question is, how many of you are Black or African-American? Ok, how many of you are American Indian or Native Alaskan? So, how many of you are Asian? And how many of you are White? How many of you are Latinx? How many of you are Native Hawaiian or Pacific Islander? Well now here's the big question. How many of you are not fully one race – like you have more than one background from both of your parents? Ah, here is the thing, those categories came from the SAT exams. You see how I just categorized a group of you all into different sections? Well, that's what society is like especially for a mixed kid growing up. Now, for example I am half of two Latinx groups, Mexican and Puerto Rican and born in the United States, so you would think that's enough to be part of a culture that I can call my own, but no. Many people have said to me, "tú eres diferente. No eres una mexicana o aveces dicen que no soy una verdadera puertorriqueña", which for those who don't know what I said it basically means that I'm different and not a Mexican or real Puerto Rican. But being born in America or not having enough of an experience in one culture shouldn't stop you from being part of that side of your culture or not learning it. So in my class we will focus on you finding yourselves when you are not fully seen in your history. That's why here I hope we can learn our real history and others as well to get a better, more complete understanding of the world. Now let's learn about how certain words hold different meanings in different countries.

(School bell rings.)

You become the system

MIKE: I'm, you know, I'm African-American. Um, I was in the eighth grade. I was in Middle School. We had an English teacher, ah, and we read a book on the Holocaust. And at the end of the book – I went to school in the Midwest by the way, in a small town in the Midwest- and at the end of the book, she posed a question to the class that was,

TEACHER: Could something like that, like what we just read about, happen here in America?

MIKE: And, you know, basically everybody in the class said,

STUDENTS: No, that could never happen here!

MIKE: and my answer was, "Yeah it could *definitely* happen here!" And the teacher was shocked and she was like,

TEACHER: Why would you-? Why would you say something like that could happen here?

MIKE: And I said, "Because it- it already did." You know, if you look at the Transatlantic Slave Trade you have ten to twelve million people who are stolen, who are forcibly removed from their culture, who are ripped from everything that they've ever known. Who are sent to South America, to the Caribbean, to the U.S. where they're raped and brutalized and killed and forced into labor and- and that experience laid the foundation of the country- not just the Southern United States, but the entire country – and you're asking me whether something like could happen here? Yeah, even as a middle school student, as an eighth grader, I was like, "Yeah something like that could happen." But that wasn't part of my teacher's world view: she didn't see that. And so she was shocked and the rest of the class was shocked because that's not something that they were exposed to and because it wasn't part of the curriculum that meant that they had that hole in their knowledge even about their own country.

SHINO: So my younger one took AP US History this last year as a junior. And... The white male teacher who's... pretty clueless, but he tries... uhm at one point... he was talking about... Japanese internment. And in his effort to be... not culturally relevant, but he was trying to—so his big thing is he wants to present different perspectives on every issue, which is a good thing, so that you're not just looking at... an issue from one perspective. But when they're talking about Japanese internment, and also, the Holocaust uhm he went down this road of

TEACHER: So what could have been the benefit of concentration camps— whether it's Japanese interment or the Holocaust in Germany?

SHINO: So... yeah that was highly problematic. There are some things that have no benefits.

JOEY: And okay, so I'm just gonna tell a story because... we're at this point. So I took this course called uhm.... "Prada Chanel Ferrari" right? and it's this idea of looking at fashion theory. And this professor... she was this like old Italian immigrant, right? So she was like the cute little white lady who has like this pretty Italian accent, and we were talking about Muslim fashion because like that's like a very significant portion of like the fashion industry. And she gave us a challenge, which I thought was super interesting, which was this idea of... If you're a student. So— as a student in this class, to develop empathy for another culture, wear a hijab around campus for 24 hours... (*longer pause*) Right! Right? So, it's this idea of like... So... After she said that, I think about five hands went up. And these were my five like students of color in the class. And I thought— well, this was like an auditorium with like 200 people right? And like we ended up having this 30 minute discussion about this where like, you know, we told her "we're like not gonna do that." Right? And like some of the white kids were like-

STUDENTS: Yeah—we'll–rrr–whatever!

JOEY: And this is like–this idea that like white people really think they can do whatever the hell they want. Uhm. So I think like that's just like one example of like, how like, these white professors and white teachers have like impacted our lives. And like, just imagine... 200 students walking around a campus wearing hijabs. And like most of the people in that class were like white students. Well, most of my school is white, so... Anyways. That's fun.

NATASHA: So my son, he was in first grade. His teacher – a Caribbean woman. They were teaching those poems that, you know, like that – like it's a word and you do it the long way and then you use each letter to spell out – it's called a thing but I don't know. I remember she used, "AFRICA" cause you know, Black and Brown school. Aiiight! So I go in there and I see the first "A" was for "Africa" and I'm like well that's not all that creative but whatever. And the last one was "AIDS". And I was like – *(Pause.)* Now however old first graders are – six? seven? I was like – So then my kid comes home and asks me about AIDS. And I was like – well this wasn't a conversation I was expecting to have with you this young. Um…. But it was so hurtful because one: I had gone to that elementary school and I loved it, but two: both of my parents had died of AIDS. And it was just… so heart-wrenching that we – and it was just so – I can't. That one: now that was something that was placed in the brains of like six year olds and then it was like, let me tell you about your dead grandparents and how they died of AIDS. And then having to relive it myself, but then also being like – if this is your first time hearing about this entire continent, you now have an association between this entire continent and AIDS, right? Like we never do Europe and like attribute it to plague or small pox, right? But I just like – how dare you? Like there are so many "A" words. It could've been Awesome. It could've been A-mazing. It could've been Artistic. It could've been so many things. But we go – because it's "The Dark Continent" right – we go to AIDS. At some point, I was just like "F" should've been "Famine." "R" should've been "Refugees." Right? If we're gonna do it, let's DO it. Right? But for six year olds? Why aren't we filling them about places in the world with glee and excitement and curiosity versus fear. And then we're like, "Americans don't travel! Black people don't travel!" Well damn, y'all done spent twelve years telling us that every place we want to go got AIDS, and they got wars, and can't nobody eat in Ethiopia, and there's flies and malaria, and – well why *would* I want to go there? I don't want malaria. And it was just so shocking. And this was from a Black woman – a Black *Caribbean* woman, right? So when I say like – We become the system. And it's easy. And she's a veteran – like she's been teaching for like thirty years! You become the system if you're not careful. Even Black and Brown folks perpetuate systemic racism every day. We internalize it. You ain't got no choice. You've been drinking racism water since the day we were born. Right? And it's just like – I was just like – I was blown away. I swear to God I remember it on the board like it was yesterday and it was all them years ago.

(A long tone proceeds a Principal's announcement over a loudspeaker. Liana stands at the front of a classroom and listens to the announcement with a pained expression.)

PRINCIPAL HICKS (V.O.): Good morning students of Oliver R. White High School, this is your Principal Michael Hicks with an important announcement. Yo what's good? This Friday we'll be celebrating Black History Month. The cafeteria will be serving fried chicken nuggets and grape soda. The after-school gaming club will be playing man hunt. They'll be a special assembly featuring the American Pride Chorus singing "All the Stars" from the Black Panther soundtrack. That's all for me brothas and sistas. Have a great day and remember: Education!

Liana's lesson

LIANA: Hello class, my name is Liana and today we are going to be talking about the disconnect between Dominicans and Haitians. I am a person who is both of Dominican and Haitian descent. I grew up Never learning my Haitian culture and only taught my Dominican culture. I was also never taught the language of my people, either it being Spanish or French. Not knowing my history sparked a Curiosity to know more. So I learned and now it's your turn. In 1492 Christopher Columbus came upon the Caribbean Island which later would be called Hispaniola. He colonized it and killed most of the Taino natives with violence and diseases. By 1777 the island became divided by a French controlled west and a Spanish controlled East. The many years of colonialism caused these two Caribbean countries to hate each other. Haitians and Dominicans both come from Africa but Most Dominicans think they come from Spain. This is a prime effect of colonialism. Some people forget where they came from and that gets passed down from generations. It is important that we know where we come from and we learn our history. Take out your reading for today about The Parsley Massacre.

(School bell rings. A long tone proceeds a Principal's announcement over a loudspeaker. Alyssa stands at the front of a classroom and listens to the announcement with a pained expression.)

PRINCIPAL HICKS (V.O.): Good morning students of Oliver R. White High School, this is your Principal Michael Hicks with an important announcement. Hola! Happy Day of the Dead! This Monday we'll be celebrating Cinco De Mayo. The cafeteria will be serving white flour tortilla tacos, nachos with white cheese sauce, and White Malta. The after-school gaming club will be playing Uno.

(Over the loud speaker, we hear the sound of a door opening and slamming shut and a group of students chanting:)

ALL STUDENTS (V.O.): Food fairs and festivals are not acceptable! Food fairs and festivals are not acceptable! Food fairs and festivals are not acceptable!

PRINCIPAL (V.O.): Wait! What do you guys even want? Burritos?

LISA (V.O.): Are you serious right now? Is he seriously offering us burritos?

MARIA (V.O.): We don't want your bland-ass burritos

JASMINE (V.O.): We want ethnic studies. Real ethnic studies.

ALL STUDENTS (V.O.): Ethnic studies hear our voice, civil rights are not a
  choice! Ethnic studies hear our voice, civil rights are not a choice!

(The audio suddenly cuts out.)

Alyssa's lesson

ALYSSA: Hello class. What's good? Ni hou. ¡Hola senors y senoras! Boker tov.
  Eh, eh, what's de scene? I'm your teacher Alyssa, a multicultural young
  woman. Welcome to the first day of our ethnic studies class. In this class
  we will explore questions such as: who am I and where am I from? What
  is your culture and its history? Where am I now and where am I going?
  And finally, how has a Euro-centric default culture impacted the way
  that people of color have internalized racism? But first I'd like to know
  you all a lot better.

(Alyssa calls on someone from the audience and asks them these questions:)

> What's your name?
> What culture do you identify yourself as?
> What do you know about your culture?
> What would you like everyone else to know about your culture?
> Thank you *(insert name here)*.

This quarter's essential question is how has a Euro-centric or white default
culture impacted the way that we as people of color have internalized racism?
And the first way we'll explore this topic is through beauty standards.

(School bell rings.)

The town hall

SUPERINTENDENT: Welcome to our School District meeting. The first
  order of business will be to address the incident at Oliver R. White
  High School. The students are walking out of classes. This is not like
  the well-organized student walk-outs the district sponsored around
  Parkland. This is real. The students are calling for change and want ethnic studies courses. The first question is: What difference does it make
  to students if the curriculum reflects the history, experiences and knowledge of their communities and families?
PATRICIA: The difference that it makes is that school would exist as a con-
  tinuation of their life rather than the separate place that's disconnected
  from what they know or what they've experienced in their family and
  their community.
MICHAEL: The history of education in America is that the curriculum, if it's
  left unquestioned or unexamined, what it tends to do is silence or erase
  the experiences of so many different people. And you do damage to this

country. You create an environment that allows the President of the United States to tell sitting Congresswomen that they should go back to their countries.

JOEY: When we're only taught about heroic white figures, yeah we're gonna think that like white people are the ones with the power, right? And when you look at ethnic studies curriculum it really breaks down these power structures and like teaches us about all peoples and not just white people, right?

SHINO: In high school, I have to say, nobody taught me about the history of Asians in this country.

SADYE: So I was born in El Salvador and I never once learned about El Salvador, growing up. It wasn't in my textbooks, it wasn't in ah somebody we could aspire to, there was no leader that I learned about. In fact, what happened as a result of that was that people would say "You're from nothing and you came here". Right? And I bought into that narrative. You know, I'm from nothing.

NATASHA: If you only see yourself through these deficit lenses or not at all then how do you know where you fit in the world? Do you believe that you actually *do* fit in the world?

MICHAEL: If we're not telling the whole story then it affects all of us. It weakens everyone, not just students from a particular background. If I don't know women's history and LGBTQ history then I am a worse person for it, even though I am neither one of those things.

NATASHA: So much of it is like how do we give humanity back to all of the people that white supremacy has said, "You are not human." If I don't understand the fight of indigenous people in this country and across the Americas but I've learned how great Columbus is, how do I understand the world? And Columbus was not great at all – he was a dick!

SUPERINTENDENT: Does Ethnic Studies have to be taught by teachers of color?

NATASHA: Whooo! Dang! I should've – I should've had a drink before this!

MICHAEL: Ooooooh. Ho. Aaaah? Aaaah.? *(Beat.)* No. Ah. They don't have to. It's wonderful if they do, but I don't think that's it's a prerequisite and here's why I say that. If it was a prerequisite then we would have no ethnic studies movement because 80 percent of teachers are white. Right? So if you want to have ethnic studies taught with the teacher population that we have now, then you better be ready to teach white teachers how to do it.

JAVIER: I don't think that should be the case. I think white folks can teach social justice and I think that's good, but when you look at the history of getting Ethnic Studies into colleges, it was about supporting professors who represented the communities teaching those classes and so to honor the history of that it really should be representative.

MICHAEL: I think that insisting that ethnic studies be taught by somebody who is from that ethnicity is a cop out for white educators. It allows them to say – it allows schools to say, "Well you know um, we've got our Black teacher- *they* do ethnic studies and that means *we* don't have to deal with it."

HALLEY: There's a lot of research that students of color benefit from having teachers of color. There's also evidence that teachers of color on average set higher expectations for students of color.

PATRICIA: We have to destruct the way it is now that we have almost all white teachers teaching all subjects.

NATASHA: I should be able to go into the school and feel like – I should feel like this is still New York. Like I shouldn't be walking into school and feel like – where is everybody else from?

PATRICIA: We can't say that all white teachers will do a bad job of teaching African-American Studies, but each teacher whose going to teach African-American Studies or Latinx Studies or whatever it is that they're teaching has to look at their own life experience and how that connects to what they're teaching and what work do they need to do to be able to do a good job of delivering that material.

AMY: That's why I think the Ethnic Studies piece is so important because if you give a white middle-age teacher who's been teaching a long time a curriculum and like ask them to read those historical accounts and read these biographies and read these completely different ways of understanding pieces of American History that you thought you knew, I think that would automatically make that teacher more culturally relevant. You hear white people say a lot when they're exposed to an Ethnic Studies curriculum, "Why did I never know that?" And it has to change the lens through which they see the world.

CASSANDRA: Doesn't matter what the ethnic background is. There's a lot of teachers out there doing harmful things and possibly doing it in the name of "Oh I'm teaching about ethnic studies and culture, and all that," but their own personal beliefs are steeped in segregation. And, you know, whiteness—it can be present in a room without white people being around.

PATRICIA: One of the greatest ways to perpetuate oppression is to keep youth disconnected from society.

NATASHA: The master's tools will never dismantle the master's house.

ALL: I demand an education that is…

LIANA: Safe.

SHAENA: Diverse.

LUAN: Free.

ALYSSA: The truth.

MILADYS: Equal.

ALL: I demand an education.

END OF PLAY

27 Perfect Circle

Commissioned by Legal Momentum and Legal Services NYC
Researched and written by Khaliek Bethune, Marasia Coates-Peña,
Haqieqat Jawando, Pamela Piña, Mekhi Tudor, and Kayla Villanueva

(The ensemble forms a tableau – ANGEL sits on a chair surrounded by CONSCIENCE, FACTS, and DEFENSE. KHALIEK positions himself with the audience. The ensemble takes a deep breath in and out before Khaliek speaks to us:)

KHALIEK: *I* am the student who is being discriminated against.
ANGEL: *I* am the character representation of the student who is being discriminated against.
CONSCIENCE: *I* am this character's Conscience.
FACTS: *I* am this character's Facts.
DEFENSE: *I* am this character's Defense.

(The ensemble takes a sharp breath in.)

KHALIEK: Do you guys know the story of the Good Samaritan? I feel like that's my life. Jesus said, "Love your neighbor as yourself." But then he was questioned "Who is my neighbor?"

(The tableau shifts with ANGEL, CONSCIENCE, FACTS, and, DEFENSE forming a single line.)

ANGEL: Okay Angel, all you have to do is go to school, it won't be too bad today.
FACTS: Make sure I don't forget, pens, paper, notebooks, and my bookbag.
CONSCIENCE: I'm gonna be late if I don't hurry up! Do I look – man enough?
DEFENSE: They will live in that school if I'm late. A nadie le importa. Why put the extra effort?
ANGEL: Esperate…What's going to happen to me today? Is Mr. Alecander going to stare at my chest? Where should I go to the bathroom? Are those guys going to bother me again?
DEFENSE: Mom said "You're just going to have to fight back. I work and can't always be there, I can't trust the school to protect you. You're on your own. PERIOD."

DOI: 10.4324/9781003079835-28

CONSCIENCE: But what Mom doesn't know is I can't speak up. They don't take my gender seriously. I'm a man and all they see is a girl.

FACTS: You have to go to school today, you haven't been to school in a week and a half. You miss one more day and they're going to call ACS.

(The ensemble takes another deep breath.)

ANGEL: Okay, got everything,

ANGEL, FACTS, DEFENSE, CONSCIENCE: Let's start another day in hell.

(The ensemble shifts. One of the students becomes a sign that reads "This is a Bully-Free Zone")

ZONE: Don't worry...**this** is a bully free zone.

(BULLIED crosses the space talking on a cell phone.)

BULLIED: Yo I'm HELLA hungry so imma bout to get a chop cheese on a roll get some jalapenos on that American cheese no onions, cause those are disgusting, with lettuce tomato mayo and bbq sauce.

(A BULLY who has been listening the entire time walks in.)

BULLY: Give me the money you boutta buy that chop cheese with – jalapenos, American cheese, lettuce, tomato, mayo, and bbq sauce, and you right – no onions – they trash.

(BULLIED hangs up their phone.)

BULLIED: You ain't finna take my money.

(BULLY pushes BULLY into ZONE.)

ZONE: Hey! Stop foolin' for I pop on you!

(BULLY pulls BULLIED a few feet away from ZONE. ZONE stares at BULLY. BULLY pulls BULLIED a few more feet away from ZONE. ZONE still stares at BULLY. BULLY pulls BULLIED a few more feet away from ZONE.)

ZONE: Proceed. *(BULLY raises his fist to punch BULLIED. They freeze in this position.)*

KHALIEK: It's funny. But that's not bullying. I know that now that I'm out of high school. Bullying is based on unequal systems, it's based on an unequal power dynamic where there is either explicit or implicit bias driving that bullying. So it's discrimination. It's a violation of our rights.

And it's usually rooted in one of a variety of categories. Race, ethnicity, religion, sex, sexual orientation…those are the big ones. And what we have to understand is that schools, in terms of discrimination, have… failed….so…

INTERVIEWER: SO then – what parameters does the public school system take in order to protect students' rights?

LAWYER 1: Title IX, that's federal law. I am a lawyer. It's what I do. And the New York State Legislature implemented DASA or the Dignity for All Students Act which translates to New York City's "Respect for All," implemented to protect students' rights.

INTERVIEWER: But is it efficient?

KHALIEK: NO! Who do you talk to? Do you talk to the principal? Do you talk to the teacher? Do you file a complaint with the Department of Education? Do you call 311? And when you go on the DOE's website… I don't know, have any of you looked at the DOE's website. It's not like there is a big flashing sign that says…

ALL: Click on here if you've been bullied!

KHALIEK: You have to like, search for the Respect for All email that's on like the sixth page on the bottom. But we don't know where those emails go. So it's like this big black hole.

(The ensemble looks confused, muttering to themselves.)

KHALIEK: Like, you can click on it and your mom can fill it out and who the hell knows where it's going. And then what steps are being taken to address not only the bullying that's happening but the impact that it's having on you after it happens? Because like everything else in this day and age, if something happens to you it isn't just over and it's done. It reverberates. It has like, an echo, it follows you.

INTERVIEWER: What rights do students even have in schools?

LAWYER 2: I am a lawyer. I think the essential right is you have to be in a position where you are safe. You can't learn if you don't feel safe.

PARENT: I am a parent. Students should have the same rights in schools as outside! And, in fact, what SHOULD happen, is that this should be an even more protected place. When my student goes to school – I mean, the school takes my ownership, and so they should at this point, take my role as the parent, and protect them in an even more just way.

INTERVIEWER: Do Principals agree?

PRINCIPAL: I am a Principal. Kids come in with, uh, I feel, the right to be seen, to be known, and, to, uh, to be welcomed and held within the community for as long as we can do that.

LAWYER 2: Our core constitutional rights were set by the founding fathers in, you know, the seventeen hundreds. Who couldn't really contemplate the way we were going to live…300 years later, right? Like, they…could they have envisioned Facebook and cyberbullying?

PARENT: But what we are actually seeing is this, this BUBBLE, this place where – it – it – the opposite occurs, and we are often seeing schools PROTECT this, and so it can be an incredibly unsafe environment.

LAWYER 2: The first amendment applies. Right? You should have freedom of speech, and actually we should be fostering that in schools. Like, we shouldn't be suppressing someone's voice while their a student and then sending you out in the world and saying "No! Use your voice!" Even though you never got to practice that. And LEGALLY, the first amendment does apply.

AMY: But what, what other freedoms are they sacrificing to make sure that happens?

TEACHER: I am a teacher. And it's a double edged sword this whole freedom of speech thing, right? Um, on the one hand it's great that we don't have to be censored, right, we can say what's on our minds. Um, but people take it to the next level and they use it to be offensive with the intent to hurt, with the intent to discriminate. And I think that's hard to (*pause*) prove. It's hard to prove intent – someone can say some things and be just completely oblivious, right, because they grew up in like… in a vacuum.

PARENT: Everyone wants to feel like they belong. That they are free from judgment.

KHALIEK: One of the greatest ways to perpetuate oppression is to keep youth disconnected from society, right? So, they keep you busy doing things that don't mean anything. And that's, you know, one of the ways that the system is designed – to prevent students from connecting to meaningful change in the world.

So, Good Samaritan, right? Neighbors? Jesus answered the question, "A man was walking from Grand Concourse to Gun Hill. He was set upon by bullies, who robbed him of his dignity and left him broken and alone." And all of these adults walked past me, didn't seem to see me, and talked and talked and talked about students' rights.

(The ensemble takes a deep breath in and out.)

KHALIEK & **ANGEL**: But nothing changed.

(ZONE appears.)

ZONE: Bully free zone!

(BULLY grabs BULLY and is about to punch them.)

BULLY: You such a Bi–

(ZONE turns to look at BULLY.)

BULLY: Biiiii…beautiful person that…

(ZONE looks away and BULLY again raises a fist.)

BULLY: that should roll over an DIE-

(ZONE turns back to look at BULLY.)

BULLY: Die… die… dye, did you dye your hair?

(ZONE looks away and BULLY again raises a fist.)

BULLY: You such a waste of TIME-

(ZONE turns back to look at BULLY.)

BULLY: Time… time… time for me to go because I have class….ha…ha…ha

(BULLIED looks at ZONE. ZONE looks at the audience.)

KHALIEK: I remember in high school I had these three friends.
ANGEL: High School isn't completely terrible. I have these three amazing friends. There's Erin, who's fierce. You really couldn't get in her way. And Wilson,

(KHALIEK steps onstage to play WILSON.)

KHALIEK: *(to audience)* Oh, sorry, I have to play a character in this scene –
ANGEL: She's a little less shy than me but she's more playful. Yon's really smart. she always takes the chance to educate someone.
YON: I think in reality adults in school get away with a lot of bullying. OK, let's be for real.
ERIN/WILSON: For real.
YON: You ever have that teacher who just has kind that sarcastic way of being, and says things that, you know…and they think they can get away with that, and the students, they take it, yeah, they take it, but – it cuts you DOWN. Right? It hurts. So, no – I don't think – I think when teachers do that, a lot of people don't think that's bullying, but that adult has a lot of power over that young person, so that, for me, you know, that's a bullying situation. So in the first part of Mr. Alecander's class-
ERIN/WILSON: Mr. Alecander.
YON: It was all about court cases, and these court cases were all about people of color, and the class was made up of students of color ENTIRELY, and

he's this white man, he's new, he's QUITE young, in a sense, younger than most teachers, and he liked to talk about it a lot.

WILSON: And he's from Staten Island.

ERIN: He made that clear.

WILSON: And the first day–

ERIN: And the first day, the FIRST day, this man came, and he was like "alright", and this classroom of young, Black, Hispanic

YON: And mostly women, it was mostly women in that class, it was like five boys, five males, and the rest of us were girls, and all seniors, we were ALL seniors.

ERIN: He just looked at us and was like

ERIN, YON, WILSON: "How many of you guys have kids?"

YON: He was like "raise your hand, raise your hand if you have kids."

ERIN: And he really WANTED to know. To some students it went right over their head but to me I was like "uh huh, this white man coming in, asking us, how many of us have kids." And he really waiting for us to be like,

ERIN, YON, WILSON: Yeah I have two. Tiana and the boy.

WILSON: The thing about making us uncomfortable—it started when he got really comfortable with us. So I'd be sitting, with my arm on the edge of the chair, and he would come, and his pelvis would be RIGHT THERE, and I'm like

ERIN, YON, WILSON: Dude, PERSONAL SPACE. You never heard of boundaries?!

WILSON: And he'd be like

ERIN: How's your work?

YON: How're you doing?

WILSON: And I'd be like

ERIN, YON, WILSON: Get out of my space!

ERIN: I guess it was entertaining at first. And I don't remember ever complaining to the principal or the vice principal about the race comments, but when it turned into, like, our BODIES being involved, I think that's when a lot of us began to like

ERIN, YON, WILSON: No, that's not OK.

YON: Once I step on your school grounds, I'm young, it's your responsibility to take care of me. To make me feel safe.

WILSON: I have the right. I have the right to not have my body violated in any sort of way.

ERIN: I don't know what kind of rights we have as students because honestly, it's like the school system is its own state, our schools are part of their own separate state called the DOE.

ANGEL: (to the audience) They're comfortable talking about it. I'm not but that's because I've realized that –

KHALIEK: –every single time that I fought for myself, it came off to them as me complaining.

ANGEL: I'm just tired of telling my story, you know?

KHALIEK/ANGEL: So, yeah...

ERIN, YON, WILSON: It started off him trying to be like one of us.

ERIN: He'll rock a gold chain

YON: And some new kicks

WILSON: Maybe even walk funny

ERIN: talking with a slaaaang

YON: thinking he's slick

WILSON: Then he started to bust out jokes in class

YON: He's a white boy from Staten Island,

ERIN, YON, WILSON: so that alone made us laugh

WILSON: He asked us

MR. ALECANDER: How many of you have a criminal record? How many of you guys have been stopped by the police?

YON: Every time I think of that question, I think of Eric Garner,

ERIN, YON, WILSON: I can't breathe *(sharp quick inhale)* I can't breathe *(sharp quick inhale)* I can't breathe.

ERIN: He also told me

MR. ALECANDER: I like your lipgloss.

ERIN: And it wasn't out of kindness because he told after I put it on.

YON: It took another white man in power to say something in order for it to stop.

ERIN: It was creepy. They were trying to cover it up like an undercover cop.

WILSON: He robbed me of my body. And entered my space

ERIN: Like back up

YON/ERIN/WILSON: You're not my freshman boyfriend who tried to get to first base.

ERIN: But the most craziest thing he ever said?

WILSON: Was when he was going to the meeting after we reported him, the rumors were spread

YON: He said

MR. ALECANDER: I don't want to go to this meeting with the Principal if the vaginas are going to be there.

WILSON: Like woooow. He really said that to another teacher??

ERIN: About us?

ERIN/YON/WILSON: Well these vaginas will get you kicked out. Take your gold chain elsewhere!!

(ANGEL is left in class alone as ERIN, YON, WILSON run off high-fiving; Mr. ALECANDER turns back to look at her.)

KHALIEK: And, they did.

KHALIEK/ANGEL: But for me –

ANGEL: Nothing changed.

KAYLA: To paraphrase Ta-Nehisi Coates, "We talk about zero-tolerance and bully-free zone signs. And these are all fine and applicable, but they understate the task and allow the adults in the school to pretend that there is a real distance between their own attitudes, and those of the bullies."

(The ensemble abruptly drop character and directly address the audience.)

MARASIA: How are you guys liking the show so far? Good, right?

PAMELA: We wrote it.

KAYLA: It's crazy because we have this idea we want to explain to you guys but it's hard. Like real f—ing hard.

PAMELA: Yeah, like really hard.

KAYLA: So bear with us.

MEKHI: It has to do with perfect circles. Can anyone here draw a perfect circle? Or does anyone want to attempt it?

(MEKHI pulls out a dry erase board and offers it to audience members to attempt to draw a circle.)

MARASIA: It's okay, don't be shy. It's theory we're testing out, you see. The Plato theory.

(MEKHI brings the board back onstage to display the audience drawings.)

PAMELA: Ok, so you see how each person drew kinda the same circle? Ok not the same exact thing but in each in their minds they had an idea of this perfect circle, so they drew it out. Yeah, that's what we call a Platonic form.

MEKHI: So basically what Pamela is saying is we all have a picture in our minds what a perfect circle is. If we try to draw the circle by hand, without mathematics, we try to subconsciously mimic or copy that perfect circle.

KAYLA: You know it, we know it. We all have this idea of a perfect circle. Knowing if we attempt to draw it, it's going to be imperfect. It's never going to match it.

PAMELA: Now take that logic and apply that to the perfect school.

MEKHI: Everyone has an idea of a perfect school but when students who don't fit in the characteristics of the perfect student for that perfect school, they often get left out.

KAYLA: They become the outcast.

PAMELA: So in a sense, the bullies think they are doing an important job.

KAYLA: They force the outcasts to fit into the idea of the perfect school.

MEKHI: It reflects what the school community wants.

MARASIA: And that's our theory on why bullying is persistent, even when everyone says they're against it.

KHALIEK: So, one of worst things – right. When I was in high school, there's just two bathrooms. "Boys" and "Girls." Where am I going to feel safe? I tried the Girls... Sorry, I have to be in this scene too, there's only five of us)...and of course it had this stupid "Bully-Free Zone" sign on the door.

(ANGEL sits in a bathroom stall and receives three text messages).

CONSCIENCE: You can't pass as a man, little girl, you're disgusting.

FACTS: Everyone sees how Mr. Alecander looks at you, you don't even say anything you must like the attention.

DEFENSE: Thirsty as hell!

TRAITOR FRIEND: It's just a message. Toughen up.

ANGEL: It's not just a message it really hurts me, but they, they don't see that.

TRAITOR FRIEND: No physical harm is being done.

CONSCIENCE: But mentally it's destroying me

DEFENSE: I'm tired of people saying cyberbullying isn't a real problem, like uh...dime no ven estos.

FACTS: Students who experienced cyberbullying are nearly 2 times more likely to attempt suicide.

ANGEL: They should see what goes on in kids' lives, not just put up these posters, actually see us.

TRAITOR FRIEND: Just go talk to the counselor or fill out an incident report.

DEFENSE: Esos estupidos informes no hacen mas que matar arboles.

ANGEL/CONSCIENCE: I'm being assaulted, harassed, but no one sees me!

DEFENSE: They don't want their "perfect" little image of school to be ruined.

DEFENSE/ANGEL: Start paying the prices

ANGEL: Help

CONSCIENCE/ANGEL: I'm getting tired of yelling out for you

ANGEL: Ayudeme!

ANGEL/FACTS: I don't wanna be another statistic

ANGEL: You don't help!

TRAITOR FRIEND: You're a freak

DEFENSE/ANGEL: I am not a freak

CONSCIENCE: Why did she call me a freak?

DEFENSE: No me importa.

FACTS: I do care.

ANGEL: You're not really my friend, are you? Two-faced –

TRAITOR FRIEND: Get out of my way before I do something.

DEFENSE: You should move little girl thinking you can tell me what to do!

CONSCIENCE: Please, I don't want to fight

FACTS: Fighting is never the answer. Bullying is usually to gain control so it's better to not sink to that level

CONSCIENCE: Should I tell the teacher? this isn't gonna end well.

TRAITOR FRIEND: What, nothing to say, you abomination?

ANGEL: I... I'm. not

TRAITOR FRIEND: Wow the abomination speaks?

DEFENSE: Este homofobico me esta poniendo a prueba.

CONSCIENCE: Maybe I am an abomination, am I an abomination?

FACTS: It's always possible to cope with this by dealing logically, turn the other cheek. Accept it.

DEFENSE: Fighting this out is the only way I'm gonna get them to stop. They wanna try me.

TRAITOR FRIEND: What are you gonna do, go tell the teacher?

FACTS: School is not structured to have that type of voice for students.

TRAITOR FRIEND: No one can help you

FACTS: They are right, no one can help you

CONSCIENCE: No one can help me?

DEFENSE: Yo me puedo ayudar yo misma.

TRAITOR FRIEND: No one would even miss you, you should be dead.

ANGEL/DEFENSE: You know what? Your nothing but a loser who thinks picking on the other "weak" kids is a way of power *Defense steps to the side with Angel. Conscience and facts are knocked backwards*

TRAITOR FRIEND: You made the biggest mistake messing with me

DEFENSE: *(raises Angel's fist)* No! YOU made the biggest mistake messing with ME –

CONSCIENCE/FACTS: Wait! Rewind…

(Scene rewinds)

TRAITOR FRIEND: No one would even miss you, you should be dead.

(Conscience steps behind her)

CONSCIENCE: Why should I fear death?
  If I am, death is not.
  If death is, I am not.
  Why should I fear that which
  Can only exist when I do not? *(CONSCIENCE and ANGEL crumble)*

DEFENSE/FACTS: Wait! Rewind…

TRAITOR FRIEND: No one would even miss you, you should be dead.

FACTS : *(steps behind Angel)* You know what, bully victims are between 2 to 9 times more likely to consider suicide than non-victims, according to studies by Yale University and I will not be one of them!

TRAITOR FRIEND: And by the way, I was never your friend. I just felt bad for you.

(TRAITOR FRIEND exits)

ANGEL: Bullying is killing me from the inside out.

KHALIEK: Every time something like that would happen, with a supposed friend, I'd tell someone. I'm lying in a ditch, broken and alone, and my teachers and Principal just walk on by and say –

STUDENT: I'm not just a bullied statistic
  Rules in school are not realistic
  Kids come at me, bein' mad sadistic
  Got my mind goin' hella ballistic.
  I try and tell my teachers how I feel
  They cover it up with some sort of deal.
  It's the same speech every single time
  You wonder why some kids fall behind
  It goes a little something like this...

(A chorus of teachers sing:)

TEACHERS: We love you
  We need you
  So this is what we do
  To protect you
  As a teacher I...Cover my ass!
  As a school we...Cover our ass!
  If you wanna be
  the best you need to be
  Cover your ass.
  It's a code see
  N.Y.D.O.E
  Cover, cover, cover, cover your ass!

Student

  I couldn't believe what I was hearing
  All my safety slowly disappearing.
  They only care about their reputation
  Using us as a demonstration
  This is a cry for help – they really don't know how it felt
  Principals don't care cause they turn a blind eye
  Don't know how it feels having no one by their side.
  They really care more about covering ass
  Will the D.O.E gets what's coming to them at last?
  Bullying is seen but not heard
  They just keep on saying these wack-ass words

(A chorus of teachers sing:)

PRINCIPALS: This is my school
  You follow my rules
  So this is what I'm gonna do
  To protect you

As Principal I…Cover my ass!

As a school we…Cover our ass!

Cover, cover, cover, cover your ass

CHORUS: When I say "cover", you say "ass" – "Cover!" "Ass!" – "Cover!" "Ass!"
When I say "cover your ass", you say "cover your ass"!
"Cover your ass!" "Cover your ass!" "Cover your ass!" "Cover your ass!"
Cover, cover, cover, cover YOUR ASS!

KHALIEK/ANGEL: And nothing changed.

(BULLY prepares to pummel BULLIED)

BULLY: I'ma make it so you wish you weren't born.

ZONE: Hey, you bully!

BULLY: Hm?

ZONE: I'm talking to YOU. Can you not read??

BULLY: What do you —

ZONE: Are you illiterate? HMMM?? It says "Bully – Free Zoooone."

BULLY: I'm sorry–

ZONE: You should be sorry, you illiterate imbecile. No wonder you're on a
third grade reading level

BULLY: B-B-But

ZONE: But – but – nothing Mister 54 in ELA. Reading like "one-one-once
u-u-u-upon a t-t-time…"

(BULLY runs away crying)

ZONE: THIS is a bully-free zone.

KHALIEK: Look, you're laughing. Laughing at pure, outright bullying. We
find enjoyment in the belittling of others. We expect it. Especially when
someone has stepped out of line. We like it when people get their "just
rewards" You expect those who fall out of line to be forced back into the
circle. wthe cycle?

(The ensemble takes a deep breath)

KHALIEK: I wish schools had this kind of CandyLand scenario, protecting a
students rights if they are being discriminated against – it should be as
easy as picking up the phone or going to the school and saying "Principal
Schmo, you know, my son was bullied because of sexual orientation."

PAMELA: But, what are the specifics to DASA and title IX when it comes to
sexual orientation? Or transgender folks?

MEKHI: Technically….sexual orientation isn't protected in New York State
under…

KHALIEK: But in reality that's a grey area, in that right now it is being fought
in the Supreme Court for sexual orientation based discrimination to be

protected under Title XI, which it should be if we are protecting the dignity of all students.

SAMANTHA: I am a social worker. We judge, everybody judges, all the time right? I think when that, we just have to be aware of when we are taking that too far.

NILDA: I am a guidance counselor. The school is a place to develop our humanity. The outside world can be cruel, right, but we don't HAVE to be cruel in here...

SAMANTHA: How do we protect students rights against discrimination? I wish, I wish – that is the million dollar question. I wish I had an answer, then we probably wouldn't be sitting here.

NILDA: But I think adults don't always understand young people and they don't trust you, then they restrict you instead of knowing that, developmentally, students are supposed to be a little loud, and maybe sometimes a little oppositional, because you're trying to FIND, you know, you're trying to learn your way to make your stand.

TERRI: I am a Principal. And I can tell you that school is not structured to have that type of voice for students. You have to find and promote ways for students to have voice and agency within the school because, um, there are many things that the department of education will uh... stifle very quickly. I love my school, I love being the Principal, but I don't actually believe in schooling. I believe in education and I believe in learning, and I believe that schooling is normally oppressive. It's a system that wasn't built for **us**, and um, I feel like that we're going up against so many structures that aren't aligned to what would fully develop us because, uh, a cycle of oppression in the United States, that starts in American schools.

KHALIEK: I told my teachers. I spoke to the Principal. My mom filled out all the forms on the website on the sixth page on the bottom. I even called a lawyer, who took pity on me:

LAWYER: I would argue that you are a victim of a no-no touching accident. And robots, robots, are plotting against you and the boss man is doing nothing. And cyber-bullied?!? 59% of teens have been bullied or harassed online – it impacts your ability to learn, and the boss man, the boss man did –

ALL: Click

KHALIEK/ANGEL: And nothing's changed.

KHALIEK: Jesus said "Love your neighbor as yourself." But who is my neighbor?

(The ensemble takes a deep breath)

NILDA: Most schools are doing NOTHING concerning sexual orientation. NOTHING. I had a student, I was his advisor, for three years, loved him to death. This student has to use the boys' bathroom, right? And I see, one of my colleagues, she is yelling at my advisee in front of the staff bathroom. He would sneak into that staff bathroom, so I went up to him and I said "why would you do that, you know they don't allow students in there?" And he said to me "Miss. I can't USE the boy's bathroom."

KHALIEK: And so, one last time, I tried the Boys bathroom.

NILDA: He's been harassed in there, he felt intimidated in there. And more and more, as he came into himself, he was SHOWING, you know his identity, and as he came into himself, he was too afraid to go into that bathroom. And I had never given a thought to, what is our students' experience, behind those closed doors?

BULLY Z: Yo, I heard that trannies got small dicks.

BULLY X: Nah bro they won't ever be a real boy on some Pinocchio type thing.

BULLY Z: Hey look the fag is here.

ANGEL: Can you guys shut up–

BULLY Z: Oh look the little fag is speaking up for **herself**.

ANGEL: It's **him**.

(The ensemble begins a beat.)

BULLY X: Oh, I'm so sorry. It's him? My fault…

BULLY Z: Are you seriously gonna apologize to this… schmerm?

BULLY X: Nah I'm just messin' with you.

ANGEL: I'm not a schmerm asshole and can you ju–

BULLY Z: Hold up– what did you just call me?

BULLY X: I think this little faggot called you an asshole.

ANGEL: N–no I didn't mean it I was jus–

BULLY X: Yea, looks like she's finally growing some balls.

BULLY Z: Awww, is the little tranny scared now?

ANGEL: N–no of course not. I just really need to get to class.

(The ensemble's b*eat starts to get louder)*

BULLY X: C'mon do you really think we'll let you go?

BULLY Z: Yea, why not stay? The fun is just beginning and class doesn't begin for another 10 minutes.

BULLY X: And it's not like anyone is gonna come and look for you. No one even cares about you.

ANGEL: That's not true, Jesus is with me.

BULLY Z: Psh, Jesus really? You're a mistake created by Jesus, you don't belong to walk on this earth.

ANGEL: Ima need you to stop.

BULLY X: Stop what? The truth?

BULLY Z: Mmmm I don't think she understands what we mean by the truth, why don't we beat it onto her?

(The ensemble give one last heavy beat – Everyone drops.)

MEKHI: And this? This is not OK. Earlier when we were talking about the idea of a perfect circle and how if we attempt to draw it, it's going to be imperfect. So when we treat school the same way, everyone has these ideas of what the NORM is for the school community. Well, guess what? People like Angel aren't going to fit in the circle. They're not going to fit your expectations. And that's okay. It doesn't make them any less than a student. It doesn't make them any less than someone's kid. And it sure as hell doesn't make them any less than a human.

ANGEL/KHALIEK: I can't breathe *(Gasp)*

DEFENSE: Hell, I should've gotten that lawyer, taken that school all the way to the Supreme Court, sued them AND their mothers. Dile a todo el mundo como me trataron, and maybe, just maybe, I could've put an end to it.

ANGEL/KHALIEK: I can't breathe *(Gasp)*

CONSCIENCE: I should have spoke out at least once, or at the very least called the Suicide Hotline at 1–800–273–TALK, so I didn't risk becoming a statistic.

ANGEL/KHALIEK: I can't breathe *(Gasp)*

FACTS: I should have learned to just give up from the beginning, and not put my energy towards fighting this. I was never going to get justice.

ANGEL: *Me* who is human.

KHALIEK: *Me* who is trying to live.

ANGEL: *Me* who was just tryna learn who I am.

KHALIEK: *Me* who was put in the upside-*down* for making a *sound*.

ANGEL AND KHALIEK: *Me* who is just trying to be *me*.

KHALIEK: No no you don't get it!

    I tolerate racist and homophobic faces on a daily basis
    And you wonder why I throw books at bigots' faces.
    He said "oh…you gay fag"
    She said "go to hell with your two dads"
    And I'm tired of it… This school is toxic and disgusting!!
    Your lies are like knives cutting through my veins
    The veins that I slice through to cope with the pain.
    You cannot fathom how hurt I am.
    This school *(gasp)*, these people *(gasp)* I JUST WANT TO PUT THEM SHAME!
    It's like me against them…

ANGEL AND KHALIEK: So who's to blame?

ANGEL AND CONSCIENCE: My anxiety is silent,

ANGEL: You wouldn't even notice a change on the outside,

CONSCIENCE: I'm just overwhelmed in reality,

    This disservice, injustice, outrageous tragedy,

ANGEL: I don't normally say that but I'm tired of keeping it inside of me,

ANGEL AND CONSCIENCE: Please listen,

CONSCIENCE: People need to start knowing how to act and it's a fact,

    That bullying is this big ass cliche,

    That every situation is being looped on replay,

ANGEL: And everyone's feelings need to be paused because "professionals" got caught up in a delay *(Pause)* See there's a broken glass window, and as each sharp shard hits–

ANGEL AND CONSCIENCE: My pristine arms,

ANGEL: And each shard screams "screw you, kill yourself," you worthless bitch.

CONSCIENCE: They've already killed my self esteem,
Which gave birth to the oppression of

ANGEL: My body,

CONSCIENCE: And depression

ANGEL: In my mind,

CONSCIENCE, DEFENSE, AND FACTS: Are you Okay?

ANGEL AND KHALIEK: Yeah, I'm fine....

FACTS: I walk into class with my sexuality on my sleeves
Oh yeah forgot you get detention for crimes like these
you see Sexuality is not something you talk about at schools because...

ALL: *"their religion would make OTHER students feel unsafe."*

FACTS: Welp, I guess I have to educate instead of hate. 1 more to the 160,000 kids that skip school because they aren't

ALL: Cool.

FACTS: 1 more to the 4,400 suicidal teen deaths because you make them feel

ALL: disgusting.

FACTS: And baby I refuse.
The way I operate is not a malfunction to your distaste
And trust me I wish didn't waste all that time combating with the hate, and doubting my mental state.
Honestly I tried to change the culture to make my school a better place but there's only so much you can do –

(The ensemble takes a deep breath.)

ALL: when the circle never included – you.

END OF PLAY

28 Overdrive

A short descent into standardized testing

Commissioned by Amy Stuart Wells and The Public Good at Teachers College, Columbia University
  Researched and written by Rhaneil Clemmings, Jayline Diaz, Marquese Evans, Lizette Padua, and Ciara Shack
  (Four students come on stage. Sound effect: Family Feud theme song)

RHANEIL: Hi, my name is Rhaneil!
LIZETTE: I'm Lizette!
MARQUESE: Hello! I'm Marquese
JAY: Hi. My name is Jay! And we're Epic NEXT!

(Family Feud theme fades out as PROFESSOR DIAZ enters with a clipboard.)

JAY: Oh, yes, and this is Professor Diaz, a psychometrician.
MARQUESE: She's–
LIZETTE: No one important *(laughs uncomfortably)*
PROFESSOR DIAZ: Hello. It's so nice to meet you all.
RHANEIL: Today we'll be performing a show for you.
LIZETTE: And we need to give you a *small* test just to see if you meet the qualifications of a *good* audience. That'll determine the kind of show we do for you.
PROFESSOR DIAZ: The National Audience Assessment Board has come up with a set of questions to scrutinize how well the human brain can process information in a timed fashion. In return all we ask – prior to entertaining you – is that you yourselves participate by answering this set of questions. None of your answers will be recorded; this is for us to measure your own development and see how we might best serve you.
MARQUESE: Please make sure you raise your hand if you know the answer.
LIZETTE: Questions? Nobody? Then let's begin.
  Alright, question 1, Where was His Holiness the 14th Dalai Lama born?

(The correct answer is Taktser, China – if an audience member gets it right...)

PROFESSOR DIAZ *(WRITES IN HER NOTES)*: Hm. Hippie.

DOI: 10.4324/9781003079835-29

(OR If they say something other than Taktser, China, the ensemble makes a loud buzzer sound.)

ALL: **W**rong.

PROFESSOR DIAZ *(WRITES IN HER NOTES)*: The CORRECT ANSWER is TAKTSER, CHINA.

(OR if no one answers, after two seconds the ensemble makes a loud buzzer sound.)

ALL TOGETHER: Sorry, Time's Up.

RHANEIL: Again guys, remember – she's no one important.

(Everyone laughs uncomfortably except for PROFESSOR DIAZ.)

MARQUESE: Question 2, how many chakras are there?

(If no one answers, after two seconds the ensemble makes a loud buzzer sound.)

ALL: Sorry, times up

(If someone answers "7"…)

ALL: Yes!! That's it! Good one!

PROFESSOR DIAZ: Actually, although most people have HEARD of 7 Chakras, there are actually 114 in the human body – but I'll give it to them. Jesus…

JAY: She's no one important *(Smiles, clears throat)* Question 3, You're a bus driver.

RHANEIL: And the bus starts out empty.

MARQUESE: At the first stop 4 people get on. At the second stop, 8 people get on and 3 get off.

LIZETTE: At the third stop, 2 people get off and 4 get on.

JAY: The question is, what color are the bus driver's eyes?

(if they get it correct …)

PROFESSO R DIAZ: Mhmmm c1.13. Interesting.

(OR if no one answers, after two seconds the ensemble makes a loud buzzer sound.)

ALL TOGETHER: Sorry, Time's Up.

PROFESSOR DIAZ: Hm…slow…

ALL: She's no one important

MARQUESE: Question 4. A random sample of 374 United States pennies was collected, and the age of each penny was determined. According to the box plot that Professor Diaz is holding…

(PROFESSOR DIAZ very quickly flashes a look at a box plot on her clipboard)

MARQUESE: What is the approximate range of the ages?

(If someone asks to see the box plot again...)

PROFESSOR DIAZ: It's a timed test.

(After two seconds the ensemble makes a loud buzzer sound.)

ALL: Sorry, Time's Up.
RHANEIL: Final Question: What is the circumference of Timmy's belt?

(If someone asks a follow up question.)

PROFESSOR DIAZ: I can't help you. It's a test.

(After two seconds the ensemble makes a loud buzzer sound.)

ALL STUDENTS: Sorry, Time's Up.
JAY: Don't worry, you can take it again...
RHANEIL: You did great, really, it's a hard test...
LIZETTE: Last night's audience did a little bit better...
PROFESSOR DIAZ: Based on the Jonathan Clemmings strategy of standard-
    ized audience assessment from the study originally published by Harvard
    University, you have scored a... 27 out of 80.

(A long uncomfortable pause.)

ALL: She's no one important.

(The ensemble claps their hands together.)

ALL: Everybody is a Genius.
MARQUESE: But if you judge a fish
CIARA: By its ability to climb a tree
JAY: It will live its whole life
LIZETTE: Believing that it is
ALL: Stupid.

(Sound effect: Clock Ticking)

ALL: We're taking a test. We're taking a test. We're taking a test. We're taking
    a test.

(As they speak, the ensemble moves five chairs in to V formation.)

ALL: Angie.

(The ensemble sits.)

ANGIE: I can't focus it's as if my eyes try to be unblurred from the scattered letters in front of me, and my brain tries to hit the control button to transform like yours.

CINDY: I think I'm ready, no I know I'm ready, with all the resources I was given, I know I'm going to pass the test, I mean I'm smart enough. Daddy always says I'm smart enough.

VIOLET: Mama's gonna want me to do this right? What if I don't understand, what if I can't do this? Miss, Miss, I want my mama she can help me. Wait what? She can't? I have to take the test all by myself like a big girl.

JOSE: For what I gotta take this stupid judgmental test, I already know Ima fail, like I'm just another spic from the Bronx, well that's what they wanna call me, I feel like this test is useless.

LUCY: Walking into the class made me have anxiety and I haven't seen the test yet, why is my booklet in the front, shit it feels like everyone is staring at me, I feel like I'm exposed.

TEACHER: Why do they create these test that cause so much harm. These kids are so hurt, so shaky.

ANGIE: Stop worrying, just take the test, because the test is what makes you the best but its it's like playing Russian roulette, the trigger is the bubble and your finger is the pencil, now if I pull the trigger will it make me fail?

(Ticking clock sound effect stops)

AMY: These tests are very narrow in terms of the way students think. And it only rewards students who are very good at that reductive way of thinking, picking that one right answer all the time. And you might say, "sure, but some of these tests might be more valuable in some content areas or some knowledge, like, say, math" But the problem is with these policies, these federal policies like "No Child Left Behind."

DR. GORDON: No Child Left Behind had a lot of appeal for minority folk because we could finally hold the system accountable by those test scores. It didn't take me long though to realize that it was a false indicator.

AMY: We've put so much emphasis on these measures ALONE, right? So when you think about it, like when we define "what's a **good** school?" – that's often code for "that school has high test scores." When you define "what's a **good** student?" – that's often code for "a student that has high test scores."

DR. GORDON: The issue was not racial mix in schools the issue was quality education, and we even used racial mix in pursuit of an education of higher quality. To simply mix people by race doesn't ensure high quality education.

AMY: So if you're only valuing schools and their children and their teachers by these measures we have to ask what are we missing? What are we not valuing? And what are the consequences of that? You measure what you value…um what some people value, right. And then we value what we've measured.

DR. GORDON: loved the idea when it first cropped up and I came to regret having supported it.

AMY: And that's where the cycle becomes

ALL: Dangerous.

(The ensemble changes the chairs to form a desk in the PRINCIPAL's office. The PRINCIPAL is seated at her desk. PROTOCOL stands behind her facing away.)

ANGIE: Hey Miss, I heard I failed the Global Regents, and I wanted to talk to you about how that's going to affect my graduation

PRINCIPAL: It won't really affect your graduation, it's just a little thorn at your side that you need to get rid of. Like we always say, education is the passport to the Future.

ANGIE: Yeah but what if I fail again? What will happen then?

PRINCIPAL: I'm sure that won't happen again. Because you're a really intelligent kid, and I'm sure the second time will be the best. Because your future…

(PROTOCOL turns around and whispers in PRINCIPAL's ear.)

PROTOCOL: Future…

PRINCIPAL: future is bright!

ANGIE: OK, but does my future really depend on this test? Because the more that I take it, the more it doesn't make sense. Like-

PRINCIPAL: This is for your own good! If you never try, you'll always fail, and it will never matter…

PROTOCOL AND PRINCIPAL: So try again,

PROTOCOL: fail again, but fail better.

ANGIE: You giving me an IEP isn't going to change anything.

PRINCIPAL: Well with this IEP, its gives you more more time to focus. You won't have to rush through the test…

PROTOCOL: Testing is a skill. While this may come as a surprise to some people it is.

PROTOCOL AND PRINCIPAL: A simple fact.

ANGIE: What is a fact? Me having a different mindset as everyone else?

PRINCIPAL: Not intentionally I just feel like with this you can catch up with everyone else and graduate with all of your fellow comrades.

PROTOCOL AND PRINCIPAL: Because education is a passport to the...

ANGIE: FUTURE! I GET IT!! WE ALL DO! You want me and my "fellow" comrades to be the same, but we're not. You put us in a category, but we're not just letters in the alphabet that you can pick and choose from. You put us in a classroom where we all are taught the same, but what makes you think that the same knowledge is what will make us gain? Don't you understand that we're different? We all are! You can't make us take one test, on one day, to define one kid.

PROTOCOL: It will gain you the ability to move on in the real world. Because education is the passport to the future.

PRINCIPAL: Oh no, the test is what helps you, you know, it's to get you out to college, I mean everyone has a different score, It's just a test.

PROTOCOL: Because education is the passport to the future.

ANGIE: You just want us to be the same!!

PROTOCOL: Future.

ANGIE: Test.

PROTOCOL: Future.

ANGIE: Same.

PROTOCOL: Future.

ANGIE: Test.

PROTOCOL: Future.

ANGIE: Same.

ANGIE AND PROTOCOL: Brain.

DR. GORDON: These tests aren't realistic. You'll never have to take a test like this when you get a job or anywhere else in the real world. How many jobs demand that employees come up with the right answer on the spot, from memory, while the clock is ticking? How often are we forbidden to ask coworkers for help, or to depend on a larger organization for support? And when someone is going to judge the quality of your work, whether you are a sculptor, a lifeguard, a financial analyst, how common is it for you to be given a secret pencil-and-paper exam?

(The ensemble moves five chairs in to V formation.)

ALL: Jose.

JOSE: We never had the resources, so I don't think I'm in the wrong to complain, when they've given us all the same test to lose and not gain. I thought this test was to test our progress but it's not. It's whoever has the highest grade. They cost more. They'll go somewhere in life.

CINDY: I feel bad for the students in other schools that have extra time. Aren't they called "special ed"? It seems like they're a little slow, but they could pass if they wanted to.... maybe.

ANGIE: Stop it, just take the test, Angie.

VIOLET: Okay. I'll try. Question 1 how many quarts are in a gallon?

ALL: A 4, B 2, C 6, D 1

VIOLET: I don't know! Miss, can you help me?

Oh right. I gotta do this like a big girl.

But miss my stomach hurts. Can I go to the nurse?

No? Why not? Because I have to take the test or mommy might get mad at me.

ALL: Mommy might get mad at me. Mommy might get mad at me.

LUCY: I want to curl into a little ball – but I can't. My leg shakes to the seconds running out, counting...

ALL: One, two, three, four, five, six, seven, eight, nine, ten.

LUCY: This teacher is pissing me off. Can you sit down or go somewhere?! Cause you walking around looking at my paper is making me nervous, making me feel like Ima fail, but I know I'm going to fail.

JOSE: "Lowdowns" like me either become homeless or a dope addict, maybe a drug dealer. (*Pause*) How can ya think so little of me, of us? But I get it. It's okay. Ya'll think I'm shit – YO teacher I ain't taking this stupid ass test for the fourth time!!

(Jose leaves the formation and storms into the audience. PRINCIPAL and TEACHER rush him.)

PRINCIPAL AND TEACHER: Jose! Jose! Jose! Jose!

PRINCIPAL: It's gonna be okay. Don't worry we'll fix things, there must have been a grading issue the last time you took it –

TEACHER: We're gonna get to the bottom of this, You did everything right. There shouldn't be an issue with your test.

PRINCIPAL: We understand what your feeling right now, but we need you to calm down–

JOSE: No! You don't understand! I'm tired of everyone throwing their "I understand" cards in my face. My life is on the line here! What's the matter with you all? You're not doing anything. You prepared me to pass the test but I'm failing the real world and you people only seem to "understand" that I'm supposed to go with the flow because I need my diploma. If I can't be real in the real world then what's the point of school? What's the point of all of this testing, quizzing, grading if I'm not developing? I'm not good in school. I'm not good in the real world. I stay at the bottom. What the hell is the purpose of school anyway?!

(Glitching happens. TEACHER and PRINCIPAL start to gasp.)

PRINCIPAL AND TEACHER: The purpose of school. The purpose of school. The purpose of school.

(TEACHER breaks out of it)

TEACHER: The purpose of school is learning. It's, you know... it's giving the opportunity for students to grow...

PRINCIPAL: I think ah, maybe, ah, To empower students, empower children...

TEACHER: To learn responsibility. To be trustworthy. School is a career as a young kid.

PRINCIPAL: Exposing students to a realm of different ideas and possibilities.

PERSON 1: To Educate the hearts and minds of students and the adults that are engaged in the teaching process.

PERSON 2: Students–

ALL: aren't being seen as whole human beings.

PERSON 2: Schools currently are run as a way of warehousing troublesome members of society. But if we were to talk about the ideal, I think–

ALL: school ought to be about the development of the creative intellect.

PERSON 3: The purpose of schooling is a social control thing, the purpose of education is sort of the opposite of that –

ALL: It's freedom

DR. GORDON: Uh uh uh, you need to stop, brake, and breathe. You've got a whole lot in you, even though you don't feel it, or see it. There is something special about you. I see the frustration between you kids and the test, and I say to myself what in the world is wrong here? Students come in here early in the morning already with the impression that he or she Is failing, but y'all youngins have to look in a different direction. Get ya head out of your behind.

JOSE: No no. You people don't get it, man. During the test I am – people call it as – I'm special ed. I don't really process some things while taking the test and having the same test isn't really going to help. I get extra hours, extra time, but that isn't enough for me.

DR. GORDON: Your situation isn't isolated. You're not unique. It's not peculiar to you. A lot of people have that problem. Don't make a decision out of anger and do something you'll regret. Try and better understand how the tests can help you and not what tests have become. Now I'm not saying that the tests are perfect but testing could be used to cultivate, to develop our abilities, or at least to inform the process rather than just to tell you how good…How well you've done. Boy, if you walk out this school the last thing you'll grab at is any intellect at all. You have a future. Shape it wisely.

(The sound effect of a school bell ringing. The ensemble begins to hum a song under the RAPPER/NARRATOR's verse.)

RAPPER/NARRATOR: You see outside we are students,
  But inside we are patients
  They all think we're sick
  Giving tests as medication.
  Isn't school where you're supposed to learn?
  But you walk in the room
  And you're already a subject.
  You're told at an early age that these tests are critical
  To your disposition

And if you try to speak out
You're an imposition
And so taking the test becomes your only mission.
The teachers are supposed to act as the nurses
But they don't even think that this medicine is working.

TEACHER VOICE: There's nothing about this that guarantees integrity
But I'm trapped.
Because I'm supposed to have clarity
Be a role model
For all these young people that stare at me
And how would it look if I didn't follow the rules?

RAPPER/NARRATOR: But when you don't stand up, and sit in silence
You make us all fools.
You normalize it
And what you're forgetting is to us it feels like violence.
We need to escape from these hospital beds.
Got all these words in my head.
'Cause they got me on these meds.
But who's standing at the door?
Demanding we need more?
It's the Principals.
They make promises to soothe us.
Band-Aids for bullet holes.

PRINCIPAL: It's all in your head.
You'll be alright.
Just go back to bed.

RAPPER/NARRATOR: And you're back at your desk
Taking another test.
The parents want a voice, walking around like they have no choice.
Dragging their opinions like zombies.

PARENT 1: I'm aware of the situation...

PARENT 2: I never had a chance to have a good education

PARENT 1 AND PARENT 2: I just want the best for my child.

PARENT 1: I feel like I can't say anything...
if a doctor says my child has a tumor I'm not going to question it.
So if a teacher says my child needs tutoring
I'ma try to make the best of it.

PARENT 2: I know I'm pushing Cindy to the extreme.
The tests may be unfair, but I still want my kid to dream.

PARENT 1 AND PARENT 2: I just want the best for my child.

PARENT 1: They say your child needs PM school,

PARENT 2: She needs to be pushed

PARENT 1: Your child needs an IEP

PARENT 2: She needs to be rushed

PARENT 1: Your child needs medicine

PARENT 2: Your child needs medicine

PARENT 1: They know what's best.

> They went to school for that.
> They know the rules for that.
> And yeah I'm cool with that.

PARENT 2: That's the game.

> It's never gonna change.
> You gotta deal with that.
> If my child needs this to succeed I'm not going to question it.

PARENT 1: If my child needs this to survive, I'm gonna make the best of it.

PARENT 2: I understand she might hate me now

> but I hope she sees one day that I did this for her.
> 'Cause I don't want her to end up like me.

PARENT 1: If I were to go against,

> The government might make me get on my knees to repent.

PARENT 1 AND PARENT 2: I just want the best for my child.

RAPPER/NARRATOR: Yeah.

> And then you have these elected officials
> When you tell them about the situation all they get to preaching about is

ALL: Accountability

RAPPER/NARRATOR: How are you suppose to deal with me if all I hear from you is

ALL: Accountability

RAPPER/NARRATOR: That's all they have to say we could talk about this all day and all you'll get from them is

ALL: Accountability

RAPPER/NARRATOR: It's as if that's the excuse that they use as a suture

> But they're bad doctors.
> These meds only work twenty percent of the time and we think that's fine.
> Let those eighty percent be ill, they'll be alright.
> We'll give them more meds tonight.
> But then it doesn't work again
> and all you'll here from them is –

ALL: Accountability

RAPPER/NARRATOR: Prescribing us meds and trying to make us have the same mindset.

> Well, what happens when the medicine doesn't work for the rest?
> Are they still not going to be good, still not going to be the best?
> Trained medicated soldiers are measured
> At the top of these doctors folders.
> They're not being mindful that they're killing these patients cells,
> But they don't care. Don't you get it? As long as the medicine sells.
> These standardized tests
> Aren't the best

Things to assess us.
They shouldn't be
What makes or breaks us.
It's almost as if these people hate us.
These companies makes these tests
But they aren't the ones who grade us and survey us.
They don't know you. They don't me.
They don't know what we need.
'Cause right now I need sleep.
But that's what they don't see.
All they want from us is money.
We're the worker bees.
We gotta get these people their honey.
And when another year of testing is done
We step out into the summer sun–

(The ensemble joins hands and takes a deep breath together.)

RAPPER/NARRATOR: But once Labor Day passes
    We go back to Square One

(The sound effect of a school bell ringing. The ensemble begins to hum a song under the RAPPER/NARRATOR's verse.)

RAPPER/NARRATOR: You see outside we are students but inside we are patients
    And sometimes…
    When someone tells you you're sick your whole life
    It comes true.

(The hum cuts out.)

ALL: Cindy.
RAPPER/NARRATOR: I'm talking about you.

(The ensemble moves five chairs into a very tight V formation.)

ANGIE: But what happens to the people who don't grade well? Are they not good test takers or good working machines? The test being the battery, so we're being tested as if we were just things?
TEACHER 1: Why do I have to administer this?
    If the government's going to trust me to teach them,
    then the government should trust me to assess them.
CINDY: The test is what makes us the best,
    especially the student who has 90s and higher, like me.

(The ensemble lets out a violent cry.)

VIOLET: What if I can't do this? What if-? I don't know miss. I am trying miss. It's it's just too hard.

(The ensemble lets out a violent cry.)

CINDY: I'm sure I can get whatever I want, like get into the college I want,
Because I got what it takes.
But what if Kelly gets a 95 and I'm stuck with a 90?
What is dad gonna say, what am I gonna do?

(The ensemble lets out a violent cry.)

LUCY: I have not answered not a single question.
Ugh I have been looking at this question for the past 3 hours –
none of which makes sense. like when did we learn this,
Ugh I feel fucking stupid.
There's only 3 more minutes left- I-I'll just bubble in anything.

(The students rise out of their chairs and begin frantically bubbling in circles in overdrive.)

CINDY: What is dad gonna say, what am I gonna do?
ALL: This is not how I learn!
CINDY: I am not of value. My dad sees me as a grade. My family is full of people who are intellects, people who have made it to the top, while I... I have no chance to make it to the top. I'll be just like my dad – and I know he doesn't want that. Dad, I'm sorry. I can't be a number in a corrupted system anymore.

(Sound effect of a gunshot.)

LIZETTE: The suicide rate among 10 to 14 year-olds doubled between 2007 and 2014.
RHANEIL: The same period in which states have increasingly adopted new high-stakes tests.
LIZETTE: In 2014, 425 middle schoolers nationwide took their own lives.
RHANEIL: Psychologists say several factors are responsible, however, pressure from standardized testing is high on the list.
LIZETTE: Sorry.
RHANEIL: Time's up.
MRS. LOPEZ: I done lost my student. Lost her in the depths of work, fear, and to the trigger of her father's gun. I see my kids every year struggle. Every fucking year. For the past years. Ella esta muerta! She's gone! Because of a piece of *paper*. A piece of paper! She was scared. So many kids were.

How dare we try to define these students? I've been drinking for the past 2 weeks. I left my job, for Christ's sake. That's how bad it's been! This isn't a joke anymore. Like my mother says, If the flower blooms and turns grey, then that's when we know something is wrong. And this – this is wrong.

ALL: Everybody is a Genius.

MARQUESE: But if you judge a fish

CIARA: By it's ability to climb a tree...

JAY: Standardized testing can't test the idea and feeling of love.

RHANEIL: Like when you hug your mother, and she tells you she's proud of you no matter what.

JAY: It cannot test your acts of kindness.

LIZETTE: Como cuando ayudas a un hombre en la calle a conseguir comida.

JAY: Your creativity. Your passion.

CIARA: Like the time when you were eight and you got a star on your art project because you spent a whole week thinking of the meaning of "family."

JAY: Your truthfulness.

MARQUESE: Like when you told your parents you were gay.

ALL: Your pain.

JAY: Like the time you were told-

ALL: Your grades are not good enough.

JAY: Your heart, soul, good will, curiosity, judgment.

RHANEIL: Honor.

LIZETTE: Imagination.

CIARA: Hopefulness.

MARQUESE: Pride.

RHANEIL: Bravery.

LIZETTE: Dignity.

CIARA: Qualifications.

MARQUESE: Understanding.

RHANEIL: Forgiveness.

LIZETTE: Cultura.

CIARA: Dreams.

MARQUESE: Friendship.

(The ensemble forms a straight line facing the audience during JAY's next line.)

JAY: Those are things that tests cannot test. They can never test nor define...

(The ensemble joins hands.)

ALL: Us.

(The ensemble kneels together and bows their heads.)

END OF PLAY

29 Nothing About Us

Commissioned by New York Appleseed
  Researched and written by Roman Claudio, Javia Dean, Chrisaury Guzman, Esmirna Matos, Stitch Portillo, and Iris Zapata

(The student performers are pre-set in seats among the audience. An adult Epic representative addresses the audience.)

ADULT EPIC REP: This play was built through interviews. The student artists interviewed 42 education stakeholders about their views on educational segregation and they asked every one of them the same first question which was…

(Sound effect: a chime rings followed by a recorded voice over.)

ESMIRNA (V.O.): What is the purpose of school?
ADULT EPIC REP: Before we get started, I'd like to ask a few of you to share your thoughts: what is the purpose of school?

(The Adult Epic Rep calls on several audience members to provide their responses. After a few audience members have spoken, the Adult Epic Rep calls on a student-actor in the crowd.)

NIKET: Ah, it's a great question – I think, ah, I think maybe, ah, a cynical, ah, voice in my mind, might say that the purpose of school is ah, ah, to get folks to kind of, maybe assimilate or conform to, ah, a certain set of norms or, ah, set of behaviors that our society values.

(The Adult Epic Rep calls on another student-actor in the crowd.)

DR. GORDON: *(laughing lightly)* The purpose of school? *(laughing lightly)* I'm trying to decide whether to be facetious, or…serious. But even my facetious answer is serious. I think schools, currently, are run as a way of warehousing…uh…troublesome younger members of the society.

DOI: 10.4324/9781003079835-30

(The Adult Epic Rep calls on another student-actor in the crowd.)

ABRAM: Schooling, I think of as different from education. Schooling is like, we take everybody's kids for twelve years and teach them, more or less, to act the same way. The purpose of schooling is a social control thing. The purpose of education is sort of the opposite of that – it's freedom.

(CASSANDRA pops up from her seat. The Adult Epic Rep leaves the stage.)

CASSANDRA: OK, so I had a really rough childhood and school for me was a refuge. School was a place that I could really truly be myself. I really believe that the purpose of school should be to educate the hearts and minds of students and the adults that are engaged in the teaching process.

(The actors begin to move toward the stage as they continue to speak.)

JONATHAN: It's also to socialize our community so that we're not locked into our own family or own block or our own building. We get to meet and interact with other people, other kids who we might not otherwise see.

MATT G: Like, democratic equity: Like, building a better democracy. Building, like, a body of citizenry that, like, is literate and can like navigate the world. Social mobility: Like, I grew up poor. I'm the first person in my family to go to college, to get a bachelor's degree, let alone to get a master's degree. So how do I, like, elevate my social, like, status and like, how do I like, not be poor for the rest of my life?

SHINO: The purpose of schooling is to create people who are compassionate, people who have empathy, and people who are passionate about creating a just society and a just world.

MAURICE: The purpose of education is summed up in Plato's allegory of the cave. Long story short, it's this allegory about these cave dwellers who have been locked in a cave their entire lives. They've been chained to these chairs, which is supposed to represent ignorance and a lack of understanding. And one guy breaks free and he, like, climbs up to the real world and he's blinded by this light, which is the truth, but eventually he adjusts to it and goes back down and tries to tell other people, "No, there are real things out there in the world." And he acts as the teacher in that situation and walks the other cave dweller to the light and goes back and forth and tries to convert everyone and I tell my kids that story because it helps to reinforce the idea that the purpose of education is not for an adult to stand before you and to give you knowledge or wisdom, but to ask you a few questions to help you to stumble upon or discover a deeper and more thorough understanding of yourselves and of the world.

MATT D: School is a career as a young kid.

(The ensemble, now fully gathered on stage, performs a rap.)

ENSEMBLE: Segregation huh
    Why keep us all apart
    You want them to learn together
    So you shouldn't sort us out
    Segregation what
    We all the same – So what
    Just put us in together
    We're the same no matter what.
    Segregation huh
    Why keep us all apart
    You want them to learn together
    So you shouldn't sort us out
    Segregation what
    We all the same – So what
    Just put us in together
    We're the same no matter what.

(Sound effect: a chime rings followed by a recorded voice over.)

ESMIRNA (V.O.): And now… a town hall!

(A SCHOOL DISTRICT REPRESENTATIVE addresses the crowd.)

SCHOOL DISTRICT REPRESENTATIVE: [*Clearing her throat*] Thank you for coming out tonight for this meeting. As we try to address the segregation racially and economically in our schools, we have developed a proposal to change the high school admission criteria to take ELA and Math exams and demographic factors such as socio-economic status, home language, and home address into account.

(Displeased grumblings)

This will help diversify your district's schools to not only reflect the diversity of New York City but also to help make equity a cornerstone of our educational system. This is a time to hear from parents, community members, and students so that we can hear your concerns and ideas.

PARENT 1: I have children in the district and I'm concerned with this diversity plan that you are proposing. What about class sizes and the quality of special education for my child with the influx of *those* low performing students?
PARENT 2: What about the reputation of our school? The recognition of our high-test scores and our kids getting into prestigious programs and high

schools? We need to think about the donations from current and former parents. Have you all thought about that? You should because this will cause parents to move and will cause our art, music, and language programs to disappear.

PARENT 1: Let's not be naïve about the *type of students* that some schools will be receiving and the potential schools that our children are going to be forced to attend. It matters who's in the classroom. Why would I make the choice to put my children in an environment that I know will harm them?

PARENT 2: We have two choices. Fight for the seats that they want to give away or move. I choose to fight.

PARENT 3: What about us? All I hear is children who look like me being labeled as poor and underperforming.

PARENT 1: Nobody said your kids are under performing.

PARENT 3: *You* just said they were underperforming!

PARENT 1: No I didn't!

PARENT 2: Becky, you kind of did.

PARENT 1: I did? Oh damn. My bad.

PARENT 4: Those white lips hit those white ears differently than ours do.

PARENT 3: What is not being said about our children is that they are smart, caring, creative, and most importantly a potential friend to your child. *You all* see our children as one way...well I see *you all* as one way too. People who just take. You take over our neighborhoods and right now, you want to take the opportunity for our children to finally get access to the resources that should be a right for everyone.

PARENT 1: We worked hard for these opportunities. It is not about "taking" because we are not doing that. It's about earning what you worked for. We live in a meritocracy.

PARENT 4: Can we stop beating around the bush? This is going to happen. That is the hard truth here. I am a beneficiary of a desegregation program and it provided me a chance to have quality teachers and the proper resources to learn but it was hard to be at a school that did not want you. What I want to know is what are principals going to do to help the transition for the students coming into these new schools?

PARENT 1: I respect what the last woman said but my wife and I have worked and lived in under resourced areas as educators and I will add, as minorities in predominantly Black and Latino communities. I shared that to show that I am not a racist. Some of you in here believe that this is a race issue and I will be the first to say that it is not. This is an education issue. My children deserve the high-quality education that they earned through a test that everyone gets to take.

PARENT 2: It's just the system.

PARENT 1: Yes, the system. How am I supposed to prepare my kids to attend these new integrated schools?

SCHOOL DISTRICT REPRESENTATIVE: I don't know. How did you prepare your kids to attend segregated schools?

(Sound effect: a chime rings followed by a recorded voice over.)

ESMIRNA (V.O.): And now... beating around the bush!

(THE BUSH holds a sign that reads "THE BUSH")

THE BUSH: White supremacy.

(One at a time, each actor takes off a shoe and uses it to beat the floor around THE BUSH as they say their lines.)

BUSH BEATER #1: I've put my kid in a majority white school, because I think that's a better educational opportunity. I just feel more comfortable!

BUSH BEATER #2: I'm not racist! I just want my kids to be safe!

BUSH BEATER #3: Standardized tests are used because we believe they give every student a chance to achieve based on his own merit!

BUSH BEATER #4: Screened schools provide opportunities to pull students out of poverty!

BUSH BEATER #1: All our kids have an equal education!

BUSH BEATER #2: I'm not racist! I have a lot of Black friends!

BUSH BEATER #3: I'm not racist! I saw Black Panther three times!

BUSH BEATER #4: I'm not racist! I don't see color! I don't see color!

BUSH BEATER #1: My name is not Becky! My name is not Becky!

BUSH BEATER #2: All lives matter! All lives matter!

(The BUSH BEATERS stop. They pant heavily, out of breath.)

BUSH: White people. Hi! I'm white supremacy.

(The BUSH BEATERS slink away. BUSH transforms into POC.)

POC: America is built on segregation.

WHITE PERSON: We separate students so that the best compete with the best.

POC: We need to change this MONSTROSITY people call "The System"—a RACIALLY biased system that privileges the white and the wealthy.

WHITE PERSON: This protocol is used because we believe that each set of persons can get their education individually based on their own merit.

POC: WE HAVE BEEN "SEPARATE BUT EQUAL" BEFORE BROWN V. BOARD OF EDUCATION; BEFORE PLESSY V. FERGUSON.

WHITE PERSON: People of color don't really stand for America due to the *(clears throat)* "shade" that is being "thrown at them"

POC: "Land of the free, Home of the Brave" my ass

WHITE PERSON: Diversity is important

POC: God created us for this reason

WHITE PERSON: "All men are created equal" – Thomas Jefferson

POC: Slave owner.

(Sound effect: a chime rings followed by a recorded voice over.)

ESMIRNA (V.O.): Who benefits from educational segregation?

DONNA: I think who benefits... I don't think anyone really benefits, maybe the powers that be. Uh, the people that want to continue the status quo of oppression.

TONI: White people.

JONATHAN: White people and people with money.

NOULA: Me. Upper middle class white people. Me!

CASSANDRA: I would like to just say it's white people, but it's not just white people who benefit all the time. All skin folk ain't your kinfolk. There are people who maybe are no longer first generation American who now have access to certain things and they don't necessarily want a new wave of people to be able to have access to some of the things that *they* got so they could be where *they* are- they benefit from the system as it stands.

ABRAM: Other people benefit from highly segregated schools because they're the lucky ones that sort of get plucked out of poverty and placed into like a better life or whatever. And I think in some ways I count myself as that. I grew up very poor, but the system is set up so that someone like me that displays certain talents as a kid is able to be plucked out of that and placed into a better situation.

PATRICIA: Families and students who have access to what are often called the best schools. In order to have best schools you have to have schools to compare them to. If everybody had a great school then we wouldn't have that difference anymore. But it comes down to that idea of scarcity – If I let go of something or I don't fight for that life – there's not enough for everybody.

(Sound effect: a chime rings followed by a recorded voice over.)

ESMIRNA (V.O.): And now... the system!

(Four actors merge to form a four-headed, eight-legged monster: THE SYSTEM. A PARENT enters. THE SYSTEM actors speak in unison.)

SYSTEM (ALL): Hello. We are The System. We are committed to providing excellent educational opportunities that are open, accessible, and welcoming to all city students!

PARENT: Hi. My kid has a nut allergy. What school offers nut free lunches?

SYSTEM (ALL): Of course!

SYSTEM (ACTOR 1): Go to Room 425!

SYSTEM (ACTOR 3): A worker will assist you!

SYSTEM (ACTOR 2): Right?

SYSTEM (ACTOR 4): YES!

(PARENT crosses the stage as THE SYSTEM actors come apart and reform into another twisted shape.)

PARENT: My kid has a nut allergy! What school offers nut free lunches?
SYSTEM (ALL): Of course!
SYSTEM (ACTOR 3): A pamphlet is available
SYSTEM (ACTOR 1): In room 253
SYSTEM (ACTOR 2): Right?
SYSTEM (ACTOR 4): YES!

(PARENT crosses the stage as THE SYSTEM actors come apart and reform into another twisted shape.)

PARENT: My kid has a nut allergy! What school offers nut free lunches?
SYSTEM (ALL): Of course!
SYSTEM (ACTOR 3): Your opinion matters
SYSTEM (ACTOR 1): Go to Room 23.4
SYSTEM (ACTOR 2): Right?
SYSTEM (ACTOR 4): YES!

(PARENT crosses the stage as THE SYSTEM actors come apart and reform into another twisted shape.)

PARENT: The uh, system, sent me here.

(ACTOR 4 steps out of THE SYSTEM and whispers to THE PARENT.)

ACTOR 4: Get out.
PARENT: What?
ACTOR 4: Get out. While you can.
PARENT: What do you mean-
ACTOR 4: Systems do exactly what they're designed to do. We're never help-
   ing our kids. That's just how it is. They lie... IT lies.
PARENT: My kid has a nut allergy!
ACTOR 4: This IS nuts!
PARENT: I'm leaving.

(PARENT starts to leave. ACTOR 4 returns to their place in THE SYSTEM. The PARENT turns back.)

PARENT: NYC Public Schools are more segregated now than they were
   before Brown vs Board Of Education, how did we get here?
SYSTEM (ALL): The fitnessgram pacer test is a very efficient tool in testing
   students.
PARENT: Can you answ-

SYSTEM (ALL): Next Question.
PARENT: My child has IEP, where should I go?
SYSTEM (ACTOR 1): Office 227.
SYSTEM (ACTOR 3): Someone will be with you soon.
SYSTEM (ACTOR 2): Right?
SYSTEM (ACTOR 4): AW YEAH!!!
PARENT: Can you please address the issue of Segregation in NYC schools?
SYSTEM (ALL): Please hold!
HOLD (V.O.): We are committed to ensuring that our programs, services, and activities are accessible to all. Each of our schools or programs will be labeled as fully accessible, partially accessible, or not-
SYSTEM (ALL): Hi yes? Of course! Next question!

(PARENT addresses the audience.)

PARENT: I think sometimes when you say the system has a life of its own, it's dangerous to say that because then you're absolving the people who are in the system and who make choices in the system from responsibility and I don't want to do that.

(Sound effect: a chime rings followed by a recorded voice over.)

ESMIRNA (V.O.): How did we get here?
CASSANDRA: From the transatlantic slave trade onward. From the very establishment of the United States. Segregation is a part of the fabric of the flag of this country. *(Pause.)* I can't believe I just said that- but when in the history of the United States have we not had to combat segregation?
SHINO: Maybe after the civil rights movement in the 60's we started believing that the problems were solved. Maybe we weren't critical enough in thinking that there were still problems.
ABRAM: People with power wanted to do something and so they invented things to justify doing that. Everything we think of as racism was invented to justify one thing or another – taking someone's land, forcing them to do work for you, keeping them out of your neighborhood, creating tests that only certain people will pass – it's all invented because you want something that consolidates your power and keeps you safe.
JONATHAN: There are hundreds of years of history. Hundreds of years of colonialism. In more recent times people have been unwilling to talk about this history and unwilling to talk about segregation. People want to kind of flatten it out and talk about other things and that prevents us from having meaningful change because people aren't even recognizing the problem.
MATT G: The primary driver of segregation is white supremacy. Segregation is the child of white supremacy.
MAURICE: We have to look at the history of this country and in doing so you realize that The American Dream was never supposed to be accessible

to people of color, or to women or to queer people. That ideal wasn't created for those people. This is why we call ourselves marginalized. Education is one of the institutions that very clearly demonstrates the marginalization of the people who are not white wealthy men. So how did we get here? Very intentionally – by actualizing the American ideal. This IS the American Dream. For the people who created it, this is what it is.

(Sound effect: a chime rings followed by a recorded voice over.)

JAVIA (V.O.): And now... white lips to white ears. Episode One: The Coffee Shop.

BECKY: There's like this really great school and all I had to do was put my son's name Timmy in this lottery.

BG: What do you mean? You put Timmy's name in a lottery?

BECKY: So like uh I put his name in this lottery for Charter Chance of Greatness.

BG: What is that?

BECKY: A charter school duh.

BG: Why would you do that when you can sign in up for a public school.

BECKY: Well...

BG: Do you have any idea of what you're doing? You are basically putting your child's education in a lottery and not thinking of the consequences of how your child will work in the community or just grow in general. You are literally gambling with your child's future.

BECKY: You have like no idea on what you're talking about. I like know what's right for my child, right Dave.

DAVE: Putting your child in a lottery is dumb.

BECKY: You are absolutely right Dave.

JAVIA (V.O.): Episode Two: Falling off a cliff.

BECKY: I'm like so excited that we decided to go camping you guys. Oh look a cliff! Do you guys think I can make it to the other side.

BG: Becky don't even try it. You you are literally committing suicide from doing that. You are my friend. I wouldn't want anything to happen to you. So please don't do it. You're not made of rubber.

BECKY: You like never support me in anything. Screw you! I can totally make it, like right Dave?

DAVE: You'd freaking die.

BECKY: You're so like right Dave that was dumb of me to think. Like thank you Dave. You like saved my like life.

JAVIA (V.O.): Episode Three.

MATT G: I was camping with some friends, me and my ex partner and we were the two only people of color. I've been camping since I was a kid and there's a lot of white people in camping spaces. We're hanging out by the campfire having fun. And somehow we got to talking about white supremacy and racism. Like, for sure, probably I brought it up. So I was with one of my friends from graduate school- he's like on it – getting it. Another dude, like they get it. We're talking about this- we're all agreeing. And like, a Becky, I'm just gonna call her Becky, like I could see visibly she was feeling threatened, feeling attacked and was challenging me. And I'm always welcoming someone trying to check me on whatever I'm saying if it's problematic. Everything I was saying was very basic, like white privilege and power – whatever. Nothing controversial. Nothing personal about Becky individually. It was really about the structure that we live in. And she just felt attacked and white tears- all that good stuff. So I just tried my best to be empathetic, soft-spoken, really kind, but she just didn't get it; wouldn't get it. And then I gave up. Like alright – I lost. And then my buddy Zack and her brother – obviously white dudes just literally just like verbatim plagiarized me – everything I said and just like said it to her. And I was sitting there just watching her face and everything just unfold and just her get it. And at first I was so angry that I had to have a white spokesperson. But after reflecting on this a lot and talking to my boy Zack – I learned something that night and so did he. What he learned was that it's not my job to educate white America; he was like, "It's not Matt's job to do that – it's my job." he learned he actually has more power to do that. Now why he has that power is a whiteness thing and super problematic, but he was like, "the work I'm going to be doing is going after those people and Matt's going to inform me how best to navigate those conversations; what to read, all that good stuff". And what I learned – and it was the most liberating thing I've ever gotten, was like, "It ain't my job. My job is to work with Zack the homie to do that work but like – my job is not to convince Becky that she has white privilege."

So if I'm talking to a random white person, I make sure that I have a white ally with me. Cause those white lips hit those white ears differently than mine do.

(Sound effect: a chime rings followed by a recorded voice over.)

ESMIRNA (V.O.): What is integration?

ANETH: There are the 5 R's of Real Integration: First there's Race and enrollment – how are students being enrolled in your schools? New York City Public Schools isolate many students of color and rely on racist and classist admissions policies. We want every school to reflect the diversity of the city. Next, Resources – how are resources allocated in every school? Some schools receive new textbooks like every other year; some schools haven't received a new textbook in twenty years. Some schools have twenty sports; other schools have zero sports. Then there's Relationships: how do you interact with each other in the school building? In my school there were a lot of hostile comments said in the hallways and it was predominately white teachers and teachers would say something offensive, like they didn't know it was offensive to a student of color. They just were not made aware. So with relationships you focus on building healthy and respectful relationships with everybody in the school building.

JULISSA: Then you have Restorative justice: and that's basically focusing on the fact that some kids are criminalized in their schools with metal detectors with the fact that Black and Brown kids are suspended the most. The last one is Representation: when the DOE did try to diversify our schools there was a mass firing of Black teachers. Most of the teachers that we have now are white teachers. I think it's really important for student identities and experiences to be reflected in the staff.

SHINO: If we can implement the 5 R's of integration in our schools, that is a very big first step in dismantling racism.

JOE: Honestly, the most important educational-justice concern in New York City today isn't families sending their children to schools where most children look like them. Not even close. It is not the quest to get a few thousand more Black and Brown children into the handful of predominantly White and Asian schools. Those are all side issues.

CASSANDRA: My ideal school doesn't necessarily have to be diverse. Some of the best teaching experiences I had were not because, "Oh there's white kids here and Black kids here and Latino kids here and everybody is so happy!"

JOE: The greatest barriers to true equity are the severe under-resourcing, institutional neglect, and underestimation of New York City's predominantly Black and Brown schools.

CASSANDRA: There are a few schools in New York City, in the South Bronx, in Bed-Stuy, in part of Harlem that are just doing their *damn* thing and it's not so much about the race of the students, it's just that the teachers have gotten together and partnered with families and community-based organizations to support the kids.

JOE: Those who care about racial and socioeconomic justice and the educational rights of Black and Brown children living in poverty should be deeply troubled by the rhetoric of integration.

MATT G: When I hear a Black parent say, "I've put my kid in a majority white school, because I think that's a better educational system." For a Black or Brown parent to say that to me, like hurts my soul to say that, because it means they've internalized something about us and themselves that is supposedly inferior- which I think is wrong. That comes from a place of pain and like a traumatic experience and just listening and honoring that is the way I approach families of color because I know that I have those internalized things.

HALLEY: So there's that cynical political argument that's like, "O.K., I know we want resource equity but integration is how we're going to get there through the back door" I think the truth is that resources absolutely matter, but integration matters for reasons beyond resources as well.

SHINO: I think by spending time together is when you start to see the humanity in people who are different from you.

JOE: We will not reach the promised land by shuffling Black and Brown children away from their neighborhood schools to Whiter schools or vice versa.

MATT G: Like I don't want you guys just to get like white schools. That's insufficient for me. I want you to get like Wakanda schools.

HALLEY: Integration when it's done well should get to the goals of resource equity but gets to a vision that is much broader than that.

JOE: Do neighborhoods like Harlem, the South Bronx, and Brownsville require more White upper-middle-class families in order for families who have lived in these communities for decades to enjoy a high quality of life and self-determination?

HALLEY: School integration actually has the power to push us to have a more integrated city overall which could mean not only trying have integrated schools but having conversations around what our housing policies look like, what patterns of gentrification mean for folks in the city.

(Sound effect: a chime rings followed by a recorded voice over.)

ESMIRNA (V.O.): And now… dropping character and dropping knowledge!

(Each student performer drops character and speaks to the audience as themselves.)

CHRISSY: Is there value in hearing from students in this conversation? YES. WE GO THROUGH THE BULLSHIT SO OBVIOUSLY YOU SHOULD. And not only the "good kids" but everyone, even the ones that struggle in school. We all have voices.

ESMIRNA: If you're telling me that the choices you make to change school policies on segregation can affect my future and my learning then you bet I'm gonna be apart of the conversation.

STITCH: The students are the ones going through the school. They're the ones who deal with everything that the system has become. They're the most experienced in the way the system is set up right now.

ROMAN: Students go to school to get an education but also, they go to school to make change to the school community. Students have every right for their voices to be heard.

IRIS: When there is an issue that pertains to a group of people they should always be included in the conversation. Not including students in the conversation in my opinion is utterly stupid. It's like having brain surgeons discuss the topic of rocket science. It makes no sense. We as students are looked down upon simply because of our age, and the fact of "you lack experience", when we are the very people that are going through the things they are talking about.

(Sound effect: a chime rings followed by a recorded voice over.)

ESMIRNA (V.O.): And now... the finale!
ESMIRNA: Are we equal?
    no one knows
    even those with 20/20
    are to blind to see
    the system we in goes in
    way way deep
ALL: Segregation huh?
    Why keep us all apart?
    You want them to learn together
    So you shouldn't sort us out.
    Segregation what?
    We all the same – So what?
    Just put us in together
    We're the same no matter what.
ESMIRNA: Advancements and enhancements
    all designed for a purpose.
    Segregation at the heart of the beast
    and we all know it.
    But if we all agree then what's stopping us from stopping the quota?
    Same stuff that the schools need, money.
    We have a voice, and yet we stay running.
    Find solutions that don't work
    all because of the color of our skin
ALL: Races. Faces.
    Why we chase 'em?
    Don't adults have all the power?
    So why they messing up?
    Listen up.
    The system is fucked up.
    Schools look like jail
    And students be on cuffs
    Segregation huh?
    Why keep us all apart?
    You want them to learn together
    So you shouldn't sort us out.
    Segregation what?
    We all the same – So what?
    Just put us in together
    We're the same no matter what .

(Music Cuts Off. ESMIRNA addresses the audience.)

ESMIRNA: So are we equal? Ask yourself.
  Victims to the system that we've been dealt.
  This is a racist country and we've invested in white supremacy.
  There's a chance for change but will we take it?
  Are we equal? That's up for interpretation.
ALL: Equality.
  That's all we want.
  We have the right.
  Nothing about us without us is for us.

END OF PLAY

Conclusion

Nothing about us without us is for us.

I hope this book and these plays will inspire you to consistently remember that phrase and keep it close to your heart before you create your next lesson plan, or design your next course syllabus, or program another season of plays, or draft a new diversity and inclusion policy. If there are exercises or protocols you've found in these pages that you think might be helpful to you in your work with young people, then by all means, please do share them. The students will undoubtedly let you know if *they* find them helpful. Make sure you listen!

I hope all of this inspires you to remove the barriers to rooms where young people of color are frequently talked about but rarely allowed to enter. I hope this encourages you to always learn with and from the youth you teach and to think of students as co-conspirators in a shared experience rather than customers and consumers of your pedagogical or artistic brilliance. I hope you create a space where you all can question everything together and build something messy and beautiful and brilliant and meaningful that changes the world.

DOI: 10.4324/9781003079835-31

Index

Printed in the United States
by Baker & Taylor Publisher Services